Bed &
Breakfast
✢ California ✢

Elk Cove Inn

Bed & Breakfast
❖ California ❖

A Selective Guide

By Linda Kay Bristow

Illustrated by Linda Herman

CHRONICLE BOOKS · SAN FRANCISCO

LIBRARY OF CONGRESS CATALOGING IN PUBLICATION DATA

Bristow, Linda Kay.
  Bed and breakfast, California: a selective guide / by Linda Kay Bristow: illustrated by Linda Herman — [Expanded, updated]
      p.   cm.

  Bibliography: p.
  Includes index.
  ISBN 0-87701-489-2 (pbk.)
  1. Bed and breakfast accommodations — California — Guide-books.
2. California — Description and travel — 1981 –   — Guide-books.
I. Title.
TX907.B736 1988
647'.9479403 — dc19   87-35571

EDITING:	Heidi Fritschel
BOOK DESIGN:	Linda Herman
COVER DESIGN:	Julie Noyes
CARTOGRAPHY:	Terry Milne
COMPOSITION:	TBH/Typecast, Inc.
FRONT COVER:	Courtesy of Mill Rose Inn
	Photograph by Robert Buelteman
BACK COVER:	Courtesy of House of Seven Gables Inn
	Photograph by Manuel Balesteri Chrysalis

PHOTO CREDITS:
Page 3, courtesy of Spreckels Mansion; page 5, Russell Abraham; page 11, courtesy of The Bed and Breakfast Inn; page 15, courtesy of Monte Cristo; page 27, Patricia Bolfing; page 45, courtesy of Holly Tree Inn; page 49, courtesy of Ten Inverness Way; page 53, courtesy of Pygmalion House; page 59, courtesy of Grape Leaf Inn; page 67, Youngblood Photography, Healdsburg; page 73, Jim Beazley; page 81, Susan Spann; page 85, courtesy of Ink House; page 109, courtesy of Elk Cove Inn; page 113, courtesy of Glendeven; page 119, courtesy of Joshua Grindle Inn; 139, courtesy of Carter House Inn; page 181, courtesy of Mayfield House; page 189, courtesy of Green Gables; page 199, courtesy of Stonehouse Inn; page 219, courtesy of The Parsonage

Distributed in Canada by Raincoast Books, 112 East Third Avenue Vancouver, British Columbia V5T 1C8

10 9 8 7 6 5 4 3 2 1

Chronicle Books
San Francisco, California

Table of Contents

Preface

When I first began researching inns for *Bed and Breakfast California*, I was looking for places that fit my preconceived notion of what a bed and breakfast should be: an owner-occupied home with four to six guest rooms that cost a reasonable price, breakfast inclusive. It didn't take long to realize that looking for the definition-perfect bed and breakfast was like looking for a needle in a haystack. Inns come in all sizes, shapes, and price ranges. And they vary greatly in atmosphere, due to factors such as owner, locale, and architectural style.

In 1982 there were fifty bed and breakfasts in California. Today there are nearly seven hundred, and I hear of new ones all the time. As the industry has evolved, so have the lines of demarcation, and bed and breakfast is currently being offered to the public in three similar but distinct forms: the *homestay*—similar to the European tradition of an inexpensive night's lodging in the spare room of someone's home; the *commercial bed and breakfast inn*—three to eight guest rooms in a building either previously owned by the hosts or purchased specifically for transformation to an inn; and the *small hotel*—ten to thirty guest rooms, often in a historic building, offering breakfast as part of its package. From the traveler's point of view, the homestay affords the least amount of privacy, the small hotel, the most. The commercial bed and breakfast inn strikes a balance between the two: rooms are available with either shared or private baths; some rooms have private entrances; and breakfast can be enjoyed either in the room or at the dining table, depending on the policy of the inn.

In the following pages you'll find a review of what I consider to be some of the best bed and breakfast establishments in the state. Most are commercial b&b's in areas of scenic or historic interest: the Wine Country, the Mendocino Coast, the Gold Country, to name a few. They are housed in buildings ranging in style from turn-of-the-century Queen Anne Victorians to former hunting lodges to newly built structures of concrete and glass. They may contain as few as one guest room to as many as twenty-one. I have visited or stayed at almost all of them and have endeavored to give them a fair appraisal.

There is a certain etiquette involved with the bed and breakfast experience, and since forewarned is forearmed, here are some pointers to make you feel at home:

1. The basic modus operandi is the same as if you were staying at the home of a friend. Express appreciation for the offerings, be considerate, and don't treat the owner-innkeeper like a servant.

2. Don't hesitate to ask for what you want or need.

3. Clean up after yourself in a shared-bath situation.

4. Say goodbye when you check out, and return the key personally.

5. Follow house rules concerning check-out time, parking locations, payment arrangements, etc.

Some other points to remember: Rates are subject to change. The rate structure I've used throughout the book can be interpreted as follows: inexpensive — less than $75; moderate — $75 to $125; expensive — $125 to $175; very expensive — $175 plus. Reservations are a must. Though many inns book well in advance, last-minute cancellations do occur — don't hesitate to phone, or ask to have your name put on a waiting list. A private bath is sometimes hard to come by. Don't expect a telephone, television, or room service. Smoking is discouraged, pets are unwelcome, and children are subject to house policy. Some inns require a two-night minimum stay, especially through weekend or holiday periods.

I enjoyed the inns, as I know you will, and I'd like to take this opportunity to extend my appreciation to the innkeepers throughout the state for putting me up as well as for putting up with me. A special thanks to the members of BBINC (Bed and Breakfast Innkeepers of Northern California) for their support. Immeasurable gratitude to my dear friend and copy editor, Helga Wall, and to Gary Hanauer for his assistance with the research and writing of this book.

Spreckles Mansion

San Francisco
Bay Area

Point Richmond
East Brother Light Station
Berkeley
Gramma's

Archbishops Mansion
Bed and Breakfast Inn
Hermitage House
Mansion Hotel
Monte Cristo
Obrero Hotel
Red Victorian
Spreckels Mansion
Union Street Inn
Washington Square Inn

San Francisco

Half Moon Bay

Mill Rose Inn
Old Thyme Inn
San Benito House

Mountain View

Chateau Victorian
Cliff Crest Bed & Breakfast Inn
Ben Lomond — *Chateau Des Fleurs*

Spreckels Mansion

737 Buena Vista West
San Francisco, California 94117; (415) 861-3008

INNKEEPERS:	*Jonathan Shannon and Jeffrey Ross.*
ACCOMMODATIONS:	*Five rooms, three with private bath; double and queen-size beds. Five-room guest house.*
RESERVATIONS:	*Six weeks recommended.*
MINIMUM STAY:	*Two nights on weekends.*
DEPOSIT:	*First and last night's lodging.*
CREDIT CARDS:	*AE, MC, VISA.*
RATES:	*Expensive.*
RESTRICTIONS:	*Children discouraged. No pets.*

Jonathan Shannon likes to think of the Spreckels Mansion as "a country inn in the city." And indeed he has a point. This elegant Victorian, built in 1887 for Richard Spreckels, sits high on a hill in a quiet neighborhood overlooking San Francisco's Buena Vista Park.

Of all the bed and breakfast inns I visited in San Francisco, this is one of my favorites. The atmosphere is comfortable, the rooms are spacious, the innkeepers are delightful, and there is plenty of parking. (I mention this because in San Francisco parking space is a rare commodity.)

Each room reflects the innkeepers' philosophy that "the room is as important a part of the traveler's experience as anything else." With the exception of the San Francisco suite, all the rooms are Victorian in feeling. Each is appointed with antiques, family treasures, and quality furniture. And each features an incredible view of the city. The San Francisco suite, which takes up the whole third floor of the house, is decorated with contemporary furnishings and boasts a view of the city's skyline. The Sugar Baron suite is graced with tall fan windows, Corinthian columns, a pictorial-tile mantelpiece, and a canopied alcove that holds a queen-size bed. Its private bath is so enormous that you think you are walking into yet another suite. And what I wouldn't give for a soak in

the freestanding tub in front of the fireplace just about now.

Breakfast at the Spreckels Mansion is light Continental: croissants or pastries, orange juice, and coffee or tea. In the evening, guests (sometimes including United Nations ambassadors and Hollywood celebrities) mingle in the parlor to sip complimentary wine.

Nearby attractions include Haight Street shops and restaurants and Golden Gate Park. The inn is only fifteen minutes from downtown and the city's waterfront.

Archbishops Mansion

1000 Fulton Street
San Francisco, California 94117; (415) 563-7872

INNKEEPERS:	*Jonathan Shannon and Jeffrey Ross.*
ACCOMMODATIONS:	*Fifteen rooms, all with private bath; queen-size beds.*
RESERVATIONS:	*Three to four weeks recommended.*
MINIMUM STAY:	*Two nights on weekends.*
DEPOSIT:	*Two nights' lodging.*
CREDIT CARDS:	*AE, MC, VISA.*
RATES:	*Expensive.*
RESTRICTIONS:	*No pets.*

They've done it again, this irrepressible pair. And everyone is talking about it. (Bob and Sue Garmston, innkeepers of the Briggs House in Sacramento, spent their fifth wedding anniversary here and called it "a masterpiece"; in the guest ledger I spotted the names of other innkeepers looking for the ultimate getaway for themselves.) I could hardly complete my interview with the innkeepers, what with calls coming in from reporters and radio talk-show hosts. It's the Archbishops Mansion, San Francisco's premier bed and breakfast inn; one that renders European elegance in a style only Jonathan Shannon (impeccable taste with a touch of flamboyance) and Jeffrey Ross (exhaustive knowledge of architectural history and restoration) could achieve.

Built in 1904 to house the offices and residences of the archbishops of San Francisco, this Second Empire French building with its fifteen bedrooms and eighteen working fireplaces is one of the city's three largest homes — 30,000 square feet in all. The interior follows the classical style of the French Renaissance (Beaux-Arts), with receiving rooms located on the first floor and bedrooms occupying the second and third floors. The parlor, a buffer between the outside world and the one within, is handsomely appointed with Oriental carpets; fine oil paintings; a mix of European, Victorian, and Oriental antiques; a floor-to-ceiling gold-leaf mirror; and vases of tiger lilies

in bloom. (Take special note of the triple-vaulted ceiling, crystal chandelier, and massive carved redwood fireplace.) A magnificent oval glass dome hovers above the stairwell leading to the guest rooms, which are named after romantic operas: La Bohème, Manon, Tosca, Carmen, Don Giovanni, Turandot, and Madame Butterfly.

Same-day laundry and dry-cleaning service, room service (for snacks), and complimentary soft drinks are among the amenities seldom heard of at other inns. Champagne and wine are available for purchase; winetastings are a tradition. For breakfast the inn serves an assortment of freshly baked pastries, along with orange juice and coffee.

The Archbishops Mansion overlooks Alamo Square, one of the city's registered historic districts, which encompasses more Victorian architecture than any other neighborhood. (You may recognize the row of Victorians along Steiner Street from a well-known picture postcard.) Davies Symphony Hall, the Opera House, the Museum of Modern Art, and the Civic Center are just six blocks away. Eight blocks in the other direction is Golden Gate Park.

Hermitage House

2224 Sacramento Street
San Francisco, California 94115; (415) 921-5515

INNKEEPERS:	Marian Binkley and Jane Bertorelli.
ACCOMMODATIONS:	Six guest rooms, all with private bath; twin, queen-, and king-size beds.
RESERVATIONS:	Four to six weeks recommended.
MINIMUM STAY:	Two nights on weekends.
DEPOSIT:	First night's lodging.
CREDIT CARDS:	AE, MC, VISA.
RATES:	Moderate.
RESTRICTIONS:	No children under 7. No pets.

M arian Binkley told me that for the past several years she has enjoyed "restoring old buildings on a shoestring." But as I toured the Hermitage House with her, I was quickly convinced that this lovely home was restored on much more than a shoestring (to say nothing of many hours of hard work). In fact, I remembered the building from the mid-seventies when it housed a drug rehabilitation center, and I could hardly believe the transformation.

This four-story Greek Revival was originally built for Judge Charles Slack sometime between 1900 and 1903. The Binkleys purchased the house in 1978 with the intent of turning it into rental units. But its ten bedrooms, seven working fireplaces, and spacious common areas made the house a natural for a bed and breakfast inn.

Two flights of stairs lead to the main entrance of the all-redwood house. Inside, the entryway shows off the beautiful carved heart redwood detail of the period in the pillars, beams, and stairway scrolls. High ceilings mark the first two main stories, and intricate inlaid designs are worked into the edging of the hardwood floors in the living room. A small alcove to the right of the entry was once used as a chapel for weddings and christenings.

Another flight of stairs leads to the bedrooms, the most impressive of which are Judge Slack's Study with its redwood shakes, beamed ceiling, bookshelf-lined walls, massive king-size bed, and view of the city; and the Master Bedroom with a king-size bed, a cozy sitting area in front of a fireplace, and a footed tub in its private bath.

The other natural that makes Hermitage House such a success as a bed and breakfast inn is Marian Binkley. She not only shows genuine interest in her guests, but her philosophy that "a bed and breakfast inn should be small, cozy, and homelike with a single (and stable) guiding force behind it" shines through.

Early risers will appreciate the ample breakfast, which is served buffet style from 7:30 A.M. on (8:00 A.M. on weekends). The fare consists of freshly squeezed orange juice; an array of homemade quick breads, coffee cakes, muffins, and croissants; quiche; a ham and cheese platter; fruits of the season; cereal; and coffee, tea, and hot chocolate.

Hermitage House is one of only a few inns that make private-line telephones (and even televisions) available to guests, and it is perhaps for this reason that major corporations refer their favorite clients and top executives to the Hermitage.

The inn is located in the city's Pacific Heights district. The No. 1 California bus (which goes to the heart of the financial district) stops across the street. The Fillmore and Union Street shopping areas are within walking distance, and Japantown is just a few blocks away.

Union Street Inn

2229 Union Street
San Francisco, California 94123; (415) 346-0424

INNKEEPER:	*Helen Stewart.*
ACCOMMODATIONS:	*Five rooms, two with private bath; double, queen-, and king-size beds. Carriage House.*
RESERVATIONS:	*Six weeks recommended.*
MINIMUM STAY:	*Two nights on weekends.*
DEPOSIT:	*First and last night's lodging.*
CREDIT CARDS:	*AE, MC, VISA.*
RATES:	*Moderate to expensive.*
RESTRICTIONS:	*No children under 12. No pets.*

For Helen Stewart, owning and operating a bed and breakfast inn is a third career. As a mother she raised five children, and she has also taught school. As an innkeeper she is a natural. Helen's appealing calmness is reflected in the decor and surroundings of her Union Street Inn.

This two-story house, an Edwardian built around the turn of the century, is slightly set back from the bustle of Union Street. A few steps lead to a small front porch that opens to the reception area and downstairs parlor. The parlor, where guests gather in the late morning and early evening, has a soft apricot velvet wall covering, a brick fireplace, bay windows, and glass doors that open out to a back deck and garden. The furnishings, rich in tone and texture, are contemporary with a mix of antiques; the most unusual pieces are a pair of iron and brass chairs, with leather backs and seats, that were made in Australia. A bowl of potpourri made from the flowers in the garden sits on one of the end tables.

There are five bedrooms. Two have private baths and the other three share two bathrooms. Although the rooms range in price from $75 to $125 per night, I found one to be just as nice as the next. Wildrose (one of the least expensive) has a persimmon-mauve decor and features a double brass bed, an abundance of healthy-looking green plants, and a garden view. The Golden Gate room, with a queen-size canopy bed in contrasting shades of midnight blue and mocha cream, looks out to Union Street. To ease the shared bath situation there are sinks in every room, and bathrobes are provided.

The most recent addition is the Carriage House — a romantic hideaway with its own patio, garden, and Jacuzzi.

The morning I spent at the Union Street Inn I relaxed on the sun deck with a glass of orange juice, a steaming hot cup of coffee, and one of the most delicious croissants I've ever tasted. Helen told me that she and her staff "taste-tested" just about every croissant made in San Francisco until they finally settled on one made at a French bakery a few blocks away. Between the breakfast, the morning sun, and the gentle breeze that filled my senses with the fragrance of the many varieties of flowers in the garden, I found it difficult to leave.

Those who can manage to tear themselves away from this peaceful and visually pleasant environment will find some of the city's finest shops and restaurants just a short distance from the door. Fisherman's Wharf, Pier 39, Davies Symphony Hall, the Opera House, and downtown San Francisco are minutes away.

The Bed and Breakfast Inn

Four Charlton Court
San Francisco, California 94123; (415) 921-9784

INNKEEPERS:	*Robert and Marily Kavanaugh.*
ACCOMMODATIONS:	*Ten rooms, six with private bath; twin, double, queen-, and king-size beds.*
RESERVATIONS:	*Two to three months recommended.*
MINIMUM STAY:	*None.*
DEPOSIT:	*First night's lodging.*
CREDIT CARDS:	*Not accepted.*
RATES:	*Moderate to expensive.*
RESTRICTIONS:	*No children under 12. No pets.*

The Bed and Breakfast Inn, opened in 1976, was the first b&b in San Francisco. Many have opened since, but this is still one of the most popular in the city, evidenced by comments like this one in the inn's guest book: "In my fifteen years of coming to San Francisco this was my favorite visit because of you."

At the time of the inn's opening, the owners, Robert and Marily Kavanaugh didn't realize they had hit on an idea whose time had come. Having traveled extensively, they were anxious to open an inn patterned after those they had stayed at in Wales and Scotland. Bob's background in real estate and building and Marily's industriousness and flair for decorating led them to purchase and restore this one hundred-year-old Victorian, which is located in a quiet cul-de-sac off fashionable Union Street that reminds one of a London mews.

Although today the Kavanaughs are assisted by a friendly staff of five, Marily explained that they did every-thing themselves for the first three years they were in busi-ness. I didn't find this hard to believe, as the afternoon I arrived I found her ironing table linens while Bob was busy with odd jobs in the garden.

It is apparent that the Kavanaughs take great pride in what they do — and they do it well. On arrival, guests are greeted on a first-name basis and escorted to their room,

where personal touches such as fresh flowers and fruit are evident.

Many of the rooms, such as the Mayfair, Covent Garden, and Kensington Gardens, are named after areas of London. Each room is unique in decor; antiques and family heirlooms are judiciously scattered throughout.

My favorite room is Celebration, one of the four available with a private bath. And what a bath — complete with a sunken double tub, a hand-painted Sherle Wagner pedestal basin, plush towels, and scented soaps and bath oil. The bedroom, papered with a blue-and-white Laura Ashley print, features a love seat and a queen-size bed. Another popular guest room (and one of the two that open to the garden) is the Willows, decorated in green-and-white print accented by white wicker furniture.

The Continental breakfast, served on Wedgwood china, includes fresh-squeezed orange juice, warm croissants, freshly ground coffee, and herbal tea. Evening sherry is complimentary, current magazines and good books are plentiful, and, unlike many other b&b inns, rooms with televisions and telephones are available.

The Bed and Breakfast Inn is located between Laguna and Buchanan in the heart of Union Street's sixteen blocks of boutiques, restaurants, and antique shops.

Obrero Hotel

1208 Stockton Street
San Francisco, California 94133; (415) 989-3960

INNKEEPER:	*Bambi McDonald.*
ACCOMMODATIONS:	*Twelve rooms, all with shared bath; twin and double beds.*
RESERVATIONS:	*Two weeks recommended.*
MINIMUM STAY:	*Two nights.*
DEPOSIT:	*First and last night's lodging.*
CREDIT CARDS:	*Not accepted.*
RATES:	*Inexpensive.*
RESTRICTIONS:	*No pets. Quiet children are welcome.*

I would dub the Obrero Hotel the "no-frills bed and breakfast inn." But to use the words of the hotel's owner-innkeeper, Bambi McDonald, it is "a twelve-room (none of them perfect) European-style pension with an emphasis on cleanliness and value." And talk about value — this is certainly one of the least expensive places to stay in San Francisco (or anywhere, I might add), with prices ranging from $35 single to $52 triple occupancy.

But the Obrero is not for everyone, and it's not without its problems, as Bambi will be the first to admit. As a "for instance," the building's water heater only holds fifty gallons (I'll leave the rest to your imagination). But independent people interested in meeting similar types and in staying in the city at bargain prices find that the Obrero just fills the bill. A normal day at the hotel finds the gamut of visitors ranging from European students to bird-watchers from Bolinas, with a few filmmakers thrown in.

Because Ms. McDonald lived in Europe for several years and worked for friends who ran a pension in Amsterdam in exchange for room and board, she was not unfamiliar with the business. But striking out on her own in San Francisco wasn't as easy as she had imagined. It took three long, hard years to build up a reputation, and as she approaches her tenth year in business she still works twelve hours a day, seven days a week. In fact, she runs the whole operation with just one waitress, one maid, a strong dose of self-discipline, and a tight fist.

The hotel's twelve rooms share four baths, and the room furnishings are simple and sparse. Bambi describes a typical room as including "the best bed I could buy, a brass headboard, one chair, a dresser, a closet, and a sink with hot and cold running water."

Breakfast is served family style from 8:00 to 8:45 A.M., and it's enough to last through an entire day of sightseeing. A morning's sampling includes a four-minute egg, ham, cheese, an orange, hot sourdough bread, and tea and coffee — all included in the price of the room.

Family-style dinners featuring French Basque cuisine are served nightly. There are two entrées each night; sample fares include oxtail stew, cassoulet, Basque chicken, and shepherd's pie. Dinner comes with soup, salad, dessert, wine, and coffee — all for the bargain price of $10.50.

The hotel is conveniently located in the heart of San Francisco's Chinatown on the edge of North Beach, the Italian section of the city. Fisherman's Wharf and Union Square are just a stone's throw away.

The Monte Cristo

600 Presidio Avenue
San Francisco, California 94115; (415) 931-1875

INNKEEPER:	*Frances Allan.*
ACCOMMODATIONS:	*Fourteen rooms, thirteen with private bath; twin, double, and queen-size beds.*
RESERVATIONS:	*Three to four weeks recommended.*
MINIMUM STAY:	*Two nights on weekends.*
DEPOSIT:	*First night's lodging.*
CREDIT CARDS:	*AE, MC, VISA.*
RATES:	*Moderate to expensive.*
RESTRICTIONS:	*No pets.*

A couple from Laramie, Wyoming, described their stay at the Monte Cristo, one of San Francisco's many delightful bed and breakfast inns, as "a page from a storybook romance." And it's certain that the Monte Cristo has had many pages of romance throughout its history; originally built as a hotel in 1875, it was well known as a bordello at various times.

All that aside, today the Monte Cristo is surely at the height of its glory, thanks to the efforts of the current innkeeper, Frances Allan. Frances, a former nurse, a former Marinite, and a native of Winnipeg, Canada, is just the type you'd expect to find running an inn. Culturally sophisticated and anxious to please, she is full of tidbits on current theater performances, gallery and museum exhibits, and the area's best restaurants. Because Frances lives on the premises, she feels that each individual is a guest in her home rather than just a paying client.

The Monte Cristo has been superbly restored. And once you enter your bedroom door, you will forgive the long, narrow hallways that run the length of the building. With few exceptions, the rooms are spacious. All are quite comfortable. Furnishings are Early American and English antiques, and each room has a large silk flower arrangement color-keyed to the wallpaper. The rooms have various names and themes: the Violet Room, the Wicker

Room, and, my favorite, the English Four-Poster Room, which is done in shades of blues, mauves, and beige.

The Chinese Wedding Bed Room has an elaborate and inviting teak bed with a down comforter. If you've never heard of a Chinese wedding bed, don't feel bad. Neither had I. A wedding gift to the bride from her parents, the wedding bed is handed down in the bride's family through the years, eventually becoming an heirloom. The wealthier the family, the more elaborate the bed. And from the looks of this one, the family must have been the equivalent of America's Rockefellers. Chinese accents fill the rest of the room, and silk robes are provided for your use after a dip in the sunken tiled tub.

The Monte Cristo is one of the few inns in the city that serve a full breakfast. Everything is home baked. The orange juice is freshly squeezed. The coffee cake comes straight from the oven. I left asking for the pancake recipe (what's so special about pancakes? — wait until you've tried these).

The Monte Cristo is located at the corner of Pine and Presidio, just a short walk from the Sacramento Street shops and restaurants. Major bus lines take you to Golden Gate Park, Fisherman's Wharf, or downtown in about fifteen minutes.

The Mansion Hotel

2220 Sacramento Street
San Francisco, California 94115; (415) 929-9444

INNKEEPER:	*Robert Pritikin.*
ACCOMMODATIONS:	*Eighteen rooms, all with private bath; twin, double, and queen-size beds.*
RESERVATIONS:	*Two weeks recommended.*
MINIMUM STAY:	*None.*
DEPOSIT:	*First night's lodging.*
CREDIT CARDS:	*AE, MC, VISA.*
RATES:	*Expensive.*
RESTRICTIONS:	*No pets.*

Robert Pritikin's Mansion Hotel is one of those places I run into every once in a while that straddles the thin line dividing an inn from a small hotel. But there are certain features that move me to include it here. First of all, it's housed in a grand, twin-turreted Queen Anne Victorian that was built by Utah State Senator Richard Chambers in 1887. Second, the innkeeper's colorful personality, wit, and varied background make for lively conversation. And finally, there is an opulent breakfast served in-room each morning.

The hotel is billed as "being in the middle of everything—yet a million miles away." "Everything" includes the not-too-distant downtown, Fisherman's Wharf, and North Beach areas. The "million miles away" is actually just a step away from the front porch to the grand foyer, with its gigantic crystal chandelier and a mural depicting the romantic characters who inhabited the Mansion nearly a century ago.

To the right of the foyer is the Music Room, the setting for nightly classical concerts and weekend magic shows. The innkeeper ("America's foremost classical saw player") is your master of ceremonies. The piano here is said to have belonged to Claudia Chambers, the Mansion's legendary haunt whose invisible fingers play classical requests. (Claudia's bad manners are said to be the cause of a host of the hotel's problems and troubles. The staff snickers at the story of the night she unhinged a door that fell on the head of a guest who was being difficult.)

Another room worth noting is the Billiard Room. Beside the antique billiard table you'll find a stained-glass, nickelodeon player piano pumping out the tunes of John Philip Sousa and Scott Joplin. A collection of beaded Victorian purses is displayed on the wall above an outsized "dollhouse" that was the original set from Edward Albee's New York Broadway production of *Tiny Alice*. The glass-fronted armoires hold memorabilia.

Guest rooms occupy the second and third floors of the building. A brass plaque on the door of each room identifies the historic personage to whom the room is dedicated, and the walls of the room are alive with murals depicting the legend of that person's life. Your room may also have a marble fireplace, a private terrace, or a ceiling that slants to the floor.

Breakfast anyone? How does a French croissant, a wineglass full of fresh orange juice with a strawberry on the side, eggs and sausages, cereal, a fruit cup, and freshly ground coffee sound?

Tennis? Lafayette Park is just a block away. Sauna? There's one in-house. Afternoon sherry? It's complimentary. Dinner? The hotel has an intimate dining room that features entrées fit for royalty. There's Double Breast of Duckling Nicole, the Czar's Pasta, and Suprême of Chicken Luxembourg (a dish the late Grand Duchess would have given her tiara for, says Master Chef David Coyle). Last but not least are the front and back gardens displaying a collection of Beniamino Bufano sculptures, the most prominent of which are two towering bronze figures of Saint Francis of Assisi, the patron saint of San Francisco.

The Red Victorian

1665 Haight Street
San Francisco, California 94117; (415) 864-1978

INNKEEPER:	*Sami Sunchild.*
ACCOMMODATIONS:	*Fifteen rooms, three with private bath; twin, double, queen-, and king-size beds.*
RESERVATIONS:	*Two weeks recommended.*
MINIMUM STAY:	*None.*
DEPOSIT:	*In full.*
CREDIT CARDS:	*AE, MC, VISA.*
RATES:	*Inexpensive to moderate.*
RESTRICTIONS:	*Children by arrangement. No pets.*

S ami Sunchild is the artist-in-residence innkeeper; the Red Victorian is the grandest of all her works. This colorful upstairs bed and breakfast, located in the heart of San Francisco's ever-evolving Haight-Ashbury district, is a favorite of creative types and new age thinkers. Psychologists and architects, futurists and poets come here from as near as a block away to as far as New Zealand and the Orient.

The turn-of-the-century building was originally constructed as a resort hotel to host the many people who came by cable car to take the fresh country air of Golden Gate Park. The hotel faded into a home for alcoholics and then in the 1960s it was invaded by hippies.

Sami purchased the property in 1977 and began single-handedly restoring the place to its original splendor. Today Sami believes that part of what makes the Red Victorian what it is, is what it's not. It's not downtown. It's not in a frequented tourist area. And it's not for those who want to get away from it all or to just be alone. It is, however, conveniently located near Golden Gate Park and is on major bus lines to all parts of the city.

The inn's Pink Parlor, with its red carpet, pink walls, and lace curtains with red velvet valances, is the setting for lively discussions and occasional seminars where locals and guests meet and exchange ideas. Conversations continue for hours, friendships for years.

Sami's "Lines of Thought" gallery of calligraphic paintings decorates not only the Pink Parlor, but the second- and third-floor corridors as well. Guest rooms (located off long, narrow hallways) are moderately priced. The least expensive are the Globetrotter and Peace rooms. Best-of-the-house is the Peacock Suite with its stained-glass windows and canopied bed. The rooms are all simply furnished; some are accented by Haight Street memorabilia and old photographs of the hotel.

A Continental breakfast of croissants, muffins, fresh fruit, and tea is served from 8:30 to 10:30 each morning in the Pink Parlor.

Washington Square Inn

1660 Stockton Street
San Francisco, California 94133; (415) 981-4220

INNKEEPERS:	*Nan and Norm Rosenblatt.*
ACCOMMODATIONS:	*Fifteen rooms, ten with private bath; twin, double, queen-, and king-size beds.*
RESERVATIONS:	*Six to eight weeks recommended.*
MINIMUM STAY:	*None.*
DEPOSIT:	*First night's lodging.*
CREDIT CARDS:	*AE, MC, VISA.*
RATES:	*Moderate to expensive.*
RESTRICTIONS:	*Children discouraged. No pets.*

San Francisco's Nan and Norm Rosenblatt "got the bug" for a bed and breakfast inn of their own while traveling through Europe and staying at little inns along the way. Nan is an interior designer, Norm a financial wizard. Together they turned two dilapidated buildings that sat back to back into one fantastic inn: the Washington Square Inn.

A stay at the inn is so pleasant that it's tempting to stay inside, especially if you have one of the three rooms that overlook the square. Although the rooms are individually decorated, a European country theme prevails. Furnishings are a well-blended mix of antique and contemporary. The beds are all modern, but some have fabric canopies that blend with the soft floral-patterned drapes and bedspreads. Most rooms have a private bath and all have a telephone. Televisions are available on request. As in most of the other inns in this book, there are fresh flowers in every room.

Complimentary breakfast in bed runs to flaky croissants, scones and cheese brioches, fresh fruit, freshly squeezed orange juice, coffee (Italian, of course), and herb tea. Or if you prefer to meet and mingle with the other guests, you can enjoy breakfast at the formal dining table in the reception lobby.

Though it may be tempting, don't linger over breakfast too long. Washington Square is in the heart of the city's colorful Italian district, which offers plenty to see and do. This area, called North Beach, is a favorite of locals and visitors alike for its specialty shops, bakeries, cafés, and nightclubs, all within a few blocks' radius.

And if that's not enough, the inn's concierge can arrange a car, theater tickets, a tour of the city, a picnic, or even a stenographer if you've come here to get down to business (heaven forbid). Because the inn is midway between Fisherman's Wharf and the financial district, it appeals to tourists and businesspeople alike.

Tea, scones with whipped cream and jam, imported cheeses, and cucumber sandwiches are a complimentary afternoon affair.

Gramma's Inn

2740 Telegraph Avenue
Berkeley, California 94703; (415) 549-2145

INNKEEPERS:	*Kathy Kuhner and Liza Pedrick.*
ACCOMMODATIONS:	*Twenty-nine rooms, twenty-seven with private bath; twin, double, queen-, and king-size beds.*
RESERVATIONS:	*One month recommended for weekends.*
MINIMUM STAY:	*None.*
DEPOSIT:	*First night's lodging.*
CREDIT CARDS:	*AE, MC, VISA.*
RATES:	*Moderate to expensive.*
RESTRICTIONS:	*No pets.*

Gramma's is the perfect example of a bed and breakfast inn that has outgrown itself. Since it opened, the inn has become so popular that it is now housed in not one, not two, but *four* separate buildings. But success has not dimmed Gramma's main appeal as a place for relaxation in an urban environment.

The establishment's story goes back to 1976 when Kathy Kuhner, fresh from b&b-hopping her way across Europe, decided she wanted to open an inn of her own. It wasn't until 1979 that she found what she thought was the perfect property: a grand old estate named the Fay House that had been built around 1903. But its owner, a wealthy therapist, refused to sell.

Undaunted, Kathy felt certain that he would eventually come around, so in the meantime, she bought the house next door. By 1980, she'd renovated and made it the eleven-guest-room Main House of what is now the inn complex. She also restored the property's garden house. Finally, Kathy's waiting paid off. The Fay House, with its seven bedrooms and stained-glass windows across the top, was purchased along with its carriage house, which was converted into a three-guest-room annex.

Washed in sun and surrounded by a fragrant garden of roses and wisteria, the inn is close to the famed University of California campus but still far enough away for the surrounding neighborhood to be quiet and residential. Elsewhere in Berkeley, street vendors ply their wares on Telegraph Avenue, nature lovers explore the Berkeley Rose Garden and Tilden Regional Park, and museum hounds tour the UC Art Museum and Lawrence Hall of Science.

But a stay at Gramma's includes other bonuses too. First and foremost are the rooms, most of which have queen- or king-size brass or Murphy beds and various combinations of such amenities as armoires, fireplaces, decks, chaise longues, wicker rocking chairs, love seats, and antique furnishings. If you really want to indulge yourself, check into Jewel's Retreat, the third-floor penthouse of Mrs. Jewel Fay's former house, which even comes with its own living room.

Although Berkeley is well known for its breakfast haunts, don't even think about going out to eat if you stay here. Served from 7:30 to 10:00 A.M. on weekdays and 8:00 to 10:00 A.M. weekends, the scrumptious down-home repast includes scones, croissants, and muffins (both blueberry and bran are available), yogurt, buckets of fresh fruit, and three different kinds of cereal (Gramma's homemade granola is one). On Sundays, instead of the usual complimentary breakfast, you can pay a slight additional charge for a full champagne brunch with an ever-changing menu. (To avoid a wait, sign up for the 10:00 A.M. seating instead of those at 11:30 A.M. and 1:00 P.M.) Wine and cheese are offered in the evening; coffee and cookies are on hand all day.

Who might turn up while you're staying here? Almost anyone, including such recent patrons as John Astin (he played the father on television's "Addams Family"), actress Amy Irving, and poet Yevgeny Yevtushenko. Although I didn't see any of these personages myself, I did come away with a wonderful T-shirt emblazoned with Gramma's logo that will always remind me of my stay here, together with a photo I took of Sterling, the inn's sleek grey house cat, sprawled out in the summer sun.

East Brother Light Station

117 Park Place
Point Richmond, California 94801; (415) 233-2385 or (415) 990-5834

INNKEEPERS:	*Leigh and Linda Hurley.*
ACCOMMODATIONS:	*Four rooms, two with private bath; double and queen-size beds.*
RESERVATIONS:	*Six to eight months recommended.*
MINIMUM STAY:	*None.*
DEPOSIT:	*In full.*
CREDIT CARDS:	*Not accepted.*
RATES:	*Very expensive.*
RESTRICTIONS:	*Children by arrangement. No pets.*

"Have you stayed at East Brother Light Station?" I asked a well-respected inn book author friend of mine. "Stayed there?" she replied. "It was so exciting, I couldn't sleep!"

And so I was led to East Brother, such a favorite of bed and breakfast inn-goers that its available accommodations (four rooms, four nights a week) are almost always completely booked — sometimes up to a year in advance. Patience, my dears, it's well worth the wait.

Guests of the inn are shuttled from the San Pablo Yacht Harbor by boat to this Victorian-era, working lighthouse on an island in San Francisco Bay. For decades the lighthouse was run by full-time keepers employed by the Lighthouse Service, and in more recent years by rotating Coast Guard crews. Today it is manned by innkeepers Leigh and Linda Hurley, who have been on the island since 1983. Leigh, a former wine distributor, and Linda, a caterer by profession, conduct tours of the facilities complete with lighthouse lore.

A six-course dinner, as well as breakfast, is included in the price of the room. Candlelight sets the tone for a menu of pasta with fresh tomato sauce, carrot and tarragon soup, a green salad with nasturtiums and white herb dressing, salmon soufflé with orange hollandaise sauce, and crème brûlée. Champagne, wine, and port are poured at appropriate points throughout the meal.

Guest rooms here are both small and sparcely furnished: within them are contained brass beds, oak furniture, lace curtains, and old wooden trunks. Two of the overnight accommodations, along with the inn's living and dining rooms, are in the lighthouse itself; a guest house holds the remaining two. Homemade chocolate truffles beckon you to your room as ships glide effortlessly through the night fog.

In the morning a resplendent breakfast — say a raspberry crêpe torte accompanied by freshly squeezed orange juice, coffee, and tea — is followed by a hands-on demonstration of the diaphone foghorn and an 11:00 A.M. departure back to reality's shores.

San Benito House

356 Main Street
Half Moon Bay, California 94019; (415) 726-3425

INNKEEPER:	*Carol Mickelsen.*
ACCOMMODATIONS:	*Twelve rooms, nine with private bath; double beds (one room with twin beds).*
RESERVATIONS:	*Three weeks recommended.*
MINIMUM STAY:	*None.*
DEPOSIT:	*First night's lodging.*
CREDIT CARDS:	*AE, MC, VISA.*
RATES:	*Inexpensive to moderate.*
RESTRICTIONS:	*No pets.*

I can't wait to get back to San Benito House. This two-story, light blue building on a corner of Half Moon Bay's Main Street offers a romantic bed and breakfast getaway just thirty-five miles south of San Francisco. Carol Mickelsen, owner and chef-in-residence, oversees the whole operation, which consists of twelve guest rooms on the second floor, a downstairs restaurant that serves classic country cuisine, a Western-style saloon with "local color," and a garden deli-café.

The inn was originally built by Estanislaus Zabella at the turn of the century and was known as the Mosconi Hotel. In the 1930s it changed ownership and was renamed Domenic's. Mickelsen purchased the hostelry in 1976 and began a "three-phase" restoration project. The final phase (just completed at the time of my visit) entailed the careful restoration of each guest room to include fixtures and furnishings of the period.

The rooms are small but cozy. The one I called home was painted a forest green accented with white trim. There was a white iron bed with a fluffy comforter and an antique dresser with a huge bouquet of daisies in a wicker basket. Old photographs of the hotel and Half Moon Bay added a touch of interest, and a profusion of red geraniums in the flower box just outside the window added a splash of color. An upstairs deck provided a place to sit and look out over the ocean, and the sauna

(the only modern concession in the whole place) was heavenly.

The evening started off with drinks in the saloon followed by a superb dinner of fettuccine with fresh pesto, a garden salad, and rack of lamb ($18.95). As if that wasn't enough, I couldn't resist one of the French pastries that San Benito House is so famous for, Le Montmorency, a very rich chocolate cake with apricots.

Even though I was still feeling slightly full from dinner the night before, I came down for breakfast. And I have to admit I'm glad I did. There was a strong cup of Graffeo coffee, "fresh-from-the-oven" whole wheat bread with sweet butter and marmalade, a soft-boiled egg, and fresh fruit. Though breakfast is usually served in the dining room, it can be had out in the garden, or taken on a tray to the room for a leisurely breakfast in bed.

Half Moon Bay's Pacific Ocean setting offers uncrowded beaches and an outstanding tide pool area. There are hiking trails through a nearby redwood forest and several local wineries for touring. Whale watching, fishing, horseback riding, and bicycling are popular area activities.

Mill Rose Inn

615 Mill Street
Half Moon Bay, California 94019; (415) 726-9794

INNKEEPERS:	*Eve and Terry Baldwin.*
ACCOMMODATIONS:	*Six rooms, all with private bath; double, queen-, and king-size beds.*
RESERVATIONS:	*Four to six weeks recommended.*
MINIMUM STAY:	*Two nights on weekends and holidays.*
DEPOSIT:	*In full.*
CREDIT CARDS:	*AE, MC, VISA.*
RATES:	*Expensive.*
RESTRICTIONS:	*No children under 12. No pets.*

J ust at the end of four-block-long Mill Street is perhaps one of the most spectacular floral displays to be
found in all of San Mateo County, but most certainly
in the area of Half Moon Bay. This intense profusion of
color with an English country garden accent is the work
of ornamental horticulturist Terry Baldwin, who, with his
interior decorator wife, Eve, turned what was once a non-
descript, two-bedroom cottage into an inn that takes luxury in bed and breakfast lodging one step further.

The Baldwins' garden sports lilies, sweet peas, daisies, poppies, irises, delphiniums, lobelia, and English
lavender. In addition to the hundreds of carefully groomed
annuals and perennials, there are over two hundred different varieties of roses in bloom.

Guest rooms at Mill Rose could conceivably grace
the pages of *Architectural Digest*. All are equipped with
full-size private baths, hand-painted tile fireplaces, cable
television (hidden in the armoire), and even private-line
telephones. Not that this resembles a small hotel either—no
indeed. Rooms are also furnished with both fresh and silk
flower arrangements, fancy soaps and luxurious towels, his
and hers Japanese dressing gowns, a radio alarm clock,
and a well-stocked refrigerator. Each morning the daily
newspaper is delivered to the door.

Favorite hideaways (which now number six with the
recent addition of a four-room annex) include the Renais-

sance Rose (where I've stayed twice), Bordeaux Rose Suite, Botticelli Rose, and the Burgundy Rose Room with its claw-foot tub for two. All rooms have canopy or brass beds and European antiques. A hydrotherapy spa with high-powered jets sits inside the garden gazebo surrounded by tropical blooms and a charming brick courtyard with fragrant vines and a cascading fountain.

The evening wine and cheese hour affords the opportunity to mingle with other guests you might not have met previously, due to the fact that most of the accommodations at Mill Rose feature their own private entrances. The innkeepers are on hand to expound the joys of sightseeing in the area and to place calls for dinner reservations, as most bed and breakfast hosts do.

Half Moon Bay is a town that flows with the seasons: the annual Pumpkin Festival in late October attracts visitors from near and far; in December the area's Christmas tree farms allow you to select or cut down your own at prices that are half what you'd expect to pay in the city; the elephant seals at Año Nuevo are a big draw October through March; there's an annual Fourth of July parade with fireworks; whale-watching tours are popular in winter; and farm-fresh produce is available all year round. (Needless to say, Eve incorporates only the freshest of fruits, vegetables, and dairy products into her breakfast. Quiche Lorraine, an herb omelette, or fresh fruit crêpes comprise the entrée. Champagne accompanies each meal, as does coffee, tea, or Mexican hot chocolate.)

Mill Rose's location, just thirty-five miles south of San Francisco, makes it a prime candidate for a mid-week break for some relaxation or rest. It's also a good stopping point for a late Friday evening escape to Carmel or the Central Coast. Mill Rose is good to keep in mind, too, if you're heading up the coast on Highway 1 from Los Angeles or San Diego.

Old Thyme Inn

779 Main Street
Half Moon Bay, California 94019; (415) 726-1616

INNKEEPERS:	*Anne and Simon Lowings.*
ACCOMMODATIONS:	*Six rooms, four with private bath; twin, double, and queen-size beds.*
RESERVATIONS:	*Three to four weeks for weekends.*
MINIMUM STAY:	*None.*
DEPOSIT:	*First night's lodging.*
CREDIT CARDS:	*MC, VISA.*
RATES:	*Inexpensive to moderate.*
RESTRICTIONS:	*Children during mid-week only. Pets, negotiable.*

"Family run and friendly" was how Simon Lowings described his inn as he poured the complimentary wine for his guests that evening. But then Simon makes the breakfasts, too. One morning his treats may include fresh orange juice, fruit soup, three kinds of English cheeses, and homemade French cherry flan. Another day, breakfast may start off with melon and kiwi topped with sorbet and advance to whole wheat scones dusted with cinnamon and sugar, cold cuts, and coffee heated on an old potbellied stove.

Set in a historic Victorian built in 1899, the Lowings' Old Thyme Inn shows off six equally pleasant rooms for guest occupation along with a comfortable living room complete with wood-burning stove. The herb motif is everywhere, even in the name and tone of each room. Cozy and intimate, the Chamomile Room features an antique American double bed (as well as a twin) and shares a bath with the next-door Lavender Room. The roomier Lavender setting includes a queen-size iron bed and lavender and white Laura Ashley wallpaper. Sun pours into the Oregano Room, which, like the Chamomile, has an antique double bed, this one made in France. It also has a private bath with claw-foot tub.

For a bit more money, you can enjoy the rose and green–colored Thyme Room's luxurious canopied bed, fireplace, private bath, and double-size whirlpool tub, one of the two at the hostelry. The other is found in the Rosemary Room, which has a stained-glass window and queen-size iron bed. The all-green Mint Room catches an ocean view and features a claw-foot tub in its bath, as well as a fireplace set with logs.

The Lowings settled in Half Moon Bay in 1975 but didn't spend much time there until 1985 when Simon, a mining engineer, quit his job. Life in the mining camps of both South Africa and Wyoming gave the English-bred couple time to dream of a better, more family-oriented existence for themselves and their two children. "That was when I began to think about opening a bed and breakfast inn," Simon recalls. When they finally found this all-redwood Queen Anne practically in their own backyard, they knew it could be turned into an ideal lodge.

The party they held to celebrate their purchase of the property was no ordinary celebration. "We gave floor plans of the existing home to each of the fifty friends we invited and asked them to come up with ideas to improve the house," says Simon. "In the weeks that followed, almost everyone came through with suggestions that were promptly distilled and slapped squarely on the desk of an architect." Through the ensuing months Simon and several of his pals worked day and night to build bedrooms onto the top of the garage and construct a house in the backyard for use as the Lowings' own private residence.

Informal breakfasts, the fragrance of sweet peas and herbs from the garden, and firewood crackling into the wee hours of the night are only some of the pleasures of the "kick-back" atmosphere you'll find here. Take note: rates drop to *below* reasonable levels during the week; and, perhaps best of all, there's not the two-night minimum that some other inns require.

The Lowings are quick to answer questions about the many activities Half Moon Bay has to offer. Their personal recommendations range from a visit to nearby Fitzgerald Marine Reserve, which has some of the state's richest tide pools, or a whale-watching tour out of Princeton harbor, to horseback riding on one of the nine nearby state beaches or a stroll along the community's Main Street with its quaint country stores and boutiques.

Chateau Des Fleurs

7995 Highway Nine
Ben Lomond, California 95005; (408) 336-8943

INNKEEPERS:	*Lee and Laura Jonas.*
ACCOMMODATIONS:	*Three rooms, all with private bath; queen-size beds.*
RESERVATIONS:	*Two to three weeks recommended.*
MINIMUM STAY:	*None.*
DEPOSIT:	*First night's lodging.*
CREDIT CARDS:	*MC, VISA.*
RATES:	*Moderate.*
RESTRICTIONS:	*No children under 16. No pets.*

S nug in the Santa Cruz foothills of the Coastal Range is the newest addition to Santa Cruz County's roster of bed and breakfast inns. Chateau Des Fleurs, a late-1870s Victorian, once belonged to William Bartlett, who brought the Bartlett pear from Europe to northern California. He and his wife, Flora, derived their livelihood selling pears from their orchard to the canneries of nearby Santa Cruz. After Will died and the canneries closed down, Flora was frequently seen in her green Ford peddling pears along Highway 9, perhaps making a living the only way she knew how.

Needless to say, four Bartlett pear trees sit proudly on the property that surrounds the home today—now under the tender care of Lee and Laura Jonas. These, along with stately redwoods and large apple trees, can be viewed from a long wall of picture windows in the family room, hub of the bed and breakfast inn's activities.

This family room is packed with all sorts of games, including darts and horseshoes, plus a forty-six-inch color television, an extensive library, and a piano used for frequent sing-alongs. An adjoining parlor holds blue velvet recliners, a comfortable floral print sofa, a fireplace, and a century-old pump organ.

Lee and Laura's home features three guest rooms with queen-size beds and private baths. The Orchid Room, with its white wicker chairs, looks out onto a sunny deck. The interior is friendly: an oak dresser, a desk, a big white iron bed with down comforter, a bouquet of silk orchids, and a ceiling fan.

While lying in the Violet Room's brass-trimmed bed, you can gaze out at the tall trees through the beige Bishop Sleeve–style lace curtains. Silk wallpaper that swirls with clusters of tiny violets and a white table with a burgundy and violet flower arrangement lend the room its name. This room also contains an oak dresser and two wood and cane captain's chairs.

Rose is the color (and name) of the largest and most luxurious of the guest rooms. With rose-painted walls, rose bouquets on the dresser, and several flower-filled oil paintings, a stay here is akin to an afternoon in a garden. Even so, one of its main draws is the antique claw-foot tub enclosed by lace curtains on a raised wooden platform.

A piping hot breakfast is served at 9:00 A.M. sharp in the formal dining room downstairs. Sitting around an oblong dark oak table that seats six, with an inviting fireplace off to the side, guests are served juices, coffee, fresh fruit or baked apples, banana nut muffins with honey butter, or, if Laura feels like making an old family recipe, an almond-filled pastry called Swedish Kringler that's highly addictive. Cheese blintzes smothered with strawberries, quiche Lorraine, egg and cheese soufflé, waffles, and French custard toast are other favorites your hostess occasionally whips up.

Think of your stay in this mountain retreat as a center for exploring such nearby attractions as Santa Cruz's sandy beaches, Henry Cowell State Park (lots of hiking trails), Roaring Camp (ride the full-scale steam train and eat barbecue or bring your own picnic), and the more than twenty antique shops scattered between Lee and Laura's home and the coast.

Chateau Victorian

118 First Street
Santa Cruz, California 95060; (408) 458-9458

INNKEEPERS:	*Franz and Alice-June Benjamin.*
ACCOMMODATIONS:	*Seven rooms, all with private bath; queen-size beds.*
RESERVATIONS:	*Three to five weeks for summer weekends; two weeks off-season.*
MINIMUM STAY:	*None.*
DEPOSIT:	*First night's lodging.*
CREDIT CARDS:	*AE, MC, VISA.*
RATES:	*Moderate.*
RESTRICTIONS:	*No children. No pets.*

E ach year thousands of tourists flock to the beach at Santa Cruz. If you're one of them, and one who might enjoy a taste of gracious living at the same time, you'll be delighted to know about Chateau Victorian.

You won't have any problem spotting Chateau Victorian once you're in the neighborhood — which is crowded with motels and eateries and is just a block from the beach — it's painted bright orange (pumpkin, to be exact) with brown and white trim. A quaint Pennsylvania Dutch "Welcome" sign hangs in the front window.

One of the main attractions here are innkeepers Franz and Alice-June Benjamin, an easy-going, personable pair who fit right in with the beach's laid-back atmosphere. Of them a guest book entry raves: "You have elevated the business of innkeeping to an art form of which we are among the contented and appreciative beneficiaries."

Guest rooms have three things in common: queen-size beds, private baths, and fireplaces. One room has an ocean view; and antiques, brass beds, and window seats are much in evidence throughout. The Patio Room (so named from its private entrance off the back patio) is decorated in mauve and white, and furnished with a white iron and brass bed and an armoire. The original Victorian-era fireplace adds warmth on a cool summer's eve.

The room I occupied, Natural Bridges, was warm

and intimate with its delicately patterned beige and brown wallpaper, contrasting dark-wood ceiling beams, shuttered windows, iron and brass bed, and French armoire. As the sun set, the lights were dimmed, and the fireplace was lit, I couldn't envision a more romantic hideaway.

"It's a wonderful life, this innkeeping life," Franz remarked as he poured my first cup of coffee of the morning. "Ninety-nine point nine percent of the people who walk through that front door are happy and looking for a good time." A second cup of coffee (an aromatic Viennese roast) was accompanied with freshly baked croissants with whipped unsalted butter, cream cheese, and orange marmalade. A platter of fresh fruit (papaya, melon, strawberries, blackberries, and bananas) was also part of this help-yourself buffet breakfast, scheduled from 9:00 to 10:30. I partook in the dining room, but Franz and Alice-June were equally agreeable to guests taking their breakfast to the patio or out to the front deck.

Locally produced Bargetto wines, as well as cheese and crackers, were set out from 5:00 to 7:00 P.M. A nightcap of cognac was offered.

Besides the beach, the world-famous Santa Cruz Beach Boardwalk amusement park draws visitors from far and near. An interesting sidelight: more than twenty-five million people have ridden the boardwalk's Giant Dipper roller coaster, recognized as one of the ten best in the world. The city's annual events include a clam chowder cookoff in late February, a tug of war and volleyball tournament in May, a wharf-to-wharf (Santa Cruz to Capitola) footrace in July, and a Monarch butterfly festival in October.

Cliff Crest
Bed & Breakfast Inn

407 Cliff Street
Santa Cruz, California 95060; (408) 427-2609

INNKEEPERS:	*Bruce and Sharon Taylor.*
ACCOMMODATIONS:	*Five rooms, all with private bath; queen- and king-size beds.*
RESERVATIONS:	*One month for summer weekends.*
MINIMUM STAY:	*Two nights for holiday weekends.*
DEPOSIT:	*First night's lodging.*
CREDIT CARDS:	*AE, MC, VISA.*
RATES:	*Moderate.*
RESTRICTIONS:	*No pets.*

Just up the hill from Chateau Victorian is Cliff Crest, a bed and breakfast inn that offers a quieter location from which to enjoy Santa Cruz's sandy beaches, fishing pier, and nostalgia-filled boardwalk. But Cliff Crest is a local historical landmark as well. It's the former residence of William Jeter, lieutenant governor of California (1890) and one-time mayor of Santa Cruz.

The home's five guest rooms are graced with antiques and fresh flowers. The Empire Room, a large room with fireplace on the main floor, features a four-poster cano-pied bed, an armoire, hardwood floors with plum carpet-ing, and a garden view. A cozy upstairs hideaway is the Apricot Room, with its white antique queen-size bed. The Grey Room (shades of soft blue and pale grey) offers a French queen-size bed and a tiled shower for two. The Rose Room, a sunny upstairs room with views of Monterey Bay and the Santa Cruz Mountains, has an Eastlake Victorian bed, a sitting area, and an adjacent bath with a Victorian claw-foot tub. The Pineapple Room, named for its four-poster bed with pineapples carved on the posts, harbors an 1887 stained-glass window.

Innkeepers Bruce and Sharon Taylor describe them-selves as "friendly and easygoing." And it's evident they have gone out of their way to provide guests with the comforts of a "home away from home": a lazy hammock between the trees, an umbrella table and chairs on the terrace, stimulating games (Trivial Pursuit, Scrabble), and subscriptions to three daily newspapers (the *San Francisco Chronicle*, the *Santa Cruz Sentinel*, and the *Wall Street Journal*).

Sharon serves an inviting breakfast to the room — juices, fresh fruits in season, French toast, phyllo specialties, muffins and coffee cakes, along with coffee, tea, and hot chocolate. If preferred, breakfast can be enjoyed on the terrace or in the solarium, with its picture windows looking out to the beautifully landscaped gardens designed by Mr. Jeter's friend, John McLaren, the landscape architect of Golden Gate Park.

The Pelican Inn

Marin County

Sonoma County

Cloverdale
Ye Olde Shelford House
Campbell Ranch Inn
The Hope-Merrill House
Healdsburg
Belle de Jour
Grape Leaf Inn
Haydon House
101

Ridenhour Ranch House Inn
Guerneville

Pygmalion House
Santa Rosa

116

1 *Green Apple Inn*
Cotati
12
Chalet Bed and Breakfast
Sonoma

Tomales
Petaluma

Blackthorne Inn
Ten Inverness Way Inverness
101
37

Point Reyes
Holly Tree Inn

1 *Mountain Home Inn*
Mill Valley

Bolinas
The Pelican Inn
101

Mountain Home Inn

810 Panoramic Highway
Mill Valley, California 94941; (415) 381-9000

INNKEEPERS:	*Ed and Susan Cunningham.*
ACCOMMODATIONS:	*Ten rooms, all with private bath; queen- and king-size beds.*
RESERVATIONS:	*Four to six weeks recommended.*
MINIMUM STAY:	*Two nights over holiday periods.*
DEPOSIT:	*First night's lodging.*
CREDIT CARDS:	*AE, MC, VISA.*
RATES:	*Moderate to expensive.*
RESTRICTIONS:	*Children discouraged. No pets.*

After searching out over one hundred sites for a bed and breakfast inn in California, Ed Cunningham found Mount Tamalpais's Mountain Home Inn right in his own backyard. The inn, the last remaining commercial establishment on the mountain, is located on a scenic ridge just above Muir Woods. Originally built in 1912 by a Swiss couple homesick for their beloved Alps, it is bordered by over 340,000 acres of parklands and hiking trails.

The grand, national park hotels of the thirties, such as the Awahnee at Yosemite, the Timberline Lodge at Mount Hood, and the Glacier Park Lodge, served as inspiration for the building's three-tiered redwood, cedar, and glass reconstruction. All ten guest rooms have gorgeous views and private baths. Most have terraces; some, fireplaces and Jacuzzis. Each room is supplied with champagne as well as trailhead maps, making a guest feel equally comfortable whether dressed in evening clothes or hiking attire.

Room rates, quoted for two, include an expanded Continental breakfast. Mountain Home's chef also prepares lunches and dinners for the inn's on-premise gourmet restaurant. Cuisines from around the world are represented with fresh, local ingredients forming the base of each meal. Recharged travelers can request a picnic lunch "to go." The offerings include grilled chicken breasts or sandwiches, fresh fruit, cake, and even champagne.

Mount Tamalpais has always been an international meeting place; transplanted Europeans, tourists, and Bay Area residents alike revel in the splendor of the wilderness and the sweeping panoramas. Until 1884, the only access to Mount Tam was by cow trail. Later, a wagon road was followed by a scenic railway dubbed "the crookedest railroad in the world" because of its twenty-two trestles and 281 curves. Today's smoothly paved, two-lane road makes going up the mountainside much more pleasant.

Located at the junction of many popular hiking trails, Mountain Home Inn is also just a mile and a half from the outdoor Mountain Play Theatre, site of summertime theater productions. Scenic Muir Woods is two miles from the inn. Audubon Canyon Ranch, a sanctuary for great blue herons, and the Point Reyes Bird Observatory are no more than a twenty-minute drive. There are also nearby stables for horseback rides.

Stinson Beach, the largest beach in southwestern Marin County, is also the nearest coastal town to the inn. Stinson's many arts and crafts shops, surf equipment rental facilities, bookstore, and library are of interest. The delis in town can provide the fixings for an impromptu beach picnic.

The Pelican Inn

10 Pacific Way
Muir Beach, California 94965; (415) 383-6000

INNKEEPERS:	*Barry and Pamela Stock.*
ACCOMMODATIONS:	*Six rooms, all with private bath; queen-size beds.*
RESERVATIONS:	*Six months recommended.*
MINIMUM STAY:	*None.*
DEPOSIT:	*In full.*
CREDIT CARDS:	*MC, VISA.*
RATES:	*Moderate to expensive.*
RESTRICTIONS:	*No pets.*

For bed and breakfast in the spirit of sixteenth-century England's west country, plan to stay at the Pelican Inn. The Pelican is located at Muir Beach, scarcely twenty minutes north of the Golden Gate Bridge.

It was here on the Marin Coast that Sir Francis Drake beached his *Pelican* (the ship was renamed the *Golden Hinde* in mid-voyage) some four hundred years ago to claim California for Queen Elizabeth I and her descendants.

The inn is a weathered-looking English Tudor–style farmhouse that sits nestled between the ocean and the redwoods of the Golden Gate National Recreation Area. The main floor of the building houses a traditional English pub and a public dining room. Pub grub includes both fish 'n' chips and bangers and mash; prime rib and beef Wellington are listed among the dinner entrées. The bar, with its low beams, dart board, and good fellowship, is well stocked with imported brew (Bass, Watney, and John Courage on tap), wine, port, and sherry.

Overnight accommodations are located on the second floor. The rooms, with their low doorjambs and leaded windows, are graced with English antiques, heavily draped half-tester (canopy) beds, and Oriental rugs that cover the hardwood floors. Each room has a private bath.

Renaissance music, burning candles, and a roaring fire in the great inglenook set the tone for the proper English breakfast of bangers, bacon and eggs (any style), broiled tomatoes, toast with Scotch marmalade, orange juice, coffee, and tea. A stay of any length is like an ongoing tea party. And speaking of tea, Darjeeling tea with biscuits and "all things nice" can be had throughout the day by the fire or while curled up in bed with a good book.

Holly Tree Inn

3 Silverhills Road
Inverness Park, California
Mailing address: P.O. Box 642
Point Reyes Station, CA 94956; (415) 663-1554

INNKEEPERS:	*Diane and Tom Balogh.*
ACCOMMODATIONS:	*Four rooms, all with private bath; double, queen-, and king-size beds. Guest cottage.*
RESERVATIONS:	*Four weeks recommended.*
MINIMUM STAY:	*Two nights on weekends.*
DEPOSIT:	*In full.*
CREDIT CARDS:	*MC, VISA.*
RATES:	*Moderate.*
RESTRICTIONS:	*No pets.*

D iane Balogh relates a story about the afternoon a young couple rode up on horses to inquire about a room for the night. But this was nothing unusual as the Baloghs' inn — the Holly Tree Inn — is located just a mile or so from Point Reyes National Seashore, which offers a variety of outdoor activities, among them hiking, fishing, boating, birdwatching, beachcombing, whale watching, and, of course, horseback riding.

This comfortable and spacious two-story home reminiscent of a hunting lodge was built by a Swede in the late 1930s. The Baloghs, who had set their hearts on an inn of their own after staying at one in Maine in 1975, found the nineteen-acre estate on their first trip out with a realtor. They concluded the deal within a matter of days, moved in, and rented the downstairs as an apartment while the second-story conversion was taking shape.

Central to the inn is the light, airy living room with its huge brick fireplace and overstuffed sofas upholstered in provincial prints. This is a wonderful place for conversation, a complimentary glass of wine in the afternoon, or a daydream or two.

The living room opens up to the dining area, which also features a fireplace and a cozy setting for the 9:30 A.M.

buffet-style breakfast. One morning it might include pancakes and sausage with fresh fruit, coffee, tea, and orange juice. The next you might get a sampling of Diane's quiche or an omelette with homemade poppy seed bread.

There are four guest rooms — the Laurel Room, the Holly Room, the Ivy Room, and Mary's Garden — and a newly built guest cottage located up the valley a short way from the main house. The Laurel Room is the most private as well as the largest. Decorated in shades of pale blue and white, it has a comfortable sitting area and a king-size bed. The lace-edged sheets and white ruffled curtains set the mood in the Ivy Room, with its view of the flowery hillside and ivied latticework just outside the cottage windows. The Holly Room overlooks the front lawn with its flower-covered wishing well. Country antiques and peace and quiet are features the rooms have in common.

Unlike many other inns, the Holly Tree welcomes children. In fact the Baloghs have two very well-behaved children of their own.

Blackthorne Inn

266 Vallejo
P.O. Box 712
Inverness, California 94937; (415) 663-8621

INNKEEPERS:	Bill and Susan Wigert.
ACCOMMODATIONS:	Five rooms with shared baths; double and queen-size beds.
RESERVATIONS:	Six to eight weeks for weekends; two weeks for weekdays.
MINIMUM STAY:	Two nights on weekends and holidays.
DEPOSIT:	In full.
CREDIT CARDS:	MC, VISA.
RATES:	Moderate to expensive.
RESTRICTIONS:	No children. No pets.

*B*est described by *Sunset* magazine, Bill and Susan Wigert's Blackthorne Inn is "a carpenter's fantasy, with decks, hot tub, fireman's pole, and spiral staircase." But then Blackthorne Inn, which resembles a giant treehouse, has gotten so much press. Its Eagle's Nest, an octagonal, glassed-in tower was named "the most romantic, magical room on the coast" by Simon and Schuster's *West Coast Bed and Breakfast Guide*.

Actually, five guest rooms span the structure's four stories. The Studio, the inn's most spacious guest room, occupies part of the first floor. It offers a private entrance, a queen-size bed, and a separate sitting room with forest view, as well as a private redwood deck. The Hideaway, the other first floor room, is a must for night owls or late sleepers. It not only has a private entrance, but is situated so that it filters out the early morning light and sounds. Overlook and the Lupine Room are third-floor accommodations that share a hall bath. Stained-glass windows in the Overlook Room depict three common local wildflowers: poppy, iris, and thistle. The room also holds a queen-size bed, a beveled mirror, and an antique dresser. The Lupine Room, with its big brass bed, is connected by bridgeway to a hillside deck where the hot tub is located.

The second floor of the house is masculine, even

robust, in decor with strong lines and features. It encompasses a giant stone fireplace, a stained-glass window, skylights, and is surrounded by a 3,500-square-foot deck. Oriental area rugs cover hardwood floors; contemporary furnishings, antiques and collectibles, books, a stereo system, and menus from local restaurants fill the living room. Breakfast is served buffet style in the adjacent dining room at 9:30 A.M. Two kinds of coffee cake (apricot and poppy seed are not unusual), a home-baked quiche, tangy orange juice, fresh fruits, yogurt, and granola follow the early morning coffee and tea.

Blackthorne had its inception in 1973 when the Wigerts purchased a one-acre parcel on the northern side of Fish Hatchery Creek Canyon. "We used to hike the area," remembered Sue, "and always wished for our own place here." When they purchased the property, only a two-room cabin occupied the land. Well-meaning friends suggested that Bill add on a deck, and that was just the beginning of what turned out to be a three-year project. As the dwelling grew, room by room, from 1975 to 1978, another pal suggested that the couple turn the ever-expanding home into a bed and breakfast operation.

Located just an hour north of San Francisco, near the Point Reyes seashore, the inn offers a spectacular setting: long stretches of beach dotted with tide pools, nearby lagoons and bird sanctuaries, rolling hillside pastures, and densely wooded forests. "I think of this peninsula as primordial, prehistoric," says Sue.

Woodsy, yet elegant in its own casual fashion, what rings true about Blackthorne is this: it's very *Marin*.

Ten Inverness Way

10 Inverness Way
Inverness, California 94937; (415) 669-1648

INNKEEPER:	*Mary Davies.*
ACCOMMODATIONS:	*Four rooms, all with private bath; twin, double, and queen-size beds.*
RESERVATIONS:	*Four to six weeks recommended.*
MINIMUM STAY:	*Two nights on weekends.*
DEPOSIT:	*In full.*
CREDIT CARDS:	*MC, VISA.*
RATES:	*Moderate.*
RESTRICTIONS:	*No pets.*

Ten Inverness Way is a four-bedroom guest house that was built in 1904. The living room still has its original Douglas fir paneling and massive stone fireplace, and the guest rooms that were once family bedrooms retain that character. The entire house is furnished with what the proprietor calls "comfortable antiques," and the rooms are filled with fresh flowers (daisies, fuchsias, carnations, and poppies, to name just a few) from the garden that surrounds the house.

Mary Davies, a former Sacramento legislative director, has owned and operated Ten Inverness Way since 1979. She brings to it what might best be described as "a woman's touch": a flair for decorating, a feel for comfort, and the warmth of a friendly smile.

The living room is a great place to curl up with your favorite book. If you didn't bring one along you can choose from the wide selection that fills the bookshelf. The books (subjects range from religion to the arts, psychology to the classics) reflect the broad range of interests of the innkeeper. The player piano provides the evening's entertainment, and complimentary sherry can be enjoyed by the fire.

The bedrooms, all on the second floor, feature antique furniture, handmade rugs, and patchwork quilts. The most popular room in the house is at the top of the stairs. It's also the largest and the sunniest room; its four multipaned windows overlook the front garden.

There's a full American-style breakfast to start the day off right. Banana pancakes and cheese-scrambled eggs are the specialties. Egg-based dishes might be complemented by homemade bread one morning and freshly baked coffee cake the next. Fresh fruit, coffee, and tea come with every breakfast.

Ten Inverness Way is located just off Sir Francis Drake Boulevard (the main street that runs through town). From the inn you can reach the village shops, restaurants, and Point Reyes National Seashore on foot. Golden Gate Transit provides service between San Francisco and Inverness; the bus stop is a block from the house.

Chalet Bed and Breakfast

18935 Fifth Street West
Sonoma, California 95476; (707) 996-0190

INNKEEPERS:	*Patrick and Lolita Murphy.*
ACCOMMODATIONS:	*Four rooms share two baths; double beds. Guest cottage with wood-burning stove.*
RESERVATIONS:	*Four weeks recommended.*
MINIMUM STAY:	*None.*
DEPOSIT:	*In full.*
CREDIT CARDS:	*MC, VISA.*
RATES:	*Moderate.*
RESTRICTIONS:	*No pets.*

*I*t was late when I pulled into Sonoma. The Murphys have probably given up on me by now, I thought to myself as I fumbled around for the street map. As I crossed Fifth Street, I saw no sign of the Chalet—or anything resembling a bed and breakfast inn. I pulled the establishment's card out of my purse. ". . . overnite accommodations in a wonderful country farm setting. . . ." Fifth Street didn't look like a "country farm setting" to me. I saw trailer courts and tract houses, gas stations and shopping centers, but no sign of "the country." Exasperated, I pulled up to a pay phone in Safeway's parking lot. "Hello, Lolita? H-E-L-P!"

All's well that ends well, so they say. And let me be the first to tell you that Fifth Street ends well—well up a one-lane dirt road. And yes, the Chalet, the first bed and breakfast opened in Sonoma, is situated in a country-like setting, complete with chickens and goats.

The house is a two-story Swiss chalet built in 1940. It is furnished with a mix of country antiques and collectibles: 1920 radios, patchwork quilts, wicker furniture, cast-iron stoves, Navajo rugs, antique dolls, and California pottery.

Accommodations consist of two downstairs bedrooms that share a bath and a sitting room, and two upstairs rooms with a shared bath. The upstairs parlor has a wood-burning stove and limited kitchen facilities. There's an extra bed for a child or a third adult in one of the downstairs rooms. The overall feel reflects Lolita's personal preference for "antiques, comfort, and good food."

Speaking of good food, the innkeepers offer a hearty, farm-style breakfast that starts off with freshly squeezed orange juice, a fruit cup, sausage and eggs (or the "omelette of the day"), a home-baked walnut coffee cake, and French roast coffee. Fresh fruits and vegetables from the garden and eggs from the chickens are included in the menu.

The Chalet is located in the Valley of the Moon, a fascinating area steeped in early California history and surrounded by wineries and vineyards. Sonoma's central plaza (a great place to sightsee, shop, and picnic) is just three-quarters of a mile from the inn. The town's bakery, cheese factory, and sausage shop can supply all the makings for a picnic on the square or at nearby Jack London State Park.

Pygmalion House

331 Orange Street
Santa Rosa, California 95401; (707) 526-3407

INNKEEPER:	*Lola Wright.*
ACCOMMODATIONS:	*Five rooms, all with private bath; twin, double, queen-, and king-size beds.*
RESERVATIONS:	*Three weeks recommended.*
MINIMUM STAY:	*None.*
DEPOSIT:	*First night's lodging.*
CREDIT CARDS:	*MC, VISA.*
RATES:	*Inexpensive.*
RESTRICTIONS:	*Children by arrangement. No pets.*

S anta Rosa was never on my "top ten" list of places to visit in California. But since I was searching out bed and breakfast inns and had heard of one that opened there, I thought I'd stop by. I spotted a beautifully restored, freshly painted Victorian from the freeway and something (perhaps intuition, perhaps experience) told me that if there was a b&b in Santa Rosa this was it. I followed directions a friend had jotted down: Downtown exit from 101. Third Street to Wilson. Left turn. Two blocks to Laurel. Another left. A right onto Orange. Last house on the right. It came as no surprise that the last house on the right and the house I saw from the freeway were one and the same: Pygmalion House.

The house is a classic example of what one expects of a bed and breakfast. It exudes homeyness and history, and from a typical bed and breakfast enthusiast's point of view, it's just the right size.

Each of the five bedrooms offers a private bath, and each is named for the predominant color of its decor. The Blue Room wins my vote of approval: blue and white flowered wallpaper, plush blue carpeting, French Provincial furnishings, lace curtains, and a king-size bed. The bathroom has an old-fashioned claw-foot tub with brass fixtures.

Guests enjoy a full, hearty breakfast: corn flakes and

granola, fresh fruit in season, yogurt, ham, bacon, or sausage and eggs, a hot bread basket, coffee, and freshly squeezed orange juice. Other amenities: the morning paper, fresh flowers in the room, and sherry in the parlor in the afternoon.

Lola Wright brings to Pygmalion House twenty-five years of experience staying at b&b's throughout Europe and ten years as manager of an inn in Hawaii. Accordingly she defines her innkeeping style as incorporating European comfort and attention with southern hospitality and lots of Aloha spirit.

Pygmalion House is adjacent to Railroad Square, the historical section of Santa Rosa that is rapidly gaining popularity for its shops and fine restaurants. And, as I discovered, Santa Rosa is central to many areas of interest: the Napa and Sonoma wine country, the Russian River, San Francisco, Point Reyes National Seashore, and the ocean.

Green Apple Inn

520 Bohemian Highway
Freestone, California 95472; (707) 874-2526

INNKEEPERS:	*Rogers and Rosemary Hoffman.*
ACCOMMODATIONS:	*Four rooms share two baths; twin and double beds.*
RESERVATIONS:	*Two weeks recommended.*
MINIMUM STAY:	*Two nights on summer weekends and during holiday periods.*
DEPOSIT:	*First night's lodging.*
CREDIT CARDS:	*Not accepted.*
RATES:	*Inexpensive.*
RESTRICTIONS:	*No children under 7.*

I n the late nineteenth century two brothers, joint owners of one of the original homes in the town of Freestone, had a serious falling out. The burning issue has long since been forgotten, but the consequence remains. Showing more logic than good sense, one brother sawed off his half of the house and took it elsewhere. Astonished, the other brother rolled in another house and tacked it on to the wounded building.

Although the general consensus within the village is that this story is true, there is a strong difference of opinion about which of the Freestone homes the story applies to.

Rogers and Rosemary Hoffman, proprietors of the Green Apple Inn, invite you to note the different structural styles within their home, and they make the case that, indeed, it is this house that resulted from the historic feud.

The Hoffmans' Green Apple Inn is located on five acres of meadowland and redwood groves. Its sitting room, four guest rooms, and two baths provide an intimate atmosphere for socializing and spinning a few yarns of one's own. Heirlooms and family treasures fill the house; the most unusual of these are Rogers's great-grandfather's Civil War gun (a portrait of the late Thomas Rogers hangs above the fireplace mantel), the 100-year-old Seth Thomas mantel clock, a Japanese wood carving, a coal scuttle from the turn of the century, a French Revolution–era etching, and a 250-year-old brass coffee urn. (Guest rooms hold iron and brass beds with fluffy patchwork and floral print comforters, marble-topped dressers, wicker pieces, and wildflowers.)

As expected, apple-based dishes make up the breakfast menu at the Green Apple Inn. Typical fare includes French toast with walnuts and apples, a fresh fruit salad or baked apple in wintertime, freshly baked apple bread with homemade marmalade, and coffee.

After breakfast you can take a walking tour of Freestone's award-winning nursery; visit the local bird farm, homespun clothing store, or metal sculpture workshop; hike through the surrounding hills and valleys; or tell your troubles to Maude, the Hoffmans' pet nanny goat.

Ridenhour
Ranch House Inn

12850 River Road
Guerneville, California 95446; (707) 887-1033

INNKEEPER:	*Richard Jewell.*
ACCOMMODATIONS:	*Eight rooms, five with private bath; double and queen-size beds.*
RESERVATIONS:	*Four weeks recommended.*
MINIMUM STAY:	*Two nights on weekends and holidays.*
DEPOSIT:	*First night's lodging.*
CREDIT CARDS:	*MC, VISA.*
RATES:	*Inexpensive to moderate.*
RESTRICTIONS:	*No children under 10. No pets.*

L ouis William Ridenhour was a homesteader from Missouri who came to California in 1850 and in 1856 began to farm the Ridenhour Ranch—940 acres on both sides of the Russian River. In 1906 his son, Louis E. Ridenhour, constructed a handsome ranch house of heart redwood on 2¼ acres of the property. The younger Ridenhour's daughter Virginia, and her husband, former Assistant Surgeon General Justin K. Fuller, eventually came into possession of the house. In 1977 it was sold and remodeled into a bed and breakfast inn. Current owner is Culinary Institute of America–trained chef, Richard Jewell.

This two-story, eleven-room house has eight bedrooms, a large country kitchen, and a formal dining room. The comfortable living room beckons guests to relax, chat, read, play cards, put together a puzzle, or just sit and sip a glass of port in front of the brick fireplace.

Each bedroom is individually and tastefully appointed with country English and American antique furnishings, quilts, Oriental rugs, the finest-quality linens, flowers, and plants. The bathroom medicine cabinets are stocked with toothpaste, Band-Aids, and other essentials one might have left behind.

Rick's extraordinarily flavorful breakfast—apple and

walnut potato crêpes, eggs Benedict, or amaretto and raspberry French toast accompanied by fresh-baked muffins (strawberry, banana-coconut, and banana–peanut butter)—is just what you would expect. This, along with animal-shaped, hand-carved fresh fruit, as well as juice and tea, is served each morning in the kitchen or the dining room. Trays are available for guests to take breakfast back to their room or out to the patio.

The informally landscaped grounds invite a stroll under the redwoods and oaks. The trees of the orchard yield a variety of fruit (apples, peaches, pears, and figs) for picking and eating. A hot tub is available for guests' use. Secluded river beaches are a short walk away. One can walk to Korbel Winery for a tour of their champagne cellars.

Some things to note: the inn is closed to the public during the months of January and February. On weekends dinners and picnic lunches are available upon request.

Grape Leaf Inn

539 Johnson Street
Healdsburg, California 95448; (707) 433-8140

INNKEEPERS:	*Terry Sweet and Kathy Cookson.*
ACCOMMODATIONS:	*Seven rooms, all with private bath; queen- and king-size beds.*
RESERVATIONS:	*Two to three months recommended.*
MINIMUM STAY:	*Two nights on weekends.*
DEPOSIT:	*First night's lodging.*
CREDIT CARDS:	*MC, VISA.*
RATES:	*Moderate.*
RESTRICTIONS:	*No children under 7. No pets.*

I liked Grape Leaf Inn when it was owned by Laura Salo, but I like it even more now that the new owner, Terry Sweet, has remodeled, expanded, and transformed this cute Queen Anne into a seven-bedroom, seven-bath gem that is surely the envy of the competition.

The inn is located in the small town of Healdsburg, a short bike ride from one of California's premier grape-growing regions: the Alexander Valley.

In keeping with the natural surroundings, the proprietor has named the guest rooms after grape varietals: Merlot, Pinot Noir, Gamay Rosé. Cabernet Sauvignon has skylight windows in both bedroom and bath. The Chardonnay Suite features stained-glass windows, an antique armoire, and a separate sitting room; there's an old-fashioned pull-chain toilet and a double-sink oak vanity in the bath. Sauvignon Blanc's brass and iron bed faces a bay window with a love seat. And the Zinfandel Room has a king-size bed, an antique oak dresser, and an Oriental rug that covers the hardwood floor. (The four upstairs rooms all have sloped roofs and two-person whirlpool tub/showers.)

Innkeeper Kathy Cookson pours a sampling of Sonoma County wine to go along with the Sonoma County cheeses that are served in the front parlor late each afternoon. Books, magazines, and games are available, or one can just sit and relax on the sofa in front of the fireplace.

A collection of local artists' paintings and photographs are on display throughout the inn.

A full country breakfast is served buffet style from 9:00 to 10:00 in the dining room. Featured dishes include Mexican eggs with guacamole, bacon and broccoli frittata, or quiche Lorraine; fresh blueberry or banana-almond coffee cake (the inn's most requested recipe); cereal and milk; fresh fruit in season (baked apples in winter); freshly ground coffee; and freshly squeezed orange juice.

Within walking distance of the inn are river beaches and night-lighted tennis courts. Bicycles can be rented just three blocks away for informal tours of the Wine Country. The innkeeper will make dinner reservations or arrangements for river canoe trips and other recreational activities.

Belle de Jour

16276 Healdsburg Avenue
Healdsburg, California 95448; (707) 433-7892

INNKEEPERS:	*Tom and Brenda Hearn.*
ACCOMMODATIONS:	*Five rooms, four with private bath; double, queen-, and king-size beds.*
RESERVATIONS:	*Two weeks recommended.*
MINIMUM STAY:	*Two nights on weekends and some holidays.*
DEPOSIT:	*$50.*
CREDIT CARDS:	*MC, VISA.*
RATES:	*Moderate.*
RESTRICTIONS:	*No pets.*

L et me introduce you to the *new* Belle de Jour. Tom and Brenda Hearn are now at the helm. This energetic young couple struck out from L.A.'s fast lane for the serenity of Sonoma County and a business of their own. They purchased the property, an 1875 Italianate Victorian, from former owner-innkeeper Custis Piper in February of 1986. Out went the "working farm" atmosphere, including the sheep, rabbits, and goats. In marched four friendly felines — one the ripe old age of twenty-two.

Six acres of flower, herb, and vegetable gardens, fruit-bearing trees, and cozy little nooks set the stage for the guest accommodations: one room with double brass bed and shared bath in the main house and four separate cottages overlooking the back meadow. The cottages, freshly painted and nestled in the pines, have fireplaces and antique wood-burning stoves. All include ceiling fans, and some also come with whirlpool tubs for two. Overall, the mix of contemporary and antique pieces make up what the innkeepers call a "California country" decor.

Guests enter the main house through the kitchen, with its gleaming copper pots and pans, large commercial range, and glass-front refrigerator — all an indication that this is one couple that takes breakfast seriously. "We emphasize three things," notes Brenda of the bountiful breakfast produced here each morning and served either on the deck or in the kitchen dining room at 9:00 A.M. sharp. "Freshness, variety, and abundance."

The house blend of java and a selection of fresh juices kick off the morning meal. Home-baked breads are accompanied by waffles or egg and cheese dishes with an abundance of fresh fruit. Sleepyheads like myself appreciate the option of having a Continental breakfast basket delivered to the room anytime between 7:30 and 10:30 A.M.; the only omission is the morning's hot entrée. (Picnic baskets or box lunches brimming with Sonoma County goodness and picnic-style dinners are also available upon request.)

Belle de Jour's location seldom leaves guests with nothing to do — that is, unless it's by choice. The countryside invites a crisp morning run or a bike ride. Golf, tennis, swimming, canoeing, and even kayaking are all available nearby. Local wineries are among the finest, and the backroads offer quaint country charm. A real treat, though, is a backroads/wineries tour in the Hearns' 1923 Star touring car. The 3 ½-hour trip concludes with a palate-pleasing lunch, Wine Country style.

Belle de Jour is now open seven days a week, year-round. From Highway 101 take the Dry Creek Road off ramp. Turn right on Dry Creek to the stoplight, then left on Healdsburg Avenue, and continue for approximately one mile. The Simi Winery tasting room is on the left, the *new* Belle de Jour on the right.

Haydon House

321 Haydon Street
Healdsburg, California 95448; (707) 433-5228

INNKEEPERS:	*Richard and Joanne Claus.*
ACCOMMODATIONS:	*Eight rooms, four with private bath; twin, double, and queen-size beds.*
RESERVATIONS:	*One month recommended.*
MINIMUM STAY:	*Two nights on weekends.*
DEPOSIT:	*First night's lodging.*
CREDIT CARDS:	*MC, VISA.*
RATES:	*Inexpensive to moderate.*
RESTRICTIONS:	*No children under 10. No pets.*

Haydon House has been called the "all-American home" and a "perfect expression of Main Street, America." Others appreciate the home for its fine decor. But whatever you term Haydon House's blend of warmly appointed furniture and late Victorian and early California Craftsman architecture, you'd never guess that it was once a boys' home, a rest home, and even a Catholic convent.

For over seventy years, the two-story Queen Anne played out its history on a little tree-lined street near Healdsburg's central plaza. Then in 1983 Richard and Joanne Claus purchased the property surrounded by a white picket fence and proceeded to eradicate all the traces of "old institution." Working nearly round-the-clock for several months, the Clauses cleaned, renovated, and repainted until the walls were awash in pastels and the rich fir floors glistened. Baskets of dried and silk flowers began to fill each of the bedrooms, and French and American antiques helped restore the grand look the home must have had when it was first built in 1912.

In addition to the vintage, claw-foot tubs in three of the six bedrooms of the main house, and the baskets overflowing with luxurious towels, I particularly liked the lace curtains, custom-made down comforters and matching bed linens, and the handmade Dhurrie rugs. Careful attention to period design is evident in the antique oak, walnut, and mahogany vanities with old-fashioned sinks. Downstairs, there's a pump organ with a special history: it was saved from the convent.

Although all of the second-floor bedrooms are charming, the Attic Suite, with its sloping ceiling, skylights, sitting room, queen-size iron and brass bed, and cane rocking chair, is the standout.

Two more rooms, each with luxurious whirlpool tub and dramatic skylights that look into the trees, are in a newly completed, Victorian-style cottage in the Clauses' backyard. "The Pine Room will have a four-poster pine pencil bed and other Shaker reproductions, as well as some antique pine pieces," said Joanne, whose friendly attitude is one of the inn's major assets. "The Victorian Room will be furnished with a mahogany vanity and other antiques, along with Ralph Lauren's Victorian-style wicker bed and rocker." White pine was shipped from Vermont for the floors.

Breakfast-time at Haydon House brings forth an unlimited buffet. Joanne serves everything from scrambled eggs, frittatas, and homemade bran muffins to fresh apple cake, coffee cakes, large bowls of melon and other fresh fruits with topping, and, on Sundays, Oklahoma pancakes with sweet maple syrup in the big sunny dining room. "Best plan on eating only two meals a day while staying at Haydon House," exclaimed one visitor in a letter to the *San Francisco Examiner.*

During the afternoon, you may want to go wine tasting at the dozens of little wineries that dot the Russian River, only a few blocks from the inn, and nearby Alexander Valley. Or better still, take a stroll to the plaza. Along the way, you'll find cafés, boutiques, gift shops, antique shops, and the Healdsburg Museum, which traces the city's Indian, pioneer, and agricultural past.

When you're thoroughly relaxed and imbued with the splendor of Wine Country atmosphere, wander back to the inn. There, in one of the house's two spacious parlors, you can celebrate a perfect ending to your vacation by sipping even more complimentary wine.

Campbell Ranch Inn

1475 Canyon Road
Geyserville, California 95441; (707) 857-3476

INNKEEPERS:	*Mary Jane and Jerry Campbell.*
ACCOMMODATIONS:	*Four rooms, two with private bath; king-size beds.*
RESERVATIONS:	*Two to three weeks recommended.*
MINIMUM STAY:	*Two nights on weekends.*
DEPOSIT:	*Half of full amount.*
CREDIT CARDS:	*Not accepted.*
RATES:	*Moderate.*
RESTRICTIONS:	*No children. No pets.*

A generous man will prosper; he who refreshes others will himself be refreshed.

Proverbs 11:25

I not only feel right at home at the Campbell Ranch, I feel as though I could return again and again. This is due in part to the serenity here. Perhaps it is also due to the fact that since the Campbells' living quarters are not separate from their inn operation, one immediately feels like part of the family. Then again it might just have something to do with that delicious banana cream pie (my favorite) that is served at the kitchen table just before bedtime. But no one describes the Campbell Ranch experience better than Mary Jane when she says, "People come here to *stay!*"

There's plenty more to stay for — picturesque hilltop views of lush rolling vineyards, a well-maintained swimming pool and hot tub spa, tennis courts, Ping-Pong, and horseshoes, not to mention bicycles and peaceful country roads.

The Campbell Ranch is a modern, split-level ranch-style home with traditional furnishings. The living room's two floral-patterned sofas sit face-to-face in front of a massive brick fireplace that divides the living room from the family room, where guests find chess, checkers, jigsaw puzzles, a stereo, and yes, even a television set.

The bedroom on the lower level (Room A) affords the most privacy, as it is the sole bedroom on this floor and is equipped with a private bath. Here you will find wood-paneled walls, green plants, a desk, and a comfortable reading chair, as well as a collection of *National Geographic* magazines dating from 1959 — enough to keep an armchair traveler holed-up here for years.

My favorite room was the one I stayed in overnight — preselected from the brochure for its Baldwin piano and balcony with a view of the countryside — Room B. There was a spacious closet, a desk, ivy plants, and shelves abounding with good reading material.

Mary Jane cites her job as a maid during college and her experience as a wife and mother (three boys) as the training ground for operating a bed and breakfast inn.

"Jerry's the handyman around here," she says. "He does all the grass cutting and repairs, though he loves socializing too. He is genuinely interested in people, and a good conversationalist."

The kitchen provides the setting for breakfast, which is served until 10:00 A.M. Monday through Saturday and until 9:00 A.M. on Sundays. Selections include a choice of cantaloupe with fresh strawberries, *or* freshly squeezed orange juice, *or* orange halves, *or* sliced bananas with sugar and cream. Group B selections consist of cold cereal, a cheese omelette, fried eggs and potatoes, or the Campbell Ranch egg puff (loaded with fresh sautéed mushrooms and Monterey Jack cheese). From Group C you can choose between white toast, zucchini bread, sour cream coffee cake, homemade honey-wheat loaf, or blueberry or bran muffins. And finally, the beverages: coffee, tea, milk, or hot chocolate.

There's plenty to do after breakfast for those who aren't content to just *stay*: winery tours, a nearby dam and fish hatchery, and canoeing or tubing on the Russian River (just seven minutes away). Snoopyland, home of cartoonist Charles Shultz, is in nearby Santa Rosa. The inn also provides a central location for easy day trips to Mendocino, Napa, Sonoma, and even San Francisco.

The Hope-Merrill House

21253 Geyserville Avenue, P.O. Box 42
Geyserville, California 95441; (707) 857-3356

INNKEEPERS:	*Bob and Rosalie Hope.*
ACCOMMODATIONS:	*Five rooms, all with private bath; double and queen-size beds.*
RESERVATIONS:	*Three to four weeks recommended.*
MINIMUM STAY:	*Two nights on weekends, May through October.*
DEPOSIT:	*First night's lodging.*
CREDIT CARDS:	*MC, VISA.*
RATES:	*Moderate.*
RESTRICTIONS:	*No children. No pets.*

Victoriana buffs, arise — and head straight to Geyserville, for one of the finest overnight experiences on the bed and breakfast circuit — the Hope-Merrill House, named after the present owners-innkeepers, Bob and Rosalie Hope, and the original builder-occupant, J. P. Merrill.

This 1875-ish Eastlake/Stick–style Victorian is a virtual museum of the trends and treasures of its time, from the carefully researched and reproduced wall coverings to the period furnishings and fixtures. Of special interest is the Lincrusta-Walton wainscoting in the entranceway and upstairs hall, and the tin ceiling in the kitchen. The Hopes' collection of glassware and bric-a-brac, as well as their books on Victorian gardens, furnishings, and house building (and one on gas lighting in America), delight the eye and captivate the mind.

The reasonably priced guest accommodations include the Victorian Room with its old trunk, chaise longue, antique perfume bottles, and walnut carved headboard from the 1860s; the Peacock Room, the only downstairs bedroom with a fireplace, queen-size bed, and whirlpool bath; the Bachelor's Button, with a brass bed, chestnut dresser, and Maxfield Parrish prints; and the Carpenter Gothic and Briar Rose rooms. (The inn now

also offers a gazebo, a swimming pool, and a fun-filled stagecoach-picnic ride.)

Victoriana buffs, awake — to one of the most delicious gourmet breakfasts found on the bed and breakfast circuit. Rosalie (a caterer whose creations are highly respected by the top names in the valley) is known for her hot poached pears with ginger, fresh peaches with zabaglione, chili egg puff with salsa, French toast like no other, sour cream coffee cake, homemade apple butter, and homemade jams.

The slow-paced, rural atmosphere makes one inclined to linger, perhaps too long, while scenic views along Highway 128 and tours and tastings along the Russian River Wine Road await. Bob offers winetasting advice and cites this, along with lovemaking, as the two activities his guests seem to be most interested in. "Canoeing runs a distant third," he adds.

"Our desire was to authentically re-create a living history of the Victorian era for people to enjoy," Bob explains. Victoriana buffs, acclaim: Well done!

Ye Olde' Shelford House

29955 River Road
Cloverdale, California 95425; (707) 894-5956

INNKEEPERS:	*Al and Ina Sauder.*
ACCOMMODATIONS:	*Three rooms, two with private bath; twin, queen- and king-size beds. Carriage house.*
RESERVATIONS:	*Three to four weeks recommended for summer weekends.*
MINIMUM STAY:	*Two nights on weekends.*
DEPOSIT:	*First night's lodging.*
CREDIT CARDS:	*MC, VISA.*
RATES:	*Moderate.*
RESTRICTIONS:	*No children under 10. No pets.*

With a locale among the backroads of Cloverdale's Wine Country (where ten wineries are clustered within eleven miles of each other), a horse-drawn surrey with fringe on top, and a bicycle built for two, Ye Olde' Shelford House brims with scenic adventure possibilities.

Run by Al and Ina Sauder, Shelford House is an authentically restored 1885 Victorian, comfortably furnished with antiques, some of which were made by Al's grandfather.

The home was originally built by Eurastus Shelford on property given to him by his father, who purchased the land in 1863 as part of the Rancho Musalacon. It stayed in the Shelford family over the next 110 years, and by the time the Sauders found the two-story house after Al retired from teaching in 1984, it had been turned into a rental unit.

Many new homeowners try to modernize their properties. But not Ina and Al. "The first thing we had to do was de-modernize, starting with the downstairs bathroom," laughs Al. "Out came the new tub and toilet and in went a claw-foot tub and an antique, pull-chain water closet."

The result of this lovable couple's work is a delightful little country inn. Because the home faces acres of vineyards, the view is incredible. There are three bedrooms with lots of windows for viewing the surrounding grapevines. Each room also has beautiful homemade quilts, green plants, and fresh flowers from the surrounding gardens. One of the personalized touches here is that the bedrooms are named after Ina and Al's mothers. Some are even furnished with their parents' heirlooms.

Upstairs the Laura May Colmery Room (named after Al's adopted mother), with Laura's queen-size bed and wedding set from the 1920s, and the Helen Gabriel Linton Room (named after Ina's mom) with its antique Belgian oak bed covered with a garden-patterned quilt, share a large bathroom. The bath has family antiques as well: Laura's old washstand and an old oak potty chair. The Mary Oakes Green Room (named after Al's real mother), which features a queen-size, oak high bed and a private bath with claw-foot tub, is downstairs.

If the upstairs skylight arboretum isn't enough to captivate you, you can take a romantic dip in the inn's across-the-lawn hot tub. Closer still is the home's old-fashioned, wraparound veranda with its porch swing.

In the morning the aroma of fresh, oven-baked breakfast wafts through the house. Ina's feast starts off with a cool glass of fresh orange juice and leads on to such delights as quiche (Lorraine, seafood, or broccoli), just-made breads, jams, fresh fruit, and coffee, tea, or milk. Later in the day, a wine and cheese snack is laid out.

After breakfast, you can arrange to take a "Sip and Surrey" ride down memory lane aboard a turn-of-the-century carriage pulled by Brandy, a strawberry-roan Belgian horse, and his buddy Casey. The ride leaves the inn at 10:00 each Saturday and Sunday morning (May through October) for a leisurely jaunt down quiet country lanes to the Bandiera, Pat Paulsen, and Italian Swiss Colony wineries, all of which offer winetasting. A second ride begins with the outdoor picnic offered at Italian Swiss Colony at 12:30 P.M. Nearby, too, are Bob Trowbridge's popular canoe trips down the Russian River. Cloverdale is also the gateway to the new Lake Sonoma, which has great bass, catfish, and trout fishing, plus picnic and swim areas, and even a fish hatchery. Expect just a seven-mile, ten-minute drive from Shelford House to the lake.

Old World Inn

Napa
County

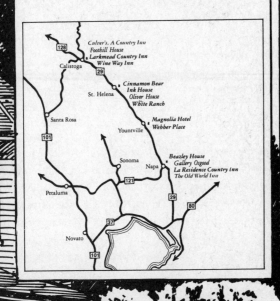

128
Calistoga

Culver's, A Country Inn
Foothill House
Larkmead Country Inn
Wine Way Inn

29

Cinnamon Bear
Ink House
Oliver House
White Ranch

St. Helena

Santa Rosa

Magnolia Hotel
Webber Place
Yountville

101

Sonoma

Beazley House
Gallery Osgood
La Residence Country Inn
The Old World Inn

Napa

121

29

Petaluma

80

37

Novato

101

Beazley House

1910 First Street
Napa, California 94559; (707) 257-1649

INNKEEPERS:	*Jim and Carol Beazley.*
ACCOMMODATIONS:	*Nine rooms, all with private bath; queen-size beds.*
RESERVATIONS:	*Two to three weeks recommended.*
MINIMUM STAY:	*Two nights on weekends.*
DEPOSIT:	*First night's lodging.*
CREDIT CARDS:	*MC, VISA.*
RATES:	*Moderate*
RESTRICTIONS:	*Children under 12 discouraged. No pets.*

F ond memories of the Beazley House: friendly people (Jim and Carol Beazley), the smell of freshly
baked muffins wafting from the kitchen, a warm
and snuggly down comforter, and one of the finest old
homes in Napa (an early California town with more than
its share of distinguished literary and business person-
alities).

This two-story, Colonial Revival–Shingle-style house
was built in 1902. Its hardwood floors, wainscoting, cove
ceilings, and stained-glass windows bespeak its Edwardian
origins. There's a large living room with a fireplace and
a window flanked by bookshelves. (The Beazleys also keep
plenty of games on hand: backgammon, chess, Yatzee, and
dominoes are all available.) To the right of the music room
is the formal dining room, where a breakfast of fresh fruits,
yogurt, cheeses or quiche, home-baked muffins, coffee and
tea, and fruit juice is served. Guest rooms are individually decorated and named according to theme. In addition
to the four accommodations in the main house, the Carriage House provides five rooms with fireplaces and private baths (all with two-person spas).

The Beazleys are as comfortable and accommodating as their house. Both are unabashedly people oriented.
Carol served as a full-time nurse for fourteen years; Jim
was a photojournalist with the *Reno Evening Gazette* and
Nevada State Journal. A tour of b&bs in England and Cali-

fornia left them with a confirmed belief in the owner-occupant philosophy of innkeeping. Many a stranger leaves Beazley House a friend — perhaps because this inn is a home as well as a business for its owners.

Beazley House is three blocks from central Napa, a city that is experiencing a rebirth as a tourist destination. It offers historic-architectural walking tours within the immediate area. There is also hot air ballooning, cycling, gliding, horseback riding, and the Robert L. Stevenson Museum, all within a few miles.

Visitors will have no difficulty finding this attractive Wine Country inn with its bright blue and white awnings, balanced symmetry, and gracefully hipped roof. But despite its impressive exterior, the best memories most people take away are of the warm and familylike atmosphere within. "We treat each individual not just as a customer," say the Beazleys, "but as a guest."

La Residence Country Inn

4066 St. Helena Highway North
Napa, California 94558; (707) 253-0337

INNKEEPERS:	*Craig Claussen and David Jackson.*
ACCOMMODATIONS:	*Nine rooms, seven with private bath; queen-size beds. Eleven-guest-room French barn.*
RESERVATIONS:	*Two to four weeks recommended.*
MINIMUM STAY:	*Two nights on weekends.*
DEPOSIT:	*First night's lodging.*
CREDIT CARDS:	*MC, VISA.*
RATES:	*Moderate to expensive.*
RESTRICTIONS:	*Children discouraged. No pets.*

Harry C. Parker was a New Orleans river pilot who caught gold fever and arrived in San Francisco in 1849. After a career as a merchant in Stockton and San Francisco, he moved to Napa County in 1865 and took up farming. In 1870 he built his dream house, a Gothic Revival with a distinctly Southern flavor. Today his home still projects this amalgamation of regional styles, and the clientele attracted by its modern-day owners reflects the adventurous spirit of its original creator and inhabitant.

There is elegance here, as befits a home built by a man from the land of magnolias. Rooms are filled with nineteenth-century antiques, chandeliers, and plantation shutters, and the majority of guest rooms also have fireplaces. The library is well stocked with mysteries, with a preponderance of the English drawing room genre. One room even boasts a small library containing the works of Robert Louis Stevenson, the nineteenth-century English literary light who lived nearby.

Bicycle enthusiasts will find a bike trail, beginning right across the road, that runs all the way to Yountville, then along the Silverado Trail to Calistoga. Runners are encouraged to enjoy the fresh Napa air and sunshine on the same trail. Balloonists frequently stay here because of the proximity of the ballooning facilities, and the proprietors are happy to recommend tours at the local wineries.

But if it's simply rest and relaxation you thirst after, you will not be disappointed. Each bedroom has its own sitting area, and the parklike setting gives the entire area a secluded and restful ambience. Its two acres boast magnolias (naturally); California live oaks; and orange, walnut, fig, apple, and pear trees. There's also a heated swimming pool, a Jacuzzi, a gazebo, and an abundance of patios and decks.

The morning's breakfast of orange juice; scrambled eggs or French toast; fresh fruit in season; pastries, muffins, breads, or caramel nut rolls; and the house blend of coffee or tea, is served from 8:30 to 10:00 in the dining room. But you may find evenings at La Residence just as enjoyable; Craig and David are especially interested in serving an international clientele. "That's the part we like best," they say. "Sitting around in the evening sharing wine and hors d'oeuvres and stories from all over the world." I'm sure the footloose Harry C. would approve.

The Old World Inn

1301 Jefferson Street
Napa, California 94559; (707) 257-0112

INNKEEPERS:	*Geoffrey and Janet Villiers.*
ACCOMMODATIONS:	*Eight rooms, all with private bath; twin, double, queen-, and king-size beds.*
RESERVATIONS:	*Two to three weeks recommended.*
MINIMUM STAY:	*Two nights on weekends.*
DEPOSIT:	*First night's lodging.*
CREDIT CARDS:	*AE, MC, VISA.*
RATES:	*Moderate.*
RESTRICTIONS:	*No children. No pets.*

When Macy's prepared to launch its China Seas linen collection, the department store chose Napa's Old World Inn to show off the new color-coordinated fabrics. So the Old World Inn interiors are courtesy of Macy's, but the Old World Inn charm is courtesy of Geoffrey and Janet Villiers, the gracious and good-humored proprietors recently transplanted here from the southwest of England.

The art of innkeeping is not new to the Villiers; in fact, you could say they perfected it at their Country House inn in Somerset County prior to settling in the Napa Valley. "Blissfully happy" is how they describe their life as innkeepers. A refreshing attitude, this — and one that is explained by the following comment: "We're retired, you see, so now we're doing exactly what we want, because we enjoy it — not because we have to."

The Villiers residence (painted a vintner's leaf green with grape trim) was built by Napa contractor E. W. Doughty in 1906. Its shingle siding, wide shady porches, clinker brick, and leaded- and beveled-glass windows reveal an eclectic combination of architectural styles.

Bright Scandinavian colors and a mix of painted Victorian and antique furniture dominate the inn's parlor and eight guest rooms, which were inspired by Swedish artist Carl Larsson. Cotton candy–colored bows, trailing vines,

and other fanciful designs are painted aroun[d]
of the walls and up the hallway, where stenciled
announces the name of each room: Carl Larsson's R[o]
Inger's Room, Anne's Room, the Mint Room, the Blu[e]
Room, the Birch Room, and the Garden Room. The most
popular room in the house is the downstairs Stockholm
Room with its multicolored striped fabric and private
entrance off the veranda.

Among the features enhancing the guests' comfort
are the air conditioning in summer and the large custom
Jacuzzi shaped like a cluster of grapes.

Tea and shortbread greet guests on arrival, a cheese
board with hot French bread is set out after 5:00, and
yummy chocolate fudge cake and homemade peppermints
satisfy that urge for a "little something" just before bedtime.

Osgood

59; (707) 224-0100

	Joan Osgood-Moehrke and Howard Moehrke.
ACCOMMODATIONS:	Three rooms, all with shared bath; double and queen-size beds.
RESERVATIONS:	Two months recommended for summer weekends.
MINIMUM STAY:	None.
DEPOSIT:	First night's lodging.
CREDIT CARDS:	AE, MC, VISA.
RATES:	Inexpensive.
RESTRICTIONS:	No children under 12. No pets.

I magine an innkeeper who's so fastidious about what she serves her guests for breakfast that no matter how many times they return, she never serves them the same item twice. Meet Joan Osgood-Moehrke, who, with her husband, Howard, operates a bed and breakfast inn in a Victorian home in central Napa. "I want each visit to be special," explains Joan, a gourmet cook who works from a collection of over four hundred cookbooks to prepare the sumptuous morning meal that she presents on sparkling china, with silver and crystal in the dining room of this 1898 Queen Anne home. Rolled shrimp pancakes with butter; wild rice and almond pancakes with sherried cream and mustard sauce; open-faced omelettes; fresh vegetable crêpes; and cheese blintzes are just some of her specialties. Each breakfast also comes with fresh juice, berries and other fresh fruit, and, during the cooler months of the year, baked apple or baked custard.

It's not just the food at Gallery Osgood that's exquisite. The all-redwood house itself is a visual masterpiece that features eleven-foot ceilings and solid finger-grained stain doors, bay windows, and a tiled fireplace with its original rosewood mantel.

The inn also reflects two of Joan and Howard's other interests: art and gardening. Outside, a sea of daffodils,

tiger lilies, roses, camellias, and irises of e[...]
brown, rust, pink, apricot, yellow, blue, white, pur[...]
even black—greet spring and summer visitors. "If J[...]
turns any more of it into flower beds, soon we won't have
a lawn," jokes Howard.

Guest rooms, too, are named after Joan's flowers. The
Poppy Room sports a queen-size iron bed with antique
mahogany accents; the Rose Room has a white iron bed
with lace tufted quilt, antique wicker vanity, and wicker
night table and chairs; and the Lupine Room, a personal
favorite, showcases the home's historic character with a walnut double bed made in the U.S. around 1880, a matching walnut dresser, and a working, handcrank Victrola with
some eighty records, circa 1890/91.

The inn overflows with pottery, woodcarving, etchings, and photography. Also a fine art and crafts gallery,
the house is full of Howard's magnificent stained-glass windows and Joan's dramatic silkscreened prints. (Look for
prime examples of the former in the Poppy and Rose
rooms; the latter are on display in the hall.)

The innkeepers encourage guests to play with Rosie,
their pet cocker spaniel. They also bubble with suggestions about where to spend the afternoon. Although you
may want to savor the beauty of the inn's quarter acre of
trees and flowers, Napa Valley bulges with enough activities to supplement a vacation of any length. Winetasting,
horseback riding, and hot air ballooning are offered by
several local firms. A glider service operates out of an airport just north of the inn. Whatever you choose, there's
plenty to do to transport you back from the inn's nineteenth-
century lifestyle to the lighter side of modern times.

). Box 2873
94599; (707) 944-8384

ery color—
ble and
an

	Diane Bartholomew and Patsy Gordon.
ACCᴏ ᴏATIONS:	*Four rooms; two with private bath; double beds.*
RESERVATIONS:	*Three weeks recommended.*
MINIMUM STAY:	*None.*
DEPOSIT:	*First night's lodging.*
CREDIT CARDS:	*MC, VISA.*
RATES:	*Inexpensive to moderate.*
RESTRICTIONS:	*No children. No pets.*

Webber Place is a 1½-story Greek Revival farmhouse. And what a farmhouse! This is the storybook clapboard farmhouse *par excellence*, complete with a delicate white picket fence. Built by Sylvester and Polly Grigsby (descendants of Capt. John Grigsby of the Bear Flag Revolt) in the 1850s, it was moved to its present station by one of the industrious Webber clan in the latter part of that decade. Loren Holte began work on this "piece of junk that nobody wanted" in the early 1970s. He reconstructed almost the entire interior of this historic rust red dwelling, while preserving many of the original accoutrements. (These include newspaper clippings from around the turn of the century, discovered during renovation, which were framed and put on the walls.)

One of several small miracles of reconstruction was the rebirth of the wood paneling on the ceiling, which had been painted over several times. During renovation, each panel was simply flipped over and carefully reattached to the wood surface. The result was the intricate tongue and groove redwood paneling that graces many of the ceilings (and one wall) of the rooms.

The town of Yountville, in which Webber Place is located, is itself a small miracle of reconstruction. It was nothing more than a sleepy village containing a Veterans Hospital until a few years ago. Then Vintage 1870 — a

charming oasis of shops and boutiques — was opened by enterprising locals with an eye to attracting more of the tourist dollar. Employment went up, and the area received a face lift that in turn drew other businesses catering to tourism. It now boasts several inns and fine restaurants and the Court of Two Sisters bakery.

Webber Place-isms I particularly liked: guests are greeted with wine from local wineries, such as Mondavi or Round Hill. There are fresh flowers in the rooms, and most rooms have old-fashioned, claw-foot bathtubs (some built for two, yet) on raised platforms, and pull-chain water closets. The lower suite is perfect for honeymooners, opening onto its private veranda with a private entrance as well. Wine and perishables may be stored in the refrigerator by guests; the Continental breakfast often includes homemade breads (the zucchini and the banana are both yummy).

Patsy Gordon and Diane Bartholomew purchased the property from Loren Holte in June of 1983, and to the delight of inngoers they established a few traditions all their own: freshly squeezed lemonade and old-fashioned sun tea, homemade oatmeal cookies, and mom's hot apple pie.

A swimming pool fashioned to look like a reflecting pond, and a hot tub are in the works. Webber Place will be an interesting inn to keep an eye on.

Magnolia Hotel

6529 Yount Street
Yountville, California 94599; (707) 944-2056

INNKEEPERS:	*Bruce and Bonnie Locken.*
ACCOMMODATIONS:	*Twelve rooms, all with private bath; double, queen-, and king-size beds.*
RESERVATIONS:	*Two to three months for weekends.*
MINIMUM STAY:	*None.*
DEPOSIT:	*In full.*
CREDIT CARDS:	*Not accepted.*
RATES:	*Moderate to expensive.*
RESTRICTIONS:	*No children under sixteen. No pets.*

I t was built as a hotel in 1873, of brick and native fieldstone — reputedly from the Silverado Trail. In the intervening years it has been a bordello, a hotel for laborers, a 4-H headquarters, and a speakeasy during Prohibition. It was rescued from oblivion by Ray and Nancy Monte (two of the creators of Vintage 1870) and is now owned by Bonnie and Bruce Locken, who have turned the Magnolia Hotel into one of the classiest and most fashionable country inns in the vineyards of California.

Class tells right from the moment one enters and spies the antique rolltop desk in the lobby. There is a formal parlor; the second floor has a very large deck, perfect for sipping wine and looking out over the surrounding vineyards. (The wine cellar is stocked with over three hundred California wines.)

Each room has its own handmade theme doll specially created by Bonnie. In the Magnolia Room I discovered a private balcony overlooking the heated pool. (I also found a welcome decanter of port.) There is a heated Jacuzzi with a redwood deck in the rear. My bedspread pattern was cleverly keyed to correspond to wall decor, and I liked the fireplace, the needlepoint chair design, and the pink lace curtains. (Other rooms have iron and brass beds, handmade quilts, and lace coverlets.) Each room has a private bath and plush towels, and it is worth noting that the Magnolia is air-conditioned during the summer.

Bruce Locken has been in the hostelry trade for thirty years serving at famous spots such as San Francisco's Clift Hotel. But he yearned for something different. "I wanted to get back to the small, intimate kind of operation — which is really how the business began," he says. He searched for eight years. In 1977 he found the Magnolia already in operation. It was love at first sight.

Bonnie is in charge of the kitchen, as one would expect of a former dietician for a chain of western hospitals.

For breakfast, enjoy French toast baked in rounds; homemade hot port wine syrup; sausage or double-thick bacon, from California Meat Company, one of the oldest sausage makers in San Francisco; eggs baked or as an omelette (try New York sharp Cheddar cheese with mushrooms and sherry wine); old-fashioned oatmeal with brown sugar, banana chips, and cream; and fresh orange juice. (The breakfast is served "family style" in the dining room.)

If you can break away from the Lockens' famous collection of cookbooks, nearby attractions include a petrified forest, over a hundred wineries, a geyser named Old Faithful after its prototype in Yellowstone, and a mud bath (yes, a mud bath). The Lockens are happy to assist with reservations. This is an operation that marries the old with the very modern and makes it work.

The Ink House

1575 St. Helena Highway
St. Helena, California 94574; (707) 963-3890

INNKEEPER:	*Lois Clark.*
ACCOMMODATIONS:	*Four rooms, all with private bath; double and queen-size beds.*
RESERVATIONS:	*Two weeks recommended.*
MINIMUM STAY:	*Two nights on weekends.*
DEPOSIT:	*Full amount.*
CREDIT CARDS:	*Not accepted.*
RATES:	*Moderate.*
RESTRICTIONS:	*No children under twelve. No pets.*

Theron H. Ink, who built this huge and decidedly Italianate Victorian, operated not one but several vineyards, as well as ranches and a livery stable. He was a landholder in Marin, Sonoma, and Napa counties, serving as a Napa County supervisor for many years.

The Ink House is still very much a private residence. (Guests use the parlor, dining room, third-floor observatory, and lounge on the wide, wraparound porch.) Proprietor Lois Clark and her husband, George, raised five children here, and it was when the children had left the nest that the bed and breakfast idea took hold. It's not hard to see why: Theron H. built this square, brown, white-trimmed residence on a palatial scale. Double stairways made it possible to divide the house in halves, one of which is for guests and the other for the Clarks.

There is no sign outside. (Lois doesn't want people who come just to gawk.) Once inside it took me some time to get used to the scale, for the ceilings are twelve feet high. In the parlor I discovered a huge antique pump organ. In the bedrooms are more antiques as well as handmade quilts.

My room was pink, with a brass-trimmed iron bed, white lace curtains, pink towels, and flowered wallpaper. The only truly modern touch here was the electric blanket—one that I genuinely appreciated.

Clever Lois keeps a book in which visitors are en-

couraged to review local restaurants, the better to inform you of which eateries are currently in favor. Lois's own Continental breakfast (served at 8:30) consists of juice, coffee, nut bread, and fruit. The bread is baked by Lois, who got in the habit of baking her own bread while she was raising her children.

Lois's most amusing moment as an innkeeper came the morning after Halloween when three young couples left a stuffed, three-armed monster at the breakfast table for her to find. She is a believer in intuition where guests are concerned: "You get a feeling for people — some want to talk, and some want to be left alone."

The Ink House is a place apart, a fascinating and pleasant curiosity. What makes it interesting is its bold combination of styles. Its monumental scale seems to promise anonymity, yet what it ultimately delivers is warm intimacy. The Ink House is finally a home, not a palace, but then Lois Clark could have told you that.

The White Ranch

707 White Lane
St. Helena, California 94574; (707) 963-4635

INNKEEPER:	*Ruth Davis.*
ACCOMMODATIONS:	*One room with private bath, double bed.*
RESERVATIONS:	*Two months recommended.*
MINIMUM STAY:	*None.*
DEPOSIT:	*First night's lodging.*
CREDIT CARDS:	*Not accepted.*
RATES:	*Moderate.*
RESTRICTIONS:	*No children. No pets.*

T alk about individual attention! You'll certainly get it here, because this delightful bed and breakfast caters to just one person (or couple) at a time. There is a private entrance to the bedroom; and although there may be only one (or two) of you, proprietor Ruth Davis maintains a dressing room and a private bath for the comfort of her visitors.

This lovely farm dwelling was built in 1865 by Asa White, a pioneer Methodist minister who arrived with his family in a covered wagon. This is deep country: you are far enough from the highway not to hear traffic sounds. You *might* hear the sound of roosters cheerfully crowing you awake of a morning, and there are plenty of other farm animals to keep you company. (There are horses pastured here, and turkeys inhabit the barn.) Ancient walnut trees in the front yard complete the bucolic scene.

Ruth's accommodations are really closer to a certain kind of European-style bed and breakfast experience than many of the others toured. (In Europe and the British Isles a bed and breakfast establishment is just as likely to be somebody's home with a spare room as an inn.) One of the objectives of this arrangement is to cut down on the expense of hotels; but it also allows the guests to find out how the people of an area or region live and think. There's no better way to get close to people than to live in their home.

Ruth embarked on her bed and breakfast adventure

when her friend Lois Clark at the Ink House called to say she had a honeymoon couple — and no room at the inn, as it were. Ruth obliged by taking them in, and she's been at it ever since.

Anyone who's ever spent time on a farm will love her porch swing. There's a picnic table on the lawn; the parlor has a fireplace and a fine Queen Anne table and chairs. The guest room is furnished with heirlooms of Ruth's family. (Her grandmother's crocheted quilt is on the bed.) I liked the oversize mirror on the dressing table, too.

There is a small porch off the bedroom with a wooden bench for those who wish to sit and drink-in the country silence. But I went to bed early, and my sleep was bone-deep and satisfying. When I woke up, refreshed and ravenous, Ruth presented me with homemade nut bread, popovers, orange juice, fresh fruit, and espresso. Delicious!

Traffic, job, crime, and noise pollution got you down? I recommend the White Ranch as the perfect antidote for your city blues.

Oliver House

2970 Silverado Trail North
St. Helena, California 94574; (707) 963-4089

INNKEEPERS:	*Richard and Clara Oliver.*
ACCOMMODATIONS:	*Four rooms, all with private bath; queen-size beds.*
RESERVATIONS:	*Three weeks recommended.*
MINIMUM STAY:	*None.*
DEPOSIT:	*First night's lodging.*
CREDIT CARDS:	*MC, VISA.*
RATES:	*Moderate to expensive.*
RESTRICTIONS:	*No children. No pets.*

Just north of the well-known restaurant Auberge du Soleil, on the Silverado Trail, is Oliver House, a three-story Swiss chalet–style home that represents a "dream come true" for its owners, Richard and Clara Oliver. "We met, fell in love, got married, and started talking about what we wanted to do," remembers Clara. "Richard, who had traveled to Switzerland, said he'd love to start a Swiss country inn right here in Napa Valley. He even scrawled out a sketch of his dream home on a little piece of paper. Then two years later, we found it."

Built in 1920, the house features four guest rooms, each with its own bath. Three of the rooms (on the second floor) have French doors that open onto balconies facing miles of vineyards. One also has an ornate 120-year-old brass bed from Scotland, English antiques, and hardwood floors. Another is filled with English antiques, antique German chairs, and a queen-size oak bed. The largest of the three is replete with an early American oak dresser, a queen-size bed with a mirror that rises from its headboard, a double shower, and a huge walkaround deck. It is also the only guest room in the house with its own stone fireplace. The third-floor Alpine Room boasts knotty pine walls, an open-beam ceiling, German antiques, a queen-size bed, and a balcony as well.

Breakfast is a leisurely 9:00 to 10:00 A.M. experience, with Richard and Clara's mouth-watering blueberry and bran muffins; rum raisin buns; custard apple rings; banana, pumpkin, and zucchini breads; homemade jams; strawberries from the garden; and blackberries "picked down the road." The Olivers' presentation is so elaborate that photographs of their meals have appeared in magazines in both the U.S. and Japan. Expect these treats to be served in the country kitchen, or, on cooler days, in the sun room.

Elsewhere around the house, expect the unexpected. The chunks of glassy, jet black rock you'll find on the Olivers' property are known as obsidian. Prized for jewelry, obsidian is so easy to spot here that the Olivers' hill, Glass Mountain, was once quarried by the Mayacamas Indians. If obsidian doesn't interest you, all you have to do to discover a genuine archaeological landmark is walk out to the front of the driveway. There next to the road is the original, 400-year-old oak tree the Indians used to sleep under between digs. It is designated California Archaeological Site Number 132.

To round out your stay, stroll to the tasting room of one of Napa Valley's wineries, just a quarter mile away, or drive or walk to any of the seven others that are within 2½ miles of Oliver House.

The Cinnamon Bear

1407 Kearney Street
St. Helena, California 94574; (707) 963-4653

INNKEEPER:	*Genny Jenkins.*
ACCOMMODATIONS:	*Three rooms, all with private bath; queen-size beds.*
RESERVATIONS:	*Two to four weeks.*
MINIMUM STAY:	*Two nights over holiday periods.*
DEPOSIT:	*Full amount.*
CREDIT CARDS:	*AE, MC, VISA.*
RATES:	*Moderate.*
RESTRICTIONS:	*No children. No pets.*

This lovely California bungalow was built in 1904 as a wedding present to Susan Smith Metzner from her father. Husband Walter Metzner was mayor of St. Helena for twenty years, and he lived with Susan in their comfortable home at 1407 Kearney Street until 1970. The present owner and creator of the Cinnamon Bear, Genny Jenkins, purchased the house in 1971 to provide a home for three growing children.

The bed and breakfast idea developed when oldest son David went to England and came back with enthusiastic reports of bed and breakfasts abroad. "So when the kids went to college," Genny says jokingly, "I changed the locks and rented out their rooms."

There was more to it than that, of course. It took tasteful, systematic remodeling of each room to provide the necessary facilities while giving each room its own character. The house had a great deal of character to begin with: broad wraparound porches — used for breakfast and general socializing in earlier days, as today — handcrafted redwood paneling, and a sitting room and dining room all testify to the quality of life of its previous owners.

Mirrored built-in cabinets, redwood beam ceilings, and ample bay windows covered by delicate lace curtains add to the homey elegance. The day I visited, there was a cheerful fire in the fireplace; plenty of sherry, games,

and good books; and a most important staple of the L
and breakfast trade—rocking chairs.

My room was similarly redolent of both taste and
comfort: Persian rugs in tones of blue and burgundy, a
white and burgundy comforter and pillow shams, and a
beige and brown private bath with a special country feeling. And, of course, bears: they are present in all sizes and
variations throughout the house, although Genny is careful not to overdo the motif.

A breakfast of homemade breads, fresh fruit, coffee
freshly ground in an antique coffee mill, and orange juice
is served either in the large dining room or on the porch
(weather permitting). A nice touch of Americana: if the
aroma of delicious food and fresh-brewed coffee doesn't
waken you, the school bell next door will.

Genny likes to tell of the time she booked a couple
over the phone and was then unexpectedly detained
downtown. "The husband literally took over. When I got
home a fire was lit, additional reservations had been
made, wine poured, cheese served, and messages taken.
Not only that—when I finally got back, he assumed I was
a guest and proceeded to show me to my room." And
where did the couple sleep? "In the basement—he'd
booked all the available rooms!"

Friendly and *welcome* are two words that describe the
Cinnamon Bear, a bed and breakfast that owes much of
its appeal to the house—but most of it to the warm and
enterprising woman who makes it a home.

mead Country Inn

ad Lane
lifornia 94515; (707) 942-5360

INNKEEPERS:	*Gene and Joan Garbarino.*
ACCOMMODATIONS:	*Four rooms, all with private bath; double and twin beds.*
RESERVATIONS:	*Four to five weeks for weekends.*
MINIMUM STAY:	*None.*
DEPOSIT:	*First night's lodging.*
CREDIT CARDS:	*Not accepted.*
RATES:	*Moderate.*
RESTRICTIONS:	*No children. No pets.*

G ene and Joan Garbarino don't have a sign out front, and they don't advertise their inn — they don't have to. Most of their bookings are repeat business, and the rest come by word of mouth. People who like this place tend to like it very much; it's not hard to see why. Classical yet simple, in a tranquil setting literally in the heart of a vineyard, perhaps the best word to describe Larkmead Country Inn is *serene*.

This inn on old Larkmead Lane, located next to famed Hanns Kornell Champagne Cellars, was built by the son of an earlier vintner on the occasion of his marriage. The house abounds with antiques, paintings, and prints from the Garbarinos' collection. Persian carpets, broad porches, wide clapboards, and a certain atmosphere of unperturbable solidity all suggest a New England inn. Until one looks out the window, that is: all rooms overlook row upon row of vineyards.

It is not particularly surprising, then, that all rooms are named after wines of the Napa Valley. The Beaujolais has an antique sewing machine and a private porch from which you see all the way to the hills on the edge of the valley on a clear and moonlit night. The Chardonnay Room features antique brass twin beds, white wicker chairs, red and white flowered spreads — and the fresh flowers and complimentary decanter of wine that all guests receive.

It so happens that my favorite room here is also my

favorite wine. The elegant Chenin Blanc Room has a chaise longue I loved, curtains and matching wallpaper, an armoire, a white wicker chair and table, and a very comfy double bed. The living room is comfortable, too; Joan's afternoon tea was especially pleasant in front of a blazing fire in the fireplace. The Garbarinos have chess, cards, puzzles, dominoes, and many books on hand to occupy idle hands and minds.

Breakfast is served on one of the porches when weather permits; mine arrived in the dining room. (And it arrived on fine china with sterling silver and linen napkins, I might add.) It consisted of fresh fruit, freshly ground coffee, and a basket of croissants, scones, and French rolls with sweet butter and homemade preserves.

Both Gene and Joan feel that their part of the Napa Valley is especially beautiful at harvest time. And both are happy to be serving the public in such a direct and personal way. "When's the last time you heard of a hotel receiving a thank-you note?" Joan asks. She adds with a touch of awe: "I've received 123!"

That's as good an indication as any I've heard of the difference between a hotel and the bed and breakfast experience.

Wine Way Inn

1019 Foothill Boulevard, Highway 29
Calistoga, California 94515; (707) 942-0680

INNKEEPERS:	*Allen and Dede Good.*
ACCOMMODATIONS:	*Six rooms, four with private bath;*
	double and queen-size beds.
RESERVATIONS:	*Four weeks recommended for weekends*
	April through November.
MINIMUM STAY:	*Two nights.*
DEPOSIT:	*Full amount.*
CREDIT CARDS:	*MC, VISA.*
RATES:	*Moderate.*
RESTRICTIONS:	*No children under 10. No pets.*

Allen and Dede Good had always wanted to work together in a joint venture, and Dede had stayed at bed and breakfasts in Europe. While vacationing in Napa Valley in 1980, they talked to a realtor. Only a few short months later, they had relocated from Los Angeles and opened their doors to the bed and breakfast public. Both are vigorous proponents of the owner-operated school of innkeeping.

Their house, built in 1915 as a family home, has many of the characteristics of a country house: the Mayacamas Mountains come right down to meet the redwood deck in back. Rooms are named after towns on Highway 29, the main Wine Country route. St. Helena — the room where I slept, and my favorite — has a bed fit for a queen (and in fact is queen-size), a private bath, an armoire, and — an especially nice touch — a basket of colored yarn compatible with the patchwork quilt on the bed. (Dede later told me it came from her home in Indiana.) There was also a candle and candlestick, a piece that more inns should consider placing in their rooms for those of us who find candlelight relaxing just before bedtime.

The comfortable living room sports a cozy fireplace, English china and pottery, an antique clock on the mantel, and, the day I was there, a decanter of excellent Napa Valley Chablis. For those who enjoy excursions, Dede is happy to prepare a "hobo picnic": everything but wi[ne] guests to take on their winery tours (including a picnic clo[th] for the table).

This poised and attractive couple get around to local restaurants, and are glad to share firsthand impressions. "We conduct a service for travelers in the area," Dede says, "and if they want help finding their way around, we provide it." Both she and her husband are quick to add that if the guest's first priority is privacy, that preference is strictly observed.

Local attractions include the Sharpsteen Museum (memorabilia, antiques, and photographs of Calistoga from its glory days as a flourishing resort of the 1860s) and a petrified forest. Why not try a mud bath? Inexpensive and relaxing, it's an experience you won't soon forget. (Just don't let friends take pictures, or you may never hear the end of it.)

Breakfast at Wine Way is Continental: fruit of the season, freshly squeezed·orange juice, homemade cakes and pastries, tea, and coffee.

's, A Country Inn

Boulevard
ifornia 94515; (707) 942-4535

INNKEEPERS:	*George Hunt and Peter Moreland.*
ACCOMMODATIONS:	*Seven rooms share three baths; twin, double, queen- and king-size beds.*
RESERVATIONS:	*Four to six weeks recommended.*
MINIMUM STAY:	*Two nights on weekends.*
DEPOSIT:	*First night's lodging.*
CREDIT CARDS:	*MC, VISA.*
RATES:	*Inexpensive to moderate.*
RESTRICTIONS:	*No children under 12. No pets.*

S am Brannan is credited with many California "firsts": he was the state's first millionaire, banker, and land developer, and he published San Francisco's first newspaper, the *California Star.* It was, in fact, a notice in Brannan's publication that drew the outside world's attention to the discovery of gold at Sutter's Mill in 1848 — and the rush was on.

In the early 1860s Brannan secured a parcel of land at the northernmost edge of what is now the renowned Napa Valley. In an attempt to persuade investors to help him develop it into a summer resort patterned after Saratoga, New York, he held a lavish dinner party. His guests were transported by boat from San Francisco to Vallejo, and by train from Vallejo to the site he had selected in the foothills of Mount St. Helena. The champagne flowed freely, and as legend has it when Sam stood up to make his formal proposal he proclaimed: "We'll make this the Calistoga of Sarafornia!"

Brannan died in 1889, but the village he founded, Calistoga, continues to this day as a resort with numerous spas, mud baths, and mineral hot springs.

An enduring historical landmark of this same genre is Culver's, a country inn located on Calistoga's Foothill Boulevard just north of Highway 29. This early 1870s Victorian was built by Maj. John Oscar Culver, a Milwaukee newspaperman who headed west for reasons unknown.

The house is carefully appointed with antiques of the period and with uniquely designed quilts. Let it not be said, however, that Culver's is without its modern conveniences. The inn boasts showers, air conditioning, a sauna, a spa, and a swimming pool.

Menus from local restaurants are available, as are guidebooks on the Napa Valley. Additional reading material includes *National Geographic*, *Time*, and *Smithsonian* magazines, as well as best-selling paperbacks. Games are found on the rolltop desk in the breakfast room. A decanter of cream sherry sits in the living room next to the player piano.

Homemade scones and sour cream coffee cake are part of the sit-down breakfast with its fresh fruit starter, served from 8:30 to 10:00.

The innkeepers are quite unobtrusive. Their objective is to provide a setting where one can reflect on people like Sam Brannan, who shaped and enlivened the history of California, and where one can engage in the activities that enrich life in California today.

Foothill House

3037 Foothill Boulevard
Calistoga, California 94515; (707) 942-6933

INNKEEPERS:	*Michael and Susan Clow.*
ACCOMMODATIONS:	*Three rooms, all with private bath; queen-size beds.*
RESERVATIONS:	*Two months recommended for weekends.*
MINIMUM STAY:	*Two nights on weekends.*
DEPOSIT:	*First night's lodging.*
CREDIT CARDS:	*MC, VISA.*
RATES:	*Moderate.*
RESTRICTIONS:	*No children. No pets.*

H igh school sweethearts Susan Parker and Michael Clow fell in love with the Napa Valley on their honeymoon back in 1974. Things were never quite the same afterward. Mike began to toy with the idea of giving up his teaching job in Wisconsin to become a winemaker, and in the interim honed his knowledge of wine by studying and sampling the area's varietals that he began importing back to the Midwest.

It wasn't long after that that the Clows first stayed at a b&b while vacationing close to home. The idea of opening a bed and breakfast in the Napa Valley seemed a natural, and thus their dream of creating an environment that would reflect the beauty of the Valley and showcase its fine wines was begun. For eight years they researched the idea, traveling and interviewing innkeepers from coast to coast. Long lists of dos and don'ts were compiled, modern furniture was exchanged for country antiques, and quilting became one of Sue's major pastimes.

For eight months the couple combed the Valley in search of the perfect home. Deals on prospective inns would sometimes close just five minutes before their offer arrived. "It was while despairing over a property that needed a bulldozer rather than a proprietor that we were shown photos of Calistoga's Franz family farmhouse," says Sue. It must have been the luck of the Irish that their offer on the property was made, and accepted, on Saint Patrick's Day.

Foothill House is comprised of three luxurious suites, each with a private entrance and bath, a fireplace, and a small refrigerator. Interiors are graced by fine antiques and four-poster beds with Sue's handmade patchwork quilts. Guests are pampered with a well-chosen, complimentary bottle of wine, a delicious Continental breakfast, and a miniature cookie jar filled with "Sweet Dreams" (homemade chocolate chip–spice cookies) by the bedside at turndown time.

Foothill House has been given many distinctions by publications and guidebooks. Most recently it was honored as one of the top 100 bed and breakfast inns in the U.S. by Frommer's guidebook. The only thing I could possibly add to this is that you can't beat the price. For what you get here, you'll pay nearly twice as much at other inns in this valley. One tip though: ask for the inn's Evergreen Suite — canopied bed, whirlpool Jacuzzi tub, and large sun deck with umbrella table and lounge chairs. (I've already lost count of the number of times I've returned to stay here ever since I found Foothill House.)

Nestled among the western foothills just north of Calistoga, the inn boasts a natural country setting distinguished by lovely old trees and scenic pastoral views. But Foothill House is still in close proximity to all the Napa Valley attractions. Calistoga itself is justly known for its health spas, mud baths, and mineral pools. Of the over one hundred wineries in the Valley to try, Cuvaison, Sterling, Chateau Montelena, Stonegate, and Hanns Kornell Champagne Cellars are all nearby.

Whitegate Inn

The Mendocino Coast

Westport

Blue Rose Inn
Country Inn
Grey Whale Inn
Pudding Creek Inn

Fort Bragg

Headlands Inn
Joshua Grindle Inn
Mendocino Village Inn

Mendocino

Rachel's Inn

Little River

Whitegate Inn

Glendeven

Albion

Victorian Farmhouse

Ukiah

101

128

Elk

Elk Cove Inn

128

Cloverdale

Old Milano Hotel
St. Orres

Gualala

Whale Watch Inn

Old Milano Hotel

38300 Highway One
Gualala, California 95445; (707) 884-3256

INNKEEPER:	*Leslie Linscheid.*
ACCOMMODATIONS:	*Nine rooms, three with private bath; double and queen-size beds.*
RESERVATIONS:	*Four weeks recommended.*
MINIMUM STAY:	*Two nights on weekends, three over holiday periods.*
DEPOSIT:	*First night's lodging.*
CREDIT CARDS:	*AE, MC, VISA.*
RATES:	*Moderate to expensive.*
RESTRICTIONS:	*No children. No pets.*

I n 1905 Bert Luccinetti built a restaurant and pub on a cliff overhanging Castle Rock, alongside what was then a busy railroad and stage road catering mainly to lumbermen. New owners turned it into a resort for fishermen in the 1920s; the 1950s saw it modernized, its Victorian heritage obscured by various layers of ticky-tacky "improvements." Today it is one of the most highly regarded inns on the northern California coast, thanks to the efforts of Leslie Linscheid, a former Macy's employee who put her business and buying skills to work in this impressive blend of old and new (now recorded in the National Registry of Historic Places).

The inn has seven rooms and two cottages. One of the cottages, actually a caboose where the old railroad once ran, has walls of sandblasted wood, a galley, and a red pot-bellied stove. Two brakemen's seats for taking in the sunsets can be reached by a ladder.

Beds, bureaus, tables, lampshades, quilts, and bric-a-brac have been chosen with loving care. Morris wallpapers, original paintings, redwood wainscoting in the halls, and old-fashioned car-sided ceilings are also featured. A Victorian-era mahogany bed highlights the Master Suite where the Luccinetti family lived. You will also see Eastlake chairs, Tiffany lamps, and a sofa that was the first Riviera bed made in 1906.

The gracious Wine Parlor is made cheerful by a great stone fireplace. Adjacent are the quieter and more reflective comforts of the Music Room, where aficionados of art books will find a fine collection. One of the more comfortable concessions to modern sensibilities is a hot tub facing the ocean. (It is encircled by an old-fashioned knob-topped fence for privacy.) The staff of the Old Milano will also arrange for you to have a massage by a certified massage practitioner, according to its brochure.

Room No. 4, with its breathtaking ocean view, was my favorite. The wallpaper design is in shades of blue, lilac, pink, and green. A comfortable overstuffed rocker faces the tumultuous Pacific, and an oval wood-framed mirror and fresh flowers in a pitcher complete the feeling of restful privacy.

The complimentary breakfast here is a full American meal: scrambled eggs, quiche, or an omelette with potatoes and fresh fruit; turnovers, poppy seed lemon muffins, or croissants with honey; creamy yogurt; a private blend of coffee; and an assortment of black and herbal teas. Guests may take their breakfast in the parlor, on the loggia, or in their room.

The Old Milano's restaurant is now back in full swing. Wednesday through Sunday night dinner entrées include fresh filet of salmon poached in a cilantro-hollandaise sauce, filet mignon, leg of lamb with spinach and goat cheese filling, and roast duck à l'orange. Am I teasing you? Best reserve early: seating capacity is only twenty-two.

I left the Old Milano revitalized. Its setting is sensational, but the main ingredients of its success are the good taste of its owner and the delicious taste of its food. There is something dreamlike in its unique compound of the Victorian and the modern. The Old Milano is like an image from art made real, and its restfulness is to a large extent due to its ability to make us feel that we are a part of another, more ordered world.

St. Orres

36601 Highway One South, P.O. Box 523
Gualala, California 95445; (707) 884-3303

INNKEEPERS:	*Ted and Eric Black; Rosemary Campiformio.*
ACCOMMODATIONS:	*Eight rooms and nine cottages, nine rooms with private bath; double and queen-size beds.*
RESERVATIONS:	*Three months for weekends.*
MINIMUM STAY:	*Two nights in cottages and ocean-view rooms on the weekends.*
DEPOSIT:	*Full amount.*
CREDIT CARDS:	*MC, VISA.*
RATES:	*Inexpensive to moderate.*
RESTRICTIONS:	*Children in cottages only. No pets.*

T he windswept isolation and wild charm of this part of the Mendocino coast are staggering. The environs (not to mention the elements) seem to demand one of two architectural styles: rigorous simplicity or the same spendthrift abandon that nature has lavished on her handiwork in the area. Master craftsman Eric Black opted for the latter. The result is a fantasy, an explosion of fine art, an architectural wonder.

It was just a few years ago that he and another carpenter bought the remains of the old Seaside Hotel (built in the 1920s) and went to work on it. Oregon red cedar was used to transform the exterior, topped off by twin domed towers, deliberately reminiscent of the homeland of the Russian trappers who settled the area. Is it any wonder that passersby stop to marvel at this audacious Russophilic beauty in the wilderness?

The fairy-tale extravagance continues inside. The entrance hall has some very fine Art Nouveau and Edwardian pieces, and highly detailed stained-glass windows. The sitting room is dominated by a castle-size fireplace that looks like it belongs in Charles Laughton's *Henry the Eighth* banquet scene. (And *six* oak doors, with stained-glass windows in each.) The dining room rises a dizzying three stories to an octagonal dome above, with row on row of windows culminating in a single rank of stained-glass panes just below its copper-domed crown.

The two front rooms have direct ocean views and French doors that open onto a balcony. Except for the cottages, most rooms share baths down the hall — a His, a Hers, and a spacious Ours with tiled tub enclosures and dual shower heads. Quilts by Gualala quilt maker Donna Bishop are lush velvet; rooms have intricate redwood paneling. (Even the telephone is paneled in redwood.)

A popular accommodation is the Tree House. This experiment in luxury contains a lovely queen-size brass bed, a tile bath with a deep sunken tub, and its own kitchenette. As if that weren't enough, there is a Franklin stove fireplace with a hand-painted tile hearth; the living room has an ocean view, with French doors leading onto a sun deck.

Other than Rosemary Campiformio's long-standing enjoyment in serving people, none of the three friends (Ted Black is Eric's uncle) had any inn or restaurant experience when they began. This has not handicapped them. Their restaurant has achieved a considerable reputation. The complimentary breakfast is served from 8:30 to 9:30 and consists of homemade pastries, yogurt with nuts and raisins, homemade granola, and fresh fruit juices. Breakfast is delivered in a basket to the cottage rooms, and served buffet style to the rest of the guests.

For me the words that best describe St. Orres are *magic* and *extravagance*. And perhaps the most wonderful part of it is the genuinely reasonable price.

Whale Watch Inn

35100 Highway One
Gualala, California 95445; (707) 884-3667

INNKEEPERS:	*Irene and Enoch Stewart.*
ACCOMMODATIONS:	*Eighteen rooms, all with private bath; queen-size beds.*
RESERVATIONS:	*Three to four weeks recommended.*
MINIMUM STAY:	*Two nights on weekends.*
DEPOSIT:	*First night's lodging.*
CREDIT CARDS:	*AE, MC, VISA.*
RATES:	*Expensive to very expensive.*
RESTRICTIONS:	*No children. No pets.*

Whale Watch Inn wasn't planned, it just "happened," according to Enoch and Irene Stewart, who purchased the two-acre property overlooking Anchor Bay and the south Mendocino coastline in 1970. Enoch, then president of an architectural design firm, built Whale Watch (a hexagonal dwelling with floor-to-ceiling windows on three sides, a central fireplace, and a magnificent view of the ever-changing Pacific) for use as the family's second home. In 1976 the Stewarts constructed a four-room addition, and October 1978 saw the official opening of the Whale Watch Inn. (Three more buildings were completed in spring 1985.)

The buildings' contemporary architecture has incorporated spacious decks, skylights, and natural-wood interiors. Some of the rooms have fireplaces, others have private spas. Four include fully equipped kitchens; and all are supplied with magazines, books, candles, wineglasses, mints, and beach towels.

The Golden Voyage Suite's contemporary furnishings and freestanding Swedish fireplace are framed by the room's many angles and high, beamed ceiling. The Country French Suite's spiral staircase leads to a sitting room where furnishings follow a French country motif. The queen-size bed features a lovely walnut and cane headboard with a matching chest; a chaise longue, upholstered in a rose and teal print, picks up the teal in the carpet and the colorful bedspread. The room also has a fireplace, a wet bar, and a window seat. There's a two-person whirlpool spa that allows you to soak in the tub and look out to sea at the same time, and the deck features yet another fantastic view of the ocean, framed by cypress trees.

Guests of the inn receive breakfast in a decorative basket at the requested hour anytime between 8:00 and 10:00. A honey-yogurt fresh fruit parfait is accompanied by the main dish of the day (mushroom phyllo turnovers, eggs Florentine, or zucchini casserole); hot breads (muffins, croissants, or scones); apple juice; and coffee, tea, hot chocolate, or milk.

Whale Watch is located at the northern edge of Anchor Bay, a protected inlet with white sandy beaches and calm waters for diving, boating, and swimming. The site's "banana belt" weather affords an escape from the usual coastal fog. Sea lions and pelicans, as well as whales, can be seen from both beach and cliff side.

Elk Cove Inn

6300 South Highway One
Elk, California 95432; (707) 877-3321

INNKEEPER:	*Hildrun-Uta Triebess.*
ACCOMMODATIONS:	*Nine rooms, seven with private bath;* *double and queen-size beds.*
RESERVATIONS:	*Two weeks recommended for weekends.*
MINIMUM STAY:	*Two nights on weekends.*
DEPOSIT:	*$50 to $100.*
CREDIT CARDS:	*Not accepted.*
RATES:	*Moderate to expensive.*
RESTRICTIONS:	*No children under 12. No pets.*

This sweet Victorian was built in the early 1890s by the L. E. White Lumber Company. (L. E. built it for his son, who was the superintendent of his mill.) From 1890 to the crash in 1929, the nearby hamlet of Elk was a booming lumber port. Now it is the quintessential sleepy coast village. And this small but charming bed and breakfast inn is the archetypical Mendocino bed and breakfast — provided you come here to get away from everything. Because there is nothing — literally *nothing* — to do here but walk, read, eat, and sleep. If it is a period of total rest you are looking for, this is definitely the place for you.

Hildrun was born in Germany but was brought to this country early in life; she is a skilled cook, specializing in European cookery (dinner is served here on Saturdays as well as breakfast). Friendly, folksy, and very amusing, Hildrun has a talent for entertaining that is a central attraction of her operation.

"What I strive for is giving people things they don't do for themselves at home," Hildrun says, "yet in a way that makes them *feel* like they are at home." Which is, by the way, perhaps the best formula for a successful bed and breakfast.

There are several choices of accommodation at Elk Cove Inn: two cabins (behind the main house where Hildrun lives) command a spectacular yet ever-changing

ocean view; an adjacent two-guest-room addition with bay windows and high beamed ceilings; and the five-bedroom Sandpiper House (originally built as an annex for visitors to the lumber company and located about a half mile away). Paths lead from both houses to private, secluded beaches.

Breakfast here is a delight. Hildrun is well known for her German egg cakes (eierkuchen) with freshly picked blackberries or huckleberries, coffee, and orange juice. For Saturday-night dinner you might be served konigsberger klops (poached meatballs in lemon-caper sauce), sauerbraten, rouladen, hasenpfeffer (rabbit in a sour cream sauce) — or any number of excellent French dishes.

Victorian Farmhouse

7001 North Highway One, P.O. Box 357
Little River, California 95456; (707) 937-0697

INNKEEPERS:	*George and Carole Molnar.*
ACCOMMODATIONS:	*Six rooms, all with private bath; queen- and king-size beds.*
RESERVATIONS:	*Three to four weeks recommended.*
MINIMUM STAY:	*Two nights on weekends.*
DEPOSIT:	*First night's lodging.*
CREDIT CARDS:	*MC, VISA.*
RATES:	*Moderate.*
RESTRICTIONS:	*No children under 16. No pets.*

I t was built in 1877 by John and Emma Dora Dennen as a private residence, which it still is. A pronounced feeling of privacy is the most striking attribute of this homey inn. But a certain atmosphere of permanence — of stability — runs it a close second. One doesn't visit here so much as reside, even if the duration of that residence is only a week or a weekend.

There are several acres — and an orchard of apple, plum, and pear trees — to ramble around in. I liked the solid triple-hung bay windows in the downstairs parlor, as well as the antique rocking horse, the Regulator clock, and the homey fireplace. Both upstairs guest rooms have ocean views, while one downstairs has a French wood-burning stove and its own sitting room. The other has an exquisite view of a small private flower garden. Quilts from the 1900s to the 1920s adorn beds in each of the rooms.

A queen-size brass bed graces the Emma Dora room; there is a white comforter draped with a quilt, white pillow shams, and a ceiling done in a tasteful (and restful) redwood design. I also liked the upstairs sitting room with its view of the rear flower gardens.

Besides innkeepers George and Carole Molnar (who purchased the property in 1985), the newest additions to the inn are the Wicker Room (antique wicker pieces, queen-size bed, ocean view, and open-front Franklin stove) and the Orchard View (pine and oak antiques and an 1815 vintage wood stove), both in a separate building located just behind the inn. A large wood deck adjoins these two accommodations to allow breakfast outdoors.

Guests are served breakfast in their rooms promptly at 8:30. Strawberry muffins or poppy seed bread, yogurt with sliced bananas, granola, fresh orange juice, and coffee, tea, or hot chocolate comprise the morning menu. Sometimes guests are served fruit fresh from the orchard outside.

Whatever you are served for breakfast, the fresh ocean breeze in these parts will make it taste better than anything you could eat in the city. The quiet pace and restful environment of this inn are most conducive to concentration and creativity—an excellent place to sort out one's thoughts and prepare emotionally for the big project back in the workaday world.

Glendeven

8221 North Highway One
Little River, California 95456; (707) 937-0083

INNKEEPERS:	*Jan and Janet deVries.*
ACCOMMODATIONS:	*Ten rooms, eight with private bath; queen-size beds.*
RESERVATIONS:	*Three months for weekends; two weeks Monday through Thursday.*
MINIMUM STAY:	*Two nights on weekends.*
DEPOSIT:	*First night's lodging.*
CREDIT CARDS:	*MC, VISA.*
RATES:	*Moderate.*
RESTRICTIONS:	*No children under 8. No pets.*

G lendeven was the country home of Isaiah Stevens, who moved here with a group of settlers from Maine. He raised and bred fine horses and cattle on his 100-acre farm, and in 1867 built a farmhouse for his bride, Rebecca Coombs. It was and is a distinctly New England–style house, typical of the architecture in the Mendocino area; many of the early settlers were from that region.

Jan deVries first saw the home on a visit to the coast in 1962. He returned later as a teacher, and married Janet Bell — and the couple then left for Portland. But the rugged North Coast (and perhaps the romance associated with their courtship) continued to exert its pull. When the deVries heard of the impending sale of the house in 1977, they returned to buy it and open it as an inn.

This is the perfect place to get over a bad case of office politics or the blahs associated with the morning headlines. The dominant note here is upbeat, and most certainly upscale. Antique furnishings sit side by side with contemporary ceramics and works of art; colorful, cheery, abstract paintings hang on the walls. The effect is quite consciously calculated to elevate the mood. And it succeeds admirably.

My favorite rooms are the Garret, a surprisingly large

eaves of the roof (with a rocking chair and a writing desk); and the Eastlin Suite, with its own sitting room, fireplace, and French rosewood bed. Guests in both rooms are invited to breakfast on a tray or to come out and mingle with the other guests. The deVries say that breakfast is "somewhere in between" full and Continental: bread or muffins, coffee cake, hard-cooked eggs, juice, and a variety of fresh fruits — including, if you are lucky, their tasty baked apples.

Exploring the sitting room, I discovered a baby grand piano and a row of large-paned windows looking out on the tended gardens with an English flavor befitting the inn's name. The light and airy feeling was enhanced by the large original barn in back (which, now remodeled, houses more guest rooms) and the lovely old cypress trees that flank and surround both structures.

Not far from Glendeven, a sense of the forest begins. But it is not Robert Frost's "lovely, dark, and deep" New England woods. Rather it is a place of laughter, a certain youthful playfulness, and the bright colors of an uncomplicated childhood. Again it is Frost who expresses this sense of childlike play: "So was I once a swinger of birches. And so I dream of going back to be."

Rachel's Inn

8200 North Highway One
Little River, California; (707) 937-0088
Mailing address: P.O. Box 134
Mendocino, California 95460

INNKEEPER:	*Rachel Binah.*
ACCOMMODATIONS:	*Five rooms, all with private bath; twin and queen-size beds.*
RESERVATIONS:	*Three to four weeks recommended.*
MINIMUM STAY:	*Two nights on weekends; three over holiday periods.*
DEPOSIT:	*First night's lodging.*
CREDIT CARDS:	*Not accepted.*
RATES:	*Moderate.*
RESTRICTIONS:	*No pets.*

A woman of many talents, Rachel Binah is credited with opening the second bed and breakfast inn ever to hit the North Coast just over fifteen years ago. (The first was Hildrun-Uta Triebess's Elk Cove Inn; Rachel and her husband Jim, from whom she is since divorced, had DeHaven Valley Farm up in Westport from 1972 to 1979.) She's back now, this time with a new inn that she simply calls Rachel's. The inn has five rooms, all exquisitely decorated, and all with private bath and queen-size beds. (Two rooms have twin accommodations for a third person.) Large, fresh flower arrangements also fill each room.

Reflecting on her life as an innkeeper, both now and then, Rachel feels that for her the main attraction of DeHaven was "having an extended family—creating a nucleus of people that you could get close to and feel warm about." Her current motivation for running an inn is to "use it as a vehicle to relate to people about issues and ideas." Rachel is highly visible and involved in the Mendocino community in a variety of ways. She's on the Executive Board for the state Democratic Party and the Central Committee for Democrats in Mendocino County. She's also involved in the offshore oil development issues affecting the northern California coast.

Rachel holds a degree in fine arts and has studied textile construction in Wales. The etchings and tapestries throughout the house are her own creations. As for the guest rooms, the inn's Parlor Suite, which has a piano in its private sitting room, is most popular. The bedroom has shuttered windows and a cushioned window bay that looks out to an ocean view. The bed is covered by a navy, burgundy, and rose-colored quilt. Another favorite is the Garden Room. Its multicolored wall tapestry sets off a platform bed. The room also has a fireplace. The Eyelet Room appeals to the feminine taste: it has a white eyelet comforter with matching pillow shams against rose carpeting and a hooked tapestry as well as a rocking chair. The Grey Room also has an ocean view, and the Blue Room steps down to a private bath with old-fashioned claw-foot tub.

Rachel's breakfasts show off her catering skills. We made our way downstairs just as the cranberry pancakes with maple syrup were being served up. An assorted fruit compote with vanilla yogurt and bacon and eggs along with a pot of steaming hot coffee also made appearances. The second morning's buffet brought forth an artichoke heart omelette with fried potatoes, homebaked corn muffins, a decadent cinnamon buttermilk streusel coffee cake, and both tomato juice and orange juice. Rachel caters lunches and dinners for groups of ten or more. It's a pity there were only two of us.

Headlands Inn

44950 Albion Street
P.O. Box 132
Mendocino, California 95460; (707) 937-4431

INNKEEPERS:	*Pat and Rod Stofle.*
ACCOMMODATIONS:	*Four rooms and a cottage, all with private bath; queen- and king-size beds.*
RESERVATIONS:	*Eight weeks recommended for weekends.*
MINIMUM STAY:	*Two nights on weekends; three during holiday periods.*
DEPOSIT:	*First night's lodging.*
CREDIT CARDS:	*Not accepted.*
RATES:	*Moderate.*
RESTRICTIONS:	*No children. No pets.*

T he Headlands Inn began as a barbershop on Main Street in the town of Mendocino in 1868. Five years later a second story was added for the barber and his family. Afterwards the dwelling was used as a saloon, a hotel annex, and a private residence. In 1883 it was moved to its present location at Howard and Albion streets.

The dwelling is three stories high, with clean, solid lines — most definitely a Victorian with a New England character. The modern conveniences are not lacking; all five rooms have private bathrooms, and all have fireplaces. Guest accommodations are named after personages that have figured prominently in the building's history. Two are attic rooms with window seats, offering the best view of the town I saw while I was there. (Look particularly for Mendocino's quaint water tower.) One room comes with a large, private balcony.

My favorite is the Bessie Strauss (named after a former owner of the home): bay windows facing the ocean, a redwood fireplace, a large mirrored armoire, a full-size sofa, lace curtains, and a wonderful king-size bed truly fit for a king.

Breakfast is comprised of fresh-baked breads and muffins, fresh fruit, a hot entrée that changes daily, hot

chocolate, coffee, and tea. It arrives on a break[...]
nished with fresh flowers. Florentine ham rolls an[...]
cious lemon yogurt bread were part of the morning m[...]
the day I was there. A copy of the San Francisco newspaper was also delivered to the door. In the afternoon complimentary wine or mineral water is served.

Local attractions are many and varied. There is an
art center, secluded sandy beaches, tide pools teeming with
marine life, hiking (three state parks are within ten miles
of Mendocino), golfing, tennis, and canoeing on Big River.
But for many, simply walking through Mendocino is
enough: it bears an astonishing resemblance to a New
England fishing village and has been used as a backdrop
for Hollywood productions. In addition, there are many
fine restaurants in the area.

rindle Inn

). Box 647
95460; (707) 937-4143

	Gwen and Bill Jacobson.
TIONS:	Ten rooms, all with private bath; twin, double, and queen-size beds.
RESERVATIONS:	Ten to twelve weeks recommended.
MINIMUM STAY:	Two nights on weekends.
DEPOSIT:	First night's lodging.
CREDIT CARDS:	Not accepted.
RATES:	Moderate.
RESTRICTIONS:	Children discouraged. No pets.

*L*ike so many others, the Grindle clan had come to the North Coast from Maine. This lovely Italianate home was built as a wedding present on the marriage of Joshua Grindle and Alice Hills in 1879 — a gift from the bride's father. Alice died in childbirth in 1882, but the house remained in the Grindle family until 1967. In 1977 Bill and Gwen Jacobson bought the house and turned it into a first-class inn.

The Jacobsons have so enhanced the "back east" tone of this exquisite bed and breakfast that it can stand up to the very best New England establishment. And it is a very romantic place; a natural, I would think, for a honeymoon.

The first things I noticed on entering were the Early American pieces in the parlor (along with the fireplace and grand piano). Colonial-era furnishings appear extensively throughout the rest of the house. All guest rooms, for example have handmade quilts from New England. The Library Room has an old-fashioned four-poster and fine handcrafted cabinets and shelves. In the dining room I found a harvest table seating ten, and Pennsylvania Dutch–style wallpaper. Impeccable taste and cleanliness add to the eastern feeling.

In back there is a cottage with two rooms, a Franklin stove, wood-beamed ceilings, and a large bath. (Both rooms are accessible by wheelchair.) A recently constructed water tower houses three additional accommodations.

The Grindle has a fine collection of old clocks that
will remind you pleasantly of all the time you have to frit-
ter away. I also liked the extensive collection of etchings,
oil paintings, and serigraphs. Two of the guest rooms in
the main house have fireplaces decorated with handcrafted
tiles made in 1870 at Ninton's, Stoke on Trent, a factory
in England. (The tiles in the Library Room illustrate *Aesop's
Fables*.)

Gwen serves an ample breakfast that includes eggs
from a nearby farm, fresh fruit, coffee cake, huckleberry
muffins, popovers, homemade breads, tea and coffee. There
are always apples and oranges in the parlor for guests, as
well as a decanter of sherry.

Whitegate Inn

499 Howard Street, P.O. Box 150
Mendocino, California 95460; (707) 937-4892

INNKEEPER:	*Patricia Patton.*
ACCOMMODATIONS:	*Five rooms, all with private bath; twin, double, and queen-size beds. Fireplaces and ocean views.*
RESERVATIONS:	*Three to four weeks recommended.*
MINIMUM STAY:	*Two nights on weekends.*
DEPOSIT:	*First night's lodging.*
CREDIT CARDS:	*Not accepted.*
RATES:	*Moderate.*
RESTRICTIONS:	*Children discouraged. No pets.*

T his house was built in 1880 by Dr. William McCornack, a local physician. He used it as his hospital,
and it retained its healing-arts association well into
living memory; it was called the McCornack Healing Center before its transformation into a bed and breakfast inn.

Many things have changed in the last hundred years
or so, but not the service orientation of the building's suc-
cession of owners — the current innkeeper is Patricia Pat-
ton, who acquired the property in May of 1986. Pat is a
savvy world traveler, who, having seen most of this planet,
now professes that "this little bit of heaven called Mendocino" is always and forever where she wants to call home.

Pat comes to the inn business from a ten-year stint
with the U.S. Department of State. Having worked in the
Foreign Service at our embassies in Austria, France, Taiwan, and Saudi Arabia, she now lets the world come to
her. Accordingly, her innkeeping style includes spending
as much time as possible with her guests and acting as
their guide through the panorama of the North Coast.

A trip to a pigmy forest, an afternoon of tidepooling at Mackerricher State Park, a horseback ride along the
beach, and an evening with the Mendocino Performing
Arts Group are some of Pat's "see and do" suggestions. She
also makes sure that her guests are aware of the movies
and TV shows that have been filmed in the area — from

Johnny Belinda (1947) to "Murder She Wrote." (Keep an eye out for Angela Lansbury when you're in town; the house used in her television series "Murder She Wrote" is on the corner of Little Lake and Ford streets.) Whitegate itself hasn't escaped Hollywood's notice. It appeared in a Bette Davis movie called *Strangers*, filmed here in the 1970s.

The house is well appointed, with gilt ceiling moldings and plaster medallions; the parlor contains a Victorian sofa, a grand Hamilton pump organ, lots of green plants, a stereo system, and a good collection of local-interest books for those curious about the area. Breakfast is served in the parlor (as is wine in the late afternoon) with silver tea and coffee service from 9:00 to 10:00 A.M. Pat makes all her own breads (carrot-pineapple or pumpkin-raisin-nut) and the granola, too. These are accompanied by sliced fresh fruit (melon, peaches, strawberries) or baked apples, yogurt, coffee, tea, and orange juice. On Sundays breakfast is extended to include walnut-cinnamon waffles with strawberry butter or rum-raisin French toast. The entire spread is served buffet style.

I slept in the Cypress Room: bay windows, an Oriental carpet, a dark oak armoire, a Franklin fireplace, white lace curtains, and a maroon down comforter with white lace-edged pillow shams. The room is sheltered by a lovely cypress tree. The largest and most popular accommodation, however, is the French Room, with its light oak French bedroom suite in the pineapple motif, Franklin fireplace, and ocean view. "A lot of honeymoons are spent here," notes Pat, who also hints at marriage proposals and romantic liaisons that no one else knows about. Wedding vows are often sealed in the gazebo outside on the lawn.

Weds nite only

Mendocino Village Inn

44860 Main Street
P.O. Box 626, Mendocino, California 95460; (707) 937-0246

INNKEEPERS:	*Tom and Sue Allen.*
ACCOMMODATIONS:	*Twelve rooms, ten with private bath; double and queen-size beds.*
RESERVATIONS:	*Three to four weeks recommended.*
MINIMUM STAY:	*Two nights on weekends.*
DEPOSIT:	*First night's lodging.*
CREDIT CARDS:	*MC, VISA.*
RATES:	*Inexpensive to moderate.*
RESTRICTIONS:	*No children under 10. No pets.*

For Tom and Sue Allen, the self-contained environment of the b&b is most appealing. After living most of their married life in New York City, their desire to "get out and do something irresponsible" was what attracted them to the coastal town of Mendocino and led them to purchase the Mendocino Village Inn. "We see bed and breakfast as an opportunity to extend our own taste and personality—to create a sort of make-believe world," said the Allens as we sat around the dining table with a cup of the house French roast and a sampling of the inn's justly famous jalapeño corn bread.

Tom is the more talkative of the two, with a subject repertoire ranging from bird species to Bach. "What we're trying to do here is turn over a bad reputation," explains Tom. "This has been an inexpensive place to stay for over thirteen years now, but it was lacking in ambience and attention to detail." "Of course there are still things to do," pipes in Sue. "Some new carpeting; wallpaper in one room."

The Allens began their restoration of the inn by going over 1890 photographs of the home with a magnifying glass to capture its architectural detail. The home, a Queen Anne Victorian, was built as the private residence of the town physician, Doctor William McCornack, in 1882. It was successively owned by four village doctors; then in the 1960s it was turned into an art gallery by Emmy Lou Packard, an artist who painted W.P.A. murals with Diego

Rivera. The house sat unoccupied for a period of years, then it once again became a family residence, and finally, a bed and breakfast inn.

The inn contains an eclectic array of theme rooms: Captain's Quarters, the Roosevelt Room, and Diamond Lil's Suite, just to name a few. Seven of the twelve rooms have fireplaces, some have ocean views, a few have private garden entrances, and ten have private baths.

The downstairs Diamond Lil is considered the best room. Its four-poster queen-size bed is covered with a crochet canopy. The room has a fireplace, a Victorian rocker, and an armoire. There's a table and chair set in the large bay window parlor, and this is one of the ten rooms that has its own private bath. Also downstairs is Captain's Quarters, also known as the Captain Lansing Room: "pineapple-post" carved bed, bull's-eye mirror (an heirloom from Tom's family), bright blue and white seashell design wallpaper, a sailing ship print, fireplace with bird's-eye redwood mantel, and a small, private bath with shower. Teddy Roosevelt's namesake is decorated with mission oak furniture; antlers hang over the bed. The brightest rooms are Miss Emily's Room and the Rosebud and Nutmeg rooms. Two attic accommodations are the least expensive offered and the only ones that share a bath. Of the three rooms with private entrances, my preference was the Quilt Cabin, with its Indian motif, willow bed, and tepee-shaped stove.

The inn's breakfast menu has undergone a major renovation too. The entrées alone are enough to make your mouth water: pain perdu (French custard toast served with blackberries and sour cream), blue cornmeal banana pancakes, Mexican strata with homemade salsa, and savory breakfast cheesecake with mushrooms, spinach, and cream cheese. But there's more. Breakfast also includes orange juice, fresh fruit, and buttermilk spice muffins or that delightful jalapeño corn bread I told you about.

An early evening wine hour is when guests convene to listen to jazz, determine foreign policy, or share Tom's thoughts on hummingbird metabolism.

Country Inn

632 North Main Street
Fort Bragg, California 95437; (707) 964-3737

INNKEEPERS:	*Don and Helen Miller.*
ACCOMMODATIONS:	*Eight rooms, all with private bath; seven queen- and one king-size bed.*
RESERVATIONS:	*Two to three weeks recommended.*
MINIMUM STAY:	*None.*
DEPOSIT:	*First night's lodging.*
CREDIT CARDS:	*MC, VISA.*
RATES:	*Inexpensive to moderate.*
RESTRICTIONS:	*No children. No pets.*

We may never know for whom this charming structure was built, but we do know it belonged to the Union Lumber Company. In 1893 it was sold to a Mr. L. A. Moody for $500 — a princely sum in those days. (A 1905 edition of the *San Francisco Examiner*, found glued to the redwood wallboards here, advertises overalls at the bargain price of 17¢ each.)

The building has passed through many hands (and lives) since then. In 1975 Don and Helen Miller moved to Fort Bragg on the craggy Mendocino County coast. Don was working as a free-lance writer, photographer, artisan, and sculptor (he calls himself a one-man advertising agency). He found himself doing a volume business writing and designing brochures for local innkeepers. It occurred to the couple that owning their own bed and breakfast inn would be an ideal way to meet people. And so it has been. (It has also given Helen a chance to pursue one of her favorite avocations: baking bread.)

This is not one of those bed and breakfasts where one is forever afraid to touch anything for fear it might break. Not that the Millers sacrifice the personal touch. Country Inn is appointed throughout with Don's photographs, sculpture, and watercolors. (The skylight in the parlor not only creates excellent light with which to view them, but accentuates the feeling of comfort and relaxation.) I liked the stairway's redwood banisters and carefully chosen wallpaper; the inn's exterior is entirely done in redwood paneling.

All of the bedrooms have plush carpeting, brass and iron beds, and wallpaper coordinated with sheets and pillowcases. Two of the rooms have fireplaces. All of the bathrooms are modern (the attic bedroom has a claw-foot tub, however); one is accessible by wheelchair with special facilities for the handicapped.

Helen makes a variety of delicious breads (sour cream nut, banana nut, and chocolate ribbon) in addition to honey-corn and honey-wheat muffins. Breakfast also includes melon wedges and slices of other fruits in season, and coffee and orange juice. Don pours complimentary wine in the evening.

Nearby attractions are surprisingly varied in Fort Bragg (a "one-taxi" town). The Footlighter Theater produces locally written musical comedy (usually old-fashioned melodramas in which the audience is encouraged to cheer the fair-haired hero; the villain makes his entrance to boos and hisses). It runs May through August. Fort Bragg is also noted for its many shops, art galleries, gardens, museums — and its award-winning gourmet ice cream.

Don and Helen speak fondly of the couple who were the first to share their accommodations. "We were mortified to find out later that we forgot to put a plug in the bathtub," Don told me. But the Millers needn't have worried — two weeks later their guests sent them a bottle of wine.

I'm not surprised. Making the great escape into total relaxation is not easy to achieve, but the congenial Millers have a formula that works.

·

Pudding Creek Inn

700 North Main Street
Fort Bragg, California 95437; (707) 964-9529

INNKEEPERS:	*Marilyn and Gene Gundersen.*
ACCOMMODATIONS:	*Ten rooms, all with private bath; twin, double, queen-, and king-size beds.*
RESERVATIONS:	*Two to three weeks recommended.*
MINIMUM STAY:	*Two nights over holidays.*
DEPOSIT:	*First night's lodging. In full during holiday periods.*
CREDIT CARDS:	*MC, VISA.*
RATES:	*Inexpensive.*
RESTRICTIONS:	*No children under 12. No pets.*

T his pretty Victorian was built in 1884 by a Russian count who fled the Old World under a cloud. He did not arrive in the New World penniless, however; some people were even so uncharitable as to suggest that he had departed with money that was not, legally speaking, his own. Ill-gotten or not, he put his spoils to good use, building seven fine homes in the Fort Bragg area.

In deference to the democratic traditions of his new homeland (and for fear of the Russian authorities, probably), our hero changed his name to the less aristocratic — and considerably more anonymous — appellation of Mr. Brown. His wedding was the occasion of considerable local interest: his bride wore the first wedding dress advertised in the Montgomery Ward catalog.

Records reveal that an equally anonymous Mr. Woods and Mrs. White later owned and lived in the count's aging home. In the 1970s it was rescued by Marilyn and Gene Gundersen and restored; in 1980 the house opened as a bed and breakfast inn, its hallways presided over by pictures of the count and his wife.

Actually there are two dwellings; both two-story buildings, connected by an enclosed garden court. (Breakfast is served here in the summer, and in the antique store–kitchen during winter.) Breakfast consists of juice, fresh fruit, homemade coffee cake, and coffee or tea. weather allows you to eat outside, you can enjoy the many varieties of fuchsias, begonias, and ferns in the garden court. (The social hour is also conducted here from 5:00 to 6:00 P.M.)

There are a total of ten guest rooms, two of which offer cozy working fireplaces. The Spinning Room is done in yellow and blue, with an old-fashioned spool-design bed. My favorite is the Interlude Room. Shades of Richard Rogers's "Blue Room": everything is blue here (including baby blue), with priscilla curtains. The king-size bed is pecan wood, and there is a spacious bathroom. Altogether a light, sunny, and very romantic room that I highly recommend.

A small country store located on the first floor of one of the dwellings offers collectibles, antiques, and gifts for sale or just for browsing. There are many shops and restaurants nearby. Tennis courts, a logging museum, and the Skunk Train depot are only a few blocks away. There is a Visitors Center in town to familiarize those who are passing through with the many sights and activities in the community.

This inn is a favorite of at least one well-known character actress. It could become your favorite too. I'm sure the roguish old count who sought refuge in the far reaches of the New World would relish the quiet good taste here — and who could help but applaud the very democratic prices associated with this modern incarnation of his nineteenth-century hideaway?

The Grey Whale Inn

615 North Main Street
Fort Bragg, California 95437; (707) 964-0640

INNKEEPERS:	*John and Colette Bailey.*
ACCOMMODATIONS:	*Fourteen rooms, all with private bath; twin, double, queen-, and king-size beds.*
RESERVATIONS:	*Three to four weeks for weekends.*
MINIMUM STAY:	*Two nights on weekends, April through October; two to three nights over holiday periods.*
DEPOSIT:	*First night's lodging; in full for holidays and April through October weekends.*
CREDIT CARDS:	*AE, MC, VISA.*
RATES:	*Inexpensive to moderate.*
RESTRICTIONS:	*No pets (local kennel accommodations).*

Fort Bragg's first (and perhaps its most distinctive) bed and breakfast inn, the Grey Whale, features spacious, comfortable rooms — all with private bath — at very affordable prices. This is an interesting establishment for several reasons, not the least of which is the discriminating staff. I found a genuine desire to please here, and considerable knowledge about the Fort Bragg area of Mendocino County.

The building itself has long been a landmark, having served from 1915, when it was built, until 1971 as the Redwood Coast Hospital, the North Coast's major health-care facility. The weathered redwood siding, completely covering the white clapboard, is trimmed with fresh colors. As more than one observer has noted, it looks as though it has always been an inn — a testament to the skill of those who designed the conversion.

John Bailey worked for Alpha Beta markets, Colette at a Veterans Hospital; both wished to go into business for themselves. They spent a year looking in northern California before they found the right place. (It was advertised in the *Wall Street Journal*.) John enjoys dealing with people in a cooperative, rather than a competitive, way.

"One gets positive feedback," Colette says. "The corporate world is a long way from Fort Bragg."

There is a wide variety of rooms here, in terms of size, decor, and views. Hallways are spacious and stairs are easy (guest rooms are on three levels); one bedroom and bath contains accommodations for the handicapped, including ramp access. The Baileys' private collection of art works is displayed throughout the building, with a strong emphasis on work by local artists. (The magnificent whale on the front grounds was carved by Byrd Baker, a leader in the Save the Whales movement.)

Guests are encouraged to let the staff know in advance of special dietary requirements. Breakfast is served from 7:30 to 10:30 A.M. each morning in the Breakfast Room. It includes homemade fruit and nut breads or coffee cake, fresh fruit, egg casseroles, yogurt or custard, juice, and hot beverages. Guests are welcome to take breakfast back to their room.

Those interested in local activities are supplied with a big book listing things to do in the area, easily the most extensive and helpful guide that I saw during my tour. There are a surprising number of attractions: Noyo Harbor with its fishing fleet, state parks and beaches, redwood forests galore, art galleries, concerts, and even good local opera at certain times of the year. Annual town festivals include the Whale Festival in March, a salmon barbecue in July, and Paul Bunyan Days in the fall.

This is one of the most successful bed and breakfast inns I visited, and it is easy to see why. It does something that many inns aim for but do not always achieve: it affords the *joie de vivre* of many people gathered under one roof in pleasant surroundings—yet still succeeds, through its conscientious attention to the needs and preferences of the individual, in making each guest feel special.

dinner Mary beth -
— Mendocino Hotel —
7 PM -

The Blue Rose Inn

520 North Main Street
Fort Bragg, California 95437; (707) 964-3477

INNKEEPER:	*Anne Samas.*
ACCOMMODATIONS:	*Five rooms, four with private bath; double and queen-size beds.*
RESERVATIONS:	*One month recommended.*
MINIMUM STAY:	*None.*
DEPOSIT:	*First night's lodging.*
CREDIT CARDS:	*AE.*
RATES:	*Inexpensive.*
RESTRICTIONS:	*No children. No pets.*

Anne Samas was raised in southwestern Pennsylvania, and she remembers clearly the popularity of the "guest house." The guest house — or tourist home, as it was sometimes called — was usually a private residence with one or more rooms available to the traveler in search of more personal (and probably less expensive) lodging. Add the breakfast — which many guest houses in Pennsylvania traditionally served — and you have the classic bed and breakfast experience as one generally finds it in Europe and the British Isles.

Anne came to Mendocino in 1962, planning to open a tourist home herself. She priced several houses, but none seemed right. It was not until 1976 that she bought the present structure. It is a 102-year-old Cape Cod Victorian, and she and her son David have done wonders with it. Her plant-filled establishment is enhanced by redwood ceilings, Tiffany and crystal chandeliers, and attractive wallpaper patterns imported from Korea, Japan, and France.

This is definitely a bed and breakfast inn rather than a private home offering bed and breakfast accommodations, but it exhibits much of the informality of a guest house. Anne's living quarters are in the rear, in an old shed she and David have transformed into a pleasant little cottage. She feels this gives guests more elbow room. "Since I'm not technically on the premises, they can do whatever they want," she says. "They have the run of the kitchen and can use the refrigerator, for example." She adds: "When guests first arrive, I spend some time with them. After that, I'm available — but I don't get in the way."

The rooms — like Anne's garden, which she modestly calls "the best garden in Fort Bragg"— are brightly hued in colors calculated to refresh as well as relax. I liked the French Provincial, which follows a color scheme of gold and lavender. The Blue Room is blue and off-white, with an antique bed of walnut, a marble-topped dresser and washstand, and a claw-foot tub in the bath. Guests relax in the Green Room, a reception area where a telephone for guest use is located. They are also welcome in the kitchen and the parlor; the latter contains rattan chairs from Taiwan and a fine hand-carved screen.)

Anne is of the opinion that when leaving the toil and turmoil of city life and the working world, one should not continue to punch the time clock. So there is no set time for breakfast: it begins at 8:00 and continues until everybody has finished. Anne sets out quiche, cinnamon-raisin bread, fruit in season, orange juice, milk, and tea and coffee. Guests are supplied with bacon and eggs, which they can make for themselves any time they feel ready for breakfast.

This distinctive laissez-faire policy is also in effect concerning one's departure. The Blue Rose has no checkout time. "Many times guests will still be sitting around the kitchen table talking with other guests over breakfast until noon or even later," Anne says. She makes it clear that this informality is one of the things that make her accommodations friendlier and more relaxed than most — and I heartily agree.

The Gingerbread Mansion

Humboldt County

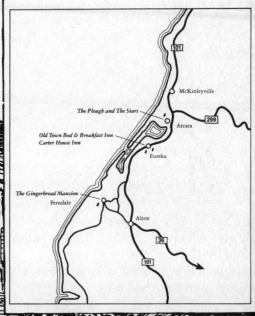

101

McKinleyville

The Plough and The Stars

299

Arcata

Old Town Bed & Breakfast Inn
Carter House Inn

Eureka

The Gingerbread Mansion
Ferndale

Alton

36

101

The Gingerbread Mansion

400 Berding Street
Ferndale, California 95536; (707) 786-4000

INNKEEPERS:	*Wendy Hatfield and Ken Torbert.*
ACCOMMODATIONS:	*Eight rooms, five with private bath; twin, double, and queen-size beds.*
RESERVATIONS:	*Three weeks recommended.*
MINIMUM STAY:	*None.*
DEPOSIT:	*Full amount.*
CREDIT CARDS:	*MC, VISA.*
RATES:	*Inexpensive to moderate.*
RESTRICTIONS:	*No children under 10. No pets.*

Watch that thirteenth step! It's taller than the rest, and purposely designed so to keep evil spirits from ascending the stairway to the upstairs bedrooms. This in strict accordance with Victorian tradition, or rather superstition, carried on to this day at the Gingerbread Mansion in Ferndale.

Billed as northern California's second-most-photographed home, this exquisitely turreted, carved, and gabled mansion with its colorfully landscaped English gardens was originally built as a residence for village physician Dr. Hogan Ring in 1899. It is a visual masterpiece — one of Ferndale's "butterfat palaces" (named for the dairy wealth that built the community), combining Queen Anne and Eastlake architectural styles with an abundance of ornamental trim.

Husband-and-wife team Ken Torbert and Wendy Hatfield purchased the home-turned-hospital-turned-apartment-house in 1982 and opened its doors as a bed and breakfast inn a year later. To date the Gingerbread Mansion has been recognized by an impressive list of publications, including *National Geographic, Sunset* magazine, and the *New York Times*.

The inn's eight bedrooms, four parlors, and formal dining room are elegantly appointed with antiques of the period. Guest rooms follow various themes and color schemes (the Fountain Room, Rose Room, Garden Room,

Lilac Room, Heron Room, Gingerbread Suite), but, surprisingly, one of the most spectacular rooms in the house is the second-floor bath, with its 200 square feet of mirrored walls and ceiling, elevated claw-foot tub, French bidet, marble-topped dresser, hanging plants, and floral pastel wallpaper with matching stained-glass window.

The inn's many "little extras" include nightly turndown service, hand-dipped chocolates by the bedside, bathrobes, luggage racks in the rooms, bicycles, a well-stocked supply of information on the area, afternoon tea and cake, and a generous Continental breakfast featuring homemade muffins and breads, assorted cheeses, fresh fruit, orange juice, coffee, and tea.

Ferndale, once known as "cream city," is today touted as "California's best-kept secret." Its well-preserved turn-of-the-century architecture and its Victorian Main Street, offering art galleries, an old-fashioned mercantile store, a blacksmith shop, and even a homemade candy "factory," give it an irresistible fairy-tale charm. Among the fairs, festivals, and parades that perpetuate the enchantment are the Scandinavian Festival, the Humboldt County Fair, the Kinetic Sculpture Race, the Ice Cream Social, and the Pet Parade.

Old Town Bed & Breakfast Inn

handwritten: 4 - 4 1/2 hrs from Ft Bragg

1521 Third Street
Eureka, California 95501; (707) 445-3951

handwritten: 50 - 65 -

INNKEEPERS:	*Leigh and Diane Benson.*
ACCOMMODATIONS:	*Five rooms, three with private bath; twin, double, queen-, and king-size beds.*
RESERVATIONS:	*Two to three weeks recommended.*
MINIMUM STAY:	*None.*
DEPOSIT:	*Full amount.*
CREDIT CARDS:	*AE, MC, VISA.*
RATES:	*Inexpensive.*
RESTRICTIONS:	*Quiet, well-behaved children only. No pets.*

Humboldt County, located in the northernmost part of California, is a region blessed with a mild climate and natural amenities based on three major resources: conifer forests, rich farmland, and an abundance of water (rivers, bays, and the Pacific Ocean). A fourth, and often unnamed, natural attraction is its people, warm and welcoming.

Eureka is Humboldt's largest city (population twenty-five thousand). An area that vividly portrays the city's importance as a major lumber, shipping, and fishing center since the 1850s is Old Town, where restored Victorian buildings on brick-paved walkways house specialty shops and restaurants. The gateway to Old Town is the renowned Carson Mansion at Second and M streets, former home of lumber baron William Carson.

Another one-time residence of the Carson family (from 1872 to 1885), and the last remaining structure of Carson's bay mill, is now a bed and breakfast inn — appropriately Old Town Bed & Breakfast Inn, located at Third and P. This is the house Mrs. Carson loved most, according to local historians, and it's easy to see why. Cute and cozy, it has a "come on in, relax awhile" feeling that is enhanced by present-day owners Leigh and Diane Benson, a couple whose affinity for old houses and new people makes for innkeeping success.

The inn's five guest rooms are decorated with antiques. Two that win my vote of confidence are the Raspberry Parfait Room (plush raspberry carpeting, delicate rose-patterned wallpaper, beige lace curtains, a ruffled comforter on the queen-size bed, and an antique dresser) and the Maxfield Parrish Room (shades of pale blue with frilly white lace curtains, a queen-size bed, and an oak armoire). Whether shared or private, bathrooms are amply stocked with the essentials even experienced travelers sometimes leave behind.

Guests convene in the wood stove–heated kitchen for a hearty breakfast complemented by lively conversation. Eggs Derelict are said to be the house specialty, although the entrée might be crab quiche one morning or cast-iron breakfast pie the next. This, along with the home-baked muffins, homemade jams and jellies, fresh fruit in season, and juice, is enough to satisfy until way past noon — which might be about the time you can expect to leave the table. As Diane says: "You never know who you're going to meet!"

- Diane -

Jerry's Room

To Humboldt -
bus -
runs from airport
to college

Carter House Inn

Third and L streets
Eureka, California 95501; (707) 445-1390

INNKEEPERS:	*Mark and Christi Carter.*
ACCOMMODATIONS:	*Seven rooms, four with private bath; six double beds and one queen-size bed.*
RESERVATIONS:	*Two to three weeks recommended.*
MINIMUM STAY:	*None.*
DEPOSIT:	*Full amount.*
CREDIT CARDS:	*AE, MC, VISA.*
RATES:	*Moderate to expensive.*
RESTRICTIONS:	*No children. No pets.*

D ear Mom and Dad,
Sophie and I are having a great time up here in Humboldt County. Yesterday we toured the lumber mill at Scotia and drove through the redwoods along the Avenue of the Giants. And you'll never guess what happened. Since we arrived in Eureka earlier than expected, we decided to walk around Old Town and get a look at the Carson Mansion (they say it's the most-photographed house in America) before locating the Carter House Inn. We parked the car and were walking down Third Street when we came alongside of one of the most magnificent Victorian structures I had ever seen. I turned to Sophie and said: "Now *there* is a place I'd like to spend a night!" As we walked around the corner to get a better look I just about died. The sign read: Carter House Inn, Bed & Breakfast.

Mark and Christi Carter are the cutest couple (she's kind of quiet, but just as sweet as can be). Mark told us he built this three-story mansion from plans taken from an 1884 San Francisco Victorian designed by Samuel and Joseph Cather Newsom (same architects as the Carson Mansion) that was destroyed in the 1906 quake. The exterior is constructed of clear heart redwood; the interior is finished in polished redwood and oak.

The first floor serves as a combination contemporary art gallery and common area for the inn. The formal din-

ing room is complete with silver service. There's an ornate wood and marble fireplace, plush velvet upholstered chairs and chaise longues in the parlor, and antiques, pottery, mantel clocks, sculpture, and paintings everywhere. The guest rooms are located on the lower level and the second and third floors. We're staying in the Burgundy Room, which is quite comfortable. Another room I like is the Pink Room, with its late-1800s European oak bedroom set.

We wanted to get over to the Samoa Cookhouse, a family-style restaurant that used to serve up to five hundred lumbermen a day, but the food's so good here there's hardly any room left—wine and hors d'oeuvres at five; tea, cookies, and cordials later in the evening. And Mom, Christi gave me her recipe for that decadent Pecan Phyllo Tart she served at breakfast this morning—along with eggs Benedict, plums with raspberry sauce, bran muffins, a smoked salmon platter, orange juice, and coffee—see what I mean? But you and Dad should really get up here yourselves, I know you'll like it too. See you soon.

Love,
Linda Kay

The Plough and the Stars Country Inn

1800 Twenty-seventh Street
Arcata, California 95521; (707) 822-8236

INNKEEPERS:	*Bill and Melissa Hans.*
ACCOMMODATIONS:	*Five rooms, two with private bath; twin, double and queen-size beds.*
RESERVATIONS:	*Two to three weeks recommended.*
MINIMUM STAY:	*Two nights over Memorial Day, Labor Day, and Thanksgiving.*
DEPOSIT:	*First night's lodging.*
CREDIT CARDS:	*Not accepted.*
RATES:	*Inexpensive.*
RESTRICTIONS:	*No children. No pets.*

*I*n the midst of all of Humboldt County's Victoriana there is a decidedly refreshing inn with a totally different ambience: The Plough and the Stars Country Inn, named after Irishman Sean O'Casey's play to reflect the proprietors' own ancestry and sentiments.

The inn is an 1860s Midwestern-style farmhouse that sits on two acres. The atmosphere is casual, and the innkeepers are a young enthusiastic pair attempting to "resurrect the proper standard of hospitality."

A series of events guided by the steady hand of fate culminated in this lifetime "dream come true" for Melissa Hans, who saw her first b&b in England at the age of seventeen. She studied hotel and restaurant management at San Francisco's City College while working part time at the Fairmont and various restaurants around town. Husband Bill, who was employed in timber management for five years, also acquired an interest in full-time innkeeping. Arcata provided the ideal spot for both to accomplish their ambitions.

Part of the attraction of The Plough and the Stars is the spontaneity and flexibility of its innkeepers. Melissa took me for a swim at the local pool, and the Hanses have been known to take guests out to the beach to watch the sunset when the mood strikes. "We're easy touches for charades and other antics," states Melissa, who has stocked the inn with a full complement of board and parlor games. Family and friends are welcome to visit guests at the inn and share a meal or join in a game of basketball, croquet, or horseshoes. Pastures, lawns, and gardens allow plenty of room for roaming, socializing, and playing, and peaceful country roads invite leisurely jaunts.

In close proximity is Arcata's town center (with one of the few remaining central plazas in California), the Humboldt State College campus, and access to Highway 101. Missy's list of "must-sees and dos" includes Redwood Park and Community Forest, Arcata's historic walking tour, Moonstone Beach, Fern Canyon, and the Mad River, a favorite fishing spot just a sand dune away. And "don'ts": pay $3 to drive through a tree at Leggett, disregard the "slow to 35 mph" signs, let anyone stick a Trees of Mystery sign on your car's bumper, or leave your swimming suit or raincoat at home.

Early risers ponder the day's activities in the spacious country kitchen over a steaming hot cup of coffee with real cream, the aroma of date-nut bread and blueberry muffins fresh from the oven, and a plate of fresh fruit with slices of cheese. Sleepyheads request breakfast in bed.

Historical, pastoral, homey: three words that merely attempt to describe a feeling too good for words. The Plough and the Stars — not just a place to sleep, rather a suitable place for awakening.

Court Street Inn

The Gold Country
Sierra

Quincy
49
The Feather Bed
20
Grandmere's
Red Castle Inn   Nevada City
Grass Valley
Murphy's Inn
80
Mayfield House
Tahoe City   Lake Tahoe
Homewood
Rockwood Lodge
Auburn
American River Inn
Georgetown
Coloma
Placerville   **50**
80
50
Briggs House
Fleming Jones Homestead
Sacramento
Mine House
Inn   **49**
16
The Foxes
Nine Eureka Street
Sutter Creek Inn
Amador City
Ione   Sutter Creek
The Heirloom
88
Jackson   *Court Street Inn*
Gate House
Inn
Dunbar House
Angels Camp
Llamahall
Guest Ranch
Sonora   **108**
4
Tuolumne
Oak Hill Ranch
Chinese Camp
108 **120**
120   *Meadow Creek*
49   Mariposa   *Ranch*

Red Castle Inn

109 Prospect Street
Nevada City, California 95959; (916) 265-5135

INNKEEPERS:	*Conley and Mary Louise Weaver.*
ACCOMMODATIONS:	*Eight rooms, six with private bath; double and queen-size beds.*
RESERVATIONS:	*Two weeks recommended.*
MINIMUM STAY:	*Two nights for Saturday and holiday period stays.*
DEPOSIT:	*Half of full amount.*
CREDIT CARDS:	*Not accepted.*
RATES:	*Moderate.*
RESTRICTIONS:	*Children discouraged. No pets.*

*I*mposing is the word for this baronial structure high on Prospect Hill, overlooking the historic Gold Rush town of Nevada City. Four stories high, it is also one of the few classic examples of Gothic Revival — as opposed to the more popular Carpenter Gothic — to be found in the western states. (Gothic Revival was an architectural fashion in the United States from 1835 to 1880; the Red Castle was built in 1859–1860.) Extensive gardens and a pond enhance the castlelike effect; a pathway on the grounds winds to the town below.

At 2,800 feet, Nevada City was one of the first towns set up by the forty-niners, who came from all parts of the world looking for the legendary quick strike in the Mother Lode (the Spanish called it the Veta Madre, and the name stuck). Some in fact did make their fortunes in gold; others prospered by furnishing the Argonauts — the name by which the gold seekers were most frequently known in the nineteenth century — with basic goods and services. One man who did both was Judge John Williams. Crossing the plains in 1849, he stayed in the booming new city long enough to become a well-known businessman, mine owner, civic leader, and finally judge. After two false starts he succeeded in erecting this monument to his industry. The Red Castle stands today as a reminder of the dreams of glory that motivated all who came to this near-wilderness and stayed to carve out a new state.

Shortly after its one-hundredth anniversary, the Red Castle was restored and later turned into an inn. Conley and Mary Louise Weaver took possession of it in January 1986. Conley, an architect by profession, not only appreciates the historical detail of the home, but vows to preserve the romantic past of this registered state landmark.

The new proprietors have followed a middle course in furnishings: authentic, but also comfortable. The bathrooms retain the old-fashioned washbasins, but stall showers have been added. The original pine floors, grain-painted doors, and ceiling moldings are exactly as Judge Williams installed them; antiques of the period have been carefully selected for each room. Guest accommodations on the second floor are "parlor suites," each containing a small sitting area as well as a bedroom. Rooms on the first floor open up onto a veranda, and there is a tastefully appointed parlor, complete with an 1880 Storey & Clark pump organ.

Breakfast is a full buffet served between 8:00 and 10:00 A.M. Included are quiches, frittatas, and soufflés; breads, muffins, and biscuits with homemade jam; and hot or cold fruit dishes. Nearby attractions include plenty of gold mines, as well as community theater, a bluegrass festival in neighboring Grass Valley, and a classical music festival. Both Tahoe National Forest and Soda Springs, a popular ski area and resort, are nearby as well.

Smithsonian magazine calls the Red Castle a "perfect restoration," and the Daughters of the Golden West have named it an important point of historical interest. It is an ideal spot to revel in the gingerbread facade and icicle trim of another era's architectural imagination, but also to relax in the comfort its new owners have created for the present.

Grandmere's Inn

449 Broad Street
Nevada City, California 95959; (916) 265-4660

INNKEEPER:	*Annette Meade.*
ACCOMMODATIONS:	*Six rooms, all with private bath; queen-size beds.*
RESERVATIONS:	*Three to four weeks recommended.*
MINIMUM STAY:	*None.*
DEPOSIT:	*First night's lodging.*
CREDIT CARDS:	*MC, VISA.*
RATES:	*Moderate to expensive.*
RESTRICTIONS:	*Children can be accommodated in one room of the inn. No pets.*

Nestled on a hill above the old downtown section of Nevada City is a white, Colonial Revival home with restrained Victorian gingerbread known as Grandmere's Inn. This six-bedroom inn is listed in the National Register of Historic Places, not just because it was built back in 1856, but because it was originally the home of Aaron Augustus Sargent, one of California's most powerful politicians. Also a lawyer, a miner, and a newspaper editor, Sargent rose to become a congressman, senator, and U.S. ambassador to Germany. He was a champion of the bill that created the transcontinental railroad, succeeding where others had failed for a decade. And it was Sargent who authored the 1878 women's rights law called the Anthony Amendment that was finally passed some forty years later, with no change in wording.

An influential suffragist of her time, Aaron's wife, Ellen, was a close friend of Susan B. Anthony, who was often a guest in this home. (When Ellen died in 1911, flags in San Francisco were lowered to half-mast for a woman for the first time in the city's history.)

Today, a small, equally intense woman with dark, sparkling eyes and an animated spirit presides over the halls of the Sargent House — Annette Meade, who bought it with a partner in 1985. Annette went from making rag rugs and quilts and studying architecture and furniture design to opening an inn that looks much the same as it did in 1856 on the outside, but has been considerably brightened and polished within.

After expanding former closets into bathrooms and adding grey and white marble floors to the entry at the bottom of the curving stairway, Annette brought in pine furniture, bright floral wallpaper, kitchen tiles made from molds designed by Julia Morgan (one of the architects of Hearst Castle), and two deep blue sofas to "warm up" the living room. Then this mother of three went to work on the bedrooms.

Devon's Room, upstairs to the back, is particularly appealing. Named for Annette's daughter, it holds a queen-size bed with a brass headboard, round nightstands topped with lace, vases of silk flowers, a big, mirrored armoire, white wicker armchairs and love seat, a double-size hide-away sofabed, and French doors that open to a sunny, glassed-in sitting room with a fine view of the garden.

Nana's Room is actually a suite with a bedroom, a sun porch, and a private bath. It has a double-size sleeper sofa, a French armoire, and a queen-size walnut bed. Papa's Room, with a mahogany four-poster, also has a private bath. John's Room has a pole pine bed; Joseph's Room, a pine four-poster. The Guest Room boasts a queen-size wicker bed as well as its own garden entrance.

If the heart of Grandmere's is its history, then the soul is its food. Guests gather around small tables for two or share the big center table for the full country meal served at 9:00 A.M. The "serve-yourself" sideboard includes such delectables as tomato frittata; curried corn or potato-cheese casserole; steaming hot croissants; bran muffins bulging with figs, coconut, and pecans; and three blends of freshly ground coffee. (Cookie jar raiding is tolerated twenty-four hours a day.)

The area has many activities to sample, as well. From an annual bluegrass festival and teddy bear convention to a Father's Day bicycle race and November quilt show, the Gold Rush town of Nevada City blossoms with excitement year-round. But perhaps nothing can top the thrill of staying in a historic home in the heart of this area that boasts such a colorful past.

Murphy's Inn

318 Neal Street
Grass Valley, California 95945; (916) 273-6873

INNKEEPERS:	*Marc and Rose Murphy.*
ACCOMMODATIONS:	*Eight rooms, six with private bath; double, queen-, and king-size beds.*
RESERVATIONS:	*Four to six weeks recommended for summer weekends.*
MINIMUM STAY:	*None.*
DEPOSIT:	*First night's lodging.*
CREDIT CARDS:	*AE, MC, VISA.*
RATES:	*Inexpensive to moderate.*
RESTRICTIONS:	*Children: negotiable. No pets.*

M urphy's Inn was originally the opulent estate of gold baron Edward Coleman, owner of the North Star and Idaho mines. Today, this show-place of the northern Gold Country, an 1866 Colonial Revival house, looks almost as it did in century-old etchings. Ivy still pours from baskets on the huge, wraparound veranda. Vines still twine up the porch's stately white columns. And a majestic sequoia tree still stands sentinel-like in the front yard.

Walking into Murphy's is like taking a step back in time. "As present and past gradually blur, today seems more of yesterday than tomorrow," notes an entry in the inn's guest book.

"Innkeeping is in my blood," says Marc Murphy, who opened the inn with a partner in 1982 and now runs it with his wife. Marc's family owns and operates a hotel in Switzerland. For seventy-five years, his great-grandmother, Theodosia, had a resort on the Russian River. With its vintage, gas-burning chandeliers, massive antique armoires, and skylights that open onto that towering sequoia, this inn reflects her delicate taste.

Crossing the threshold of the two-story building, you'll find two sitting rooms with marble and antique tile fireplaces and cherrywood and oak mantels. The pride of the three guest rooms downstairs is Theodosia's Suite, which, for honeymooners, comes with a complimentary bottle of champagne. If you arrive on a cold night, you'll be impressed to notice the fireplace already lit and the ornate, marble-topped table (between it and the seating area) graced with a bottle of chilled wine, two glasses, and a bowl of fresh fruit. The window seat holds a treasure trove of old magazines, such as a 1929 *Harpers* and a 1948 *Life*. Together with an antique vanity and a large library arranged by topic, the suite even has a king-size brass bed surrounded by lace curtains.

Of the four upstairs rooms, guest favorite is the spacious East Room, which features a mahogany four-poster bed, platform rocking chair, antique dressing table and, best of all, a skylight right in the shower. Would you prefer having an entire penthouse to yourself? Then you might consider staying in the Donation Day House, a second building the Murphys added to the inn in 1984. The sprawling top floor of the house includes French doors that separate a private sitting area from the bedroom with its king-size white iron bed and wood-burning stove.

Following a toasty night in the Gold Country, you may not even feel like leaving your room. One whiff of the inn's country breakfast, however, should be enough to lure you out. Fresh orange juice; freshly ground coffee; coddled eggs, omelettes, or eggs Benedict with hollandaise sauce; sausage; fresh fruit compote; homemade lemon or poppy seed bread; and blueberry muffins are just some of the palate-pleasers to expect. You can have your meal in the breakfast room or take it back to your bedroom.

After breakfast, if you're in the mood for a little exercise, put on your walking shoes for a historical tour of Grass Valley or take a short drive to do the same thing in nearby Nevada City. The area bulges with fine restaurants, saloons, museums, and monuments, such as Empire Mine State Park and the Malakoff Diggings.

Upon your return, you'll want to laze the rest of the day away, dividing your time between a rest in the inn's hammock (don't be surprised if Kitty, the resident cat, hops in your lap) and, if it's hot outside, a dip in the sixteen-foot-long modern swim-spa. At night, it doubles as a hot tub that will leave you so relaxed they may have to come and fish you out.

The Briggs House

2209 Capitol Avenue
Sacramento, California 95816; (916) 441-3214

INNKEEPERS:	*Bob and Sue Garmston, Barbara Stoltz, Kathy Yeates, and Paula Rawles.*
ACCOMMODATIONS:	*Seven rooms, five with private bath; twin, double, and queen-size beds.*
RESERVATIONS:	*Two to three weeks recommended.*
MINIMUM STAY:	*None.*
DEPOSIT:	*First night's lodging.*
CREDIT CARDS:	*AE, MC, VISA.*
RATES:	*Inexpensive to moderate.*
RESTRICTIONS:	*Children in Carriage House only. No pets.*

D octor William Briggs was born in Ohio, and after studying his eye, ear, nose, and throat specialty in Europe, he settled and began his practice in Sacramento. The Capital City was still something of a frontier town in those days. Technically not within the Gold Country, Sacramento, along with San Francisco, was one of the two centers of civilization the weary miners turned to when they were ready to spend their hard-won cash. But if life was hard in the mining towns, in the cities it was sometimes brutal and capricious.

But already the Gold Country was slowly turning from mining to more dependable pursuits, among them the lumber business. Dr. Briggs was one of the original organizers of the Save the Redwoods League, bitterly opposed by the lumber interests. At the same time he was becoming something of a civic leader, a friend of those in high places. In 1901, he bought this Neo-Federalist dwelling, shortly after it was built, and lived here until his death in 1931.

What luck, then, that this lively and imaginative quintet got together to restore and manage it as an inn — the first bed and breakfast to open in Sacramento. All the partners are in the same occupation (education), all have different approaches to decorating; yet somehow they managed to make the interiors compatible — despite the fact that each partner decorated a separate room.

The Heritage Suite has a queen-size bed and floor-length tieback drapes in blue, with accessories of the period (lace pillows, perfume bottles, linens, and a vintage dress hanging on the wall). My favorite was the Sunrise Room, which features a private balcony with white wicker rocker and table that catch the morning sun. It has baby blue walls, an armoire, an antique hand-carved double bed, comforter and pillows in beige lace, and a plush carpeted bath.

Guests at the Briggs House are met with baskets of fresh fruit and almonds; wine is served in the parlor in the afternoon (or mineral water, according to one's taste). Breakfast is an elaborate affair consisting of an egg-based dish (quiche or frittata), homemade muffins and breads, fresh fruits and juices.

Guests are encouraged to enjoy the large front porch, with its comfortable porch swing. In addition there are common areas where guests may relax and mingle, if they wish: a well-stocked library, the parlor (once the home's dining room), and a backyard garden — a very pleasant place with its spa and sauna, picnic table, fig and plum trees — framed by redwood lattices. Bicycles are available for pedaling around town. (Sutter's Fort, the Capitol buildings, the Railroad Museum, Old Town, and the Crocker Art Museum are all nearby.)

American River Inn

Main and Orleans streets, P.O. Box 43
Georgetown, California 95634; (916) 333-4499

INNKEEPERS:	*Will and Maria Collin.*
ACCOMMODATIONS:	*Twenty rooms, five with private bath; twin, double, and queen-size beds.*
RESERVATIONS:	*Two to three weeks recommended.*
MINIMUM STAY:	*None.*
DEPOSIT:	*$25.*
CREDIT CARDS:	*AE, MC, VISA.*
RATES:	*Inexpensive.*
RESTRICTIONS:	*No children under 10. No pets.*

Georgetown is one of those Gold Country villages that seem to exist in more than one time, the modern starkly accented by visible reminders of the Old West. Cars are parked along the main street—part of which still has the old wooden sidewalk—but it isn't unusual to see a horse tethered in front of a saloon. It was once a place of quick (if not particularly easy) money, supported by the Woodside Mine, estimated to have brought in $2 million in gold by the spring of 1853. Directly behind the mine was a spacious rooming house for miners, later a pleasure house with gambling and ladies of the night. Lola Montez, the legendary "spider dancer," once entertained here, according to local history.

The rooming house was also used as a way station by stagecoaches on the Wentworth Springs route to Tahoe. First finished in 1853, the house suffered at least three fires that razed the town during the 1880s, never quite succumbing but requiring partial renovation each time. In recent years it was a private residence and was allowed to decline.

Then it was bought by Al and Marion Podesta, who began the restoration work completed by new owners and innkeepers Will and Maria Collin.

Restoration of the historic American River Inn (formerly known as the American Hotel) turned out to be more difficult and more lengthy than anyone could have predicted. The Podestas spent seven years on the project, while the Collins managed to finish yet another year's worth of work inside of three months, with a little help from their friends. But the dream has come true. The exterior has been painted ivory with Wedgwood blue trim, and a redwood deck was added for dining *al fresco*. Inside, the red-fir floors have been stripped and refinished, and a floor-to-ceiling rock fireplace was built from native stone. Four cramped rooms downstairs were turned into two; upstairs guest rooms have been furnished with wainscoting, crown moldings, and ornamental mopboards.

Breakfast at the American River Inn is always a treat. Maria makes it a point never to serve any guest the same breakfast twice. The morning I was there I was privileged to receive quiche Lorraine, Canadian bacon, blueberry muffins, orange juice, and cinnamon coffee. (Neal and Carol La Morte, who share innkeeping duties with the Collins, have a specialty all their own: a full country breakfast with eggs "any way you like them," fresh link sausages, and country-fried potatoes.)

Guests may relax in either the dining room or the parlor with its Franklin stove and player piano. Outside is an aviary, a vegetable garden, a swimming pool, and a heated Jacuzzi. Also available for guest use are bicycles and an outdoor barbecue.

Nearby attractions include twelve lakes "up country," good fishing, and gold panning. But this is essentially a place to get away from activities, not to explore new ones. Let's just say that if you're feeling lost, the American River Inn is a place where you can begin to find your way back.

The Fleming Jones Homestead

3170 Newtown Road
Placerville, California 95667; (916) 626-5840

INNKEEPER:	*Janice Condit.*
ACCOMMODATIONS:	*Six rooms, four with private bath; single and double beds.*
RESERVATIONS:	*One month recommended for summer weekends.*
MINIMUM STAY:	*None.*
DEPOSIT:	*Full amount.*
CREDIT CARDS:	*Not accepted.*
RATES:	*Inexpensive.*
RESTRICTIONS:	*Children by arrangement. No pets.*

This delightful two-story, nineteenth-century farm-house was the first bed and breakfast inn on the western side of the Sierra foothills of El Dorado County. It's a good bet for those who seek total relaxation. No televisions, radios, not even a telephone — but there are eleven acres to relax and ramble in. Since the Fleming Jones Homestead is also a working farm, eggs and home-made preserves are for sale, pet chickens and burros roam the grounds, and pasture is available to those who want to give their horses a vacation too.

The Joneses were a pioneer family who settled in the area in the 1850s. Fleming Jones reputedly financed this home for his wife, Florence, with gambling money. She had wanted a new house for some time, when (according to family legend) Fleming came home late one night from the saloon. His cards had been lucky that night, and his pockets were full of money — which he promptly set down in front of his astonished wife. "There," he said. "Go build your house!"

Florence obeyed with alacrity. She had her new home built entirely of "clear" lumber — that is, planks without knots in them; it was completed in 1883.

When Janice Condit began to renovate the old farmhouse, she asked Fleming Jones's granddaughter if she might use his name. The granddaughter was more than happy to give the venture her blessing. It's easy to see why—this is a respectful yet very comfortable venture into the homestead's past, one that respects its tradition as a working farm. (Janice lives in an old milk house that has been imaginatively converted into living quarters, adjacent to the main dwelling.)

All rooms are decorated with country antiques. Lover's Fancy is done in tones of peach and white, with an iron and brass bed. The Oak and Rose Room looks out onto a rose garden. (The historic rose gardens, adjacent to the farmhouse, include more than two hundred rose-bushes—mostly of the "old rose" varieties such as damasks, gallicas, and rugosas.) The bed here has a hand-carved oak headboard. The Flower Basket Room opens onto the second-floor balcony, and the Bunk House is just that—rustic on the outside, as warm and charming as a cottage on the inside—decorated with all sorts of old lamps, farm implements, and homestead treasures.

The parlor beckons with two corner rockers, a pump organ, and a Steinway grand piano. Porches with swings and comfortable chairs overlook the homestead vegetable garden and adjoining meadows. Hikers can inspect the remains of mining equipment, mute testimony to the men who searched for gold here long ago.

Janice's full breakfast includes farm-fresh eggs, home-made muffins, homemade preserves, fruit breads, fresh fruit—including pears and apples from the orchard—sweet butter, and tea or fresh-ground French roast coffee. It is served at a massive oak table in the dining room that reminded me of the big tables at which my grandmother once fed my grandfather's threshing crews. If you've never had a grandmother with a farm in the country, a leisurely visit here will show you what you've missed—and once you've experienced it, you'll surely want more of the same.

Mine House Inn

South Highway 49, P.O. Box 245
Amador City, California 95601; (209) 267-5900

INNKEEPERS:	*Ann Marie and Peter Daubenspeck III.*
ACCOMMODATIONS:	*Seven rooms, all with private bath; double beds.*
RESERVATIONS:	*Two weeks recommended.*
MINIMUM STAY:	*None.*
DEPOSIT:	*First night's lodging.*
CREDIT CARDS:	*Not accepted.*
RATES:	*Inexpensive.*
RESTRICTIONS:	*No pets.*

A mador means "love of gold"— and more than half the gold mined and panned during the boom years of the Gold Rush came from Amador County. It was here in Amador City that one of the first large gold quartz mining claims was staked out, in 1850. In 1851 the Keystone Consolidated Mine was formed, its total production eventually to exceed $24 million. The Mine House Inn is located in the old mine headquarters, a solid brick structure built in 1867, during the days when any mine headquarters was a likely target for bandits and highway robbers.

Peter Daubenspeck had been in the hotel business in San Francisco for eleven years when he decided to manage the old Consolidated headquarters as an inn; the building itself had been in his family for almost three decades. It is the only inn in America housed in such a structure. It is also one of the few bed and breakfast inns in the area that accepts children, a welcome accommodation for the traveling family. And it is the only one hereabouts that has a swimming pool for the guests' enjoyment.

Peter and Ann Marie have carefully furnished their inn with antiques that all come from the Mother Lode, within a hundred-mile radius of Mine House. The decor and ambience of the rooms make this place noteworthy.

The theme of each room is keyed to its original function. In the Mill Grinding Room, for example, one finds the shaft supports still in the ceiling (these held the shafting used to drive the machinery for pulverizing the sample ore prior to assaying).

The Vault Room was actually once the huge safe in which all bullion was stored prior to shipping via Wells Fargo Stage to San Francisco. The Retort Room was where millions of dollars' worth of gold was smelted into gold bullion and carried by dumbwaiter to the vault. (The arch supporting this vault still remains.) The Stores Room with its warm red brick walls was where rock picks, tallow candles, and flasks of quicksilver were stored. The Directors' Room—with its high ceiling and private entrance to the front balcony—was where the affairs of the company were talked over, and profits were divided among mine owners and operators.

Breakfast rolls, orange juice, coffee, tea, and hot chocolate are served to the rooms each morning. The real attractions are the historical interest of the building, the reasonable rates, and the imaginative rendering of the rooms. It's also a good place for walking—Amador City has more than its share of historic buildings—and is centrally located for those who wish to explore some of the old mine sites. (In addition to Keystone Consolidated, the Plymouth Consolidated, the Central Eureka, the Kennedy, and the Argonaut mines are all within five miles of the Mine House Inn.)

The Foxes

77 Main Street
Sutter Creek, California 95685; (209) 267-5882

INNKEEPERS:	*Pete and Min Fox.*
ACCOMMODATIONS:	*Six suites, all with private bath; queen-size beds.*
RESERVATIONS:	*Three months recommended for summer weekends.*
MINIMUM STAY:	*Two nights over holiday weekends.*
DEPOSIT:	*First night's lodging.*
CREDIT CARDS:	*MC, VISA.*
RATES:	*Moderate.*
RESTRICTIONS:	*No children. No pets.*

This is one of those places that remind one of the European bed and breakfast spots. But it's more than just a couple of spare rooms; these are luxury suites, each intended to accommodate two people. (Because one is exceedingly popular with newlyweds, it is called the Honeymoon Suite. The proprietors — Pete and Min Fox — don't insist that their guests be honeymooners, but I can't think of a nicer place to spend one's honeymoon than in this intimately furnished little love nest.)

This charming two-story Victorian was once known locally as the Brinn House. It was built in 1857 and purchased by Morris Brinn and his brother in 1865. Like so many who prospered during the Gold Rush, they sought their fortunes not in mines and gold pans, but in supplying the miners with the basic necessities of life in a gold camp: they owned a dry goods store in Sutter Creek, and a fairly large one at that. Their fine home has a definite New England flavor to it, typical of many of the old homes in this area and reflecting the origins of many of the settlers.

What is remarkable is that this quintessential Gold Rush Victorian was allowed to stand vacant for twenty-five years. In the 1960s it was rescued by a couple who began its restoration; later it was owned by another couple who continued the work and served lunch in a luncheon room in the building. The Foxes have now had it for seven years, and the old Brinn residence has never looked better in its 131 years.

Their Victorian Suite consists of a sitting room, a bedroom, and a private bath. The bed has an amazing nine-foot-high headboard, and there is a matching marble-topped dresser (also nine feet tall) of walnut and walnut burl, circa 1875. The bedspread is a floral print coordinated with an antique floral-stripe wallpaper and the sheer drapes, which are tied back with a matching floral fabric. There is a Queen Anne love seat in the sitting room and another Queen Anne piece — a fine writing desk — that doubles as a breakfast table.

Breakfast at The Foxes is flexible. "Since there are only six couples to consider," Min says, "we can talk about it once they get here." A typical breakfast might include juice, fresh fruits, eggs with ham or bacon, sourdough French toast or pancakes, blueberry muffins, and a hot beverage of your choice.

Both Min and husband Pete come from Orange County. They got into the bed and breakfast business almost by accident. Pete had been in real estate for many years and envisioned the Brinn place as a possible office. The couple who were selling the house liked the Foxes' plan to open an antique shop there, but also spoke glowingly of the possibility of furnishing and renting a suite.

It was a natural. Min Fox well remembers her first customer. Jane Way of the neighboring Sutter Creek Inn called to say that a honeymoon couple had reserved the room, but in the bustle and rush of wedding arrangements had forgotten to mail their deposit. Could the Foxes put them up for a night? They could and did. The next morning the bride and bridegroom watched the annual Italian Picnic Day parade from the Foxes' porch. "They got very emotional when they left," Min recalls. "They came back for their first wedding anniversary, and have been back every year since."

There is nothing like a bed and breakfast inn to launch a new marriage — or to invigorate one that has been around a while. And there is no inn that I would recommend more highly for this than The Foxes.

Sutter Creek Inn

75 Main Street
Sutter Creek, California 95685; (209) 267-5606

INNKEEPER:	*Jane Way.*
ACCOMMODATIONS:	*Seventeen rooms, all with private bath; twin, double, and queen-size beds.*
RESERVATIONS:	*Flexible, but phone as early as possible.*
MINIMUM STAY:	*Two nights on weekends.*
DEPOSIT:	*$50 a day per room.*
CREDIT CARDS:	*Not accepted.*
RATES:	*Inexpensive to moderate.*
RESTRICTIONS:	*No children under 15. No pets.*

*H*uge lawns surround this deservedly well-known inn, and in summer garden furniture and hammocks are a delight under the redwood and laurel trees. An old and stately grape arbor is a haven for those who like to play cards during the day. Many fine restaurants are within walking distance of the inn and proprietor Jane Way keeps a book with guests' comments on local eating spots. Sutter Creek is itself a kind of living museum of architecture from 1860 to 1920. (If you wish to explore the town on foot, ask Jane for a copy of the *Stroller's Guide to Sutter Creek.*)

Sutter Creek Inn was originally built as a Greek Revival by one of the town's leading businessmen, a man named Keyes, using redwood but following the style then current in New England. (It was a wedding gift to his homesick bride, a woman from New Hampshire.) It was owned later by State Senator Edward Voorheis, who married the Keyes' daughter in 1880. It was still in the possession of the same family when it was spotted by Jane Way, on a pleasure excursion through the Gold Country with her children. She fell in love with it instantly. After two months of calling daily, she convinced the family she would be a worthy new owner of the historic building. "It's been well cared for," Jane says proudly, "and it's sturdy as a rock."

There is a large living room decorated in robin egg blue and accented with some Oriental pieces that go quite well with the country antiques. The large sofas are upholstered in floral prints, and I particularly liked the grandfather clock and the hutch with antique china. There is a very large library with current magazines and literally thousands of books, as well as a piano for the musically-inclined. Jane is a talented handwriting expert and will read your palm as well as your handwriting for character traits.

Jane is interested in psychic experiences — and it was perhaps because of that openness that she was once visited by a ghost. He was a distinguished-looking gentleman who said simply, "I will protect your inn!" and vanished. (Jane thinks he might have been Senator Voorheis.) Certainly he would be proud of her country kitchen, with its partially paneled brick walls, copper colanders, impressive collection of guns, and Oriental rug.

Many guest rooms are in what used to be outbuildings. Most have a distinctly country feeling, but bear the mark of Jane's exquisite, sophisticated taste. Some rooms have patios; most have small libraries. Many have fireplaces, and one that I particularly liked contained a table made from a bass drum. Ceiling beams, canopy beds, and samplers are the rule in other rooms. Four of the rooms have beds suspended from the ceiling.

Jane likes variation in her breakfast menu, but a typical day's fare might consist of crispy fried potatoes with bacon and onions, sliced fresh fruit, buttermilk pancakes with raw apples and walnuts, and soft scrambled eggs.

Nine Eureka Street Inn

9 Eureka Street, P.O. Box 386
Sutter Creek, California 95685; (209) 267-0342

INNKEEPERS:	*Bob and Nancy Brahmst.*
ACCOMMODATIONS:	*Five rooms, all with private bath; queen-size beds.*
RESERVATIONS:	*Flexible.*
MINIMUM STAY:	*Two nights on holiday weekends.*
DEPOSIT:	*First night's lodging.*
CREDIT CARDS:	*MC, VISA.*
RATES:	*Moderate.*
RESTRICTIONS:	*No children. No pets.*

The Lagomarsino clan were early settlers in the Gold Country, arriving in 1856. One of many industrious Italian-Americans who helped build up this area, Tobias Lagomarsino along with other family members operated a stagecoach route on the Sutter Creek, Jackson, and Volcano line. It was not until 1916, however, that the family built this modest but very nice New England–flavored dwelling in the second block of two-block-long Eureka Street, just off Main Street.

The Lagomarsino home is now operated as a very comfortable bed and breakfast by Bob and Nancy Brahmst. The rooms are individually decorated in the mode of the past, but there is also air conditioning — not a minor consideration some summer evenings. The rooms are large, the atmosphere gracious; yet the ambience remains homey. I particularly liked the large porch, with its view of the surrounding hills.

My favorite room is one that used to be a sleeping porch (now called the North Room). Windows on all three sides give it a light and airy feeling that is very refreshing.

The dining room sports chandeliers, leaded and stained-glass windows, and elm wainscoting. The sitting room (which merges into the dining area) features beamed ceilings, plush carpets, and contemporary furnishings. The sitting room closes at 10:00 P.M., but until then Bob and

Nancy invite you to "browse among the many books and revive the gentle art of conversation."

Breakfast is full and hearty: orange juice, fresh fruit (bananas and strawberries with yogurt), a zippy cheese omelette, homemade raisin-bran muffins, coffee, tea, and milk.

Sutter Creek is centrally located in the Gold Country. There is excellent fishing at the well-stocked low-elevation lakes: Camanche, Pardee, and Amador. Fairs, rodeos, and local festivals are the rule in summer. Kirkwood Meadows, one of California's best ski areas, is not far away. Or you may simply wish to drive around the back roads leading away from Highway 49. From Main Street, drive up Sutter Hill Road past the abandoned Botto Saloon and the Central Eureka Mine, or along Amador Road, past the Union-Lincoln mine site. These and other byways leading from Sutter Creek are lined with ancient stone walls and occasional crumbling stone buildings from the Mother Lode's colorful past.

Court Street Inn

215 Court Street
Jackson, California 95642; (209) 223-0416

INNKEEPER:	*Mildred Burns.*
ACCOMMODATIONS:	*Seven rooms, four with private bath; twin, double, and queen-size beds.*
RESERVATIONS:	*Two weeks recommended.*
MINIMUM STAY:	*None.*
DEPOSIT:	*First night's lodging.*
CREDIT CARDS:	*Not accepted.*
RATES:	*Inexpensive to moderate.*
RESTRICTIONS:	*No children. No pets.*

The main part of this house was built in 1870 for the Isaac Peiser family, on what was then called Corral Hill. (Apparently the area was used for grazing cattle in those early days.) Only three years later Mr. Peiser and his young son died, victims of diphtheria. The remainder of the wealthy merchant's family continued to live here until the house was sold to the Blairs, who owned the Jackson Water Works, and their daughter Grace Depue.

The Miwok Indians in this area were frequently unable to pay their water bills in cash, so they made payments in the form of baskets and other artifacts. Grace Depue kept the collection in a brick house in the back (now called the "Indian House," where two of the inn's guest rooms are located); in her will she donated it to the University of California at Berkeley, and at the time of her death it was appraised at $90,000. In this way a priceless collection of Miwok folk art was preserved for the enjoyment of all Californians.

Mildred Burns had visited the Gold Country frequently from her home in San Luis Obispo, vacationing at bed and breakfast inns. She was looking for a way to make a living, and to take care of aging parents at the same time. The present dwelling seemed to have everything: it was a home of the Victorian era, with a small house in back for her parents. Restoration began in May 1980; the first guests arrived before work was even finished, in April 1981.

That first week a woman called from Sacramento. She wanted to be married in Jackson — could she have three rooms for the wedding party? "And that was on only two days' notice," Mildred points out. "Before it was over I ended up finding a minister for them, and we had the wedding right here in the parlor. *And* the reception." It was Mildred's blunt introduction to a certain fact of life: the proprietor of a bed and breakfast inn often doubles as a social secretary.

My favorite room at Court Street (which is now on the National Register of Historic Places) is the Peiser Room. It has its own sun porch, a sitting area with wicker pieces, old quilts, and fresh flowers, and some fine Queen Anne furniture; the colors here are pink and white. (There are also ruffled pillow shams and a pitcher and washbowl.)

There are Oriental pieces throughout the house: rugs, ginger jars, and, in the larger parlor, a lovely lacquered Chinese screen. (Mildred explains that these kinds of pieces — particularly Chinese screens — were widely used during Victorian days.)

Despite what Mildred calls the "Early American Gold Rush" ambience of her carefully designed and decorated rooms, all of them are air-conditioned. Complimentary wine or tea is served in the guest rooms, sherry in the parlor. A full breakfast is served at Court Street Inn: French toast, granola, strawberries and yogurt, homemade breads (including pumpkin-banana nut), egg dishes, crêpes and quiches, orange juice, and tea or coffee. All are made especially enjoyable by the friendly company of your hostess and proprietor, a unique woman who combines vivacity with character — an admirable compound that seems especially appropriate to this very magical part of California.

Gate House Inn

1330 Jackson Gate Road
Jackson, California 95642; (209) 223-3500

INNKEEPERS:	*Frank and Ursel Walker.*
ACCOMMODATIONS:	*Five rooms, all with private bath; queen-size beds.*
RESERVATIONS:	*Two to three weeks recommended.*
MINIMUM STAY:	*Two nights on weekends, April through October.*
DEPOSIT:	*First night's lodging.*
CREDIT CARDS:	*Not accepted.*
RATES:	*Inexpensive to moderate.*
RESTRICTIONS:	*No children. No pets.*

T he Gate House seems to loom larger than life on Jackson Gate Road. Inside, its ten-foot ceilings, solid-oak parquet floors, original wall coverings, chandeliers, marble fireplace, and hints of Oriental influence bespeak Gold Country. And Gold Country it certainly is. This turn-of-the-century Victorian is located near the historic Kennedy Mine on the outskirts of Jackson, a mid–Mother Lode city and the seat of Amador County since 1854.

The two-story house, entered through a wrought-iron gate, was built by the Chichizola family, the first general merchants of the area. Structurally speaking, it is one of only two Victorians of this quality in Amador County. Frank and Ursel Walker (second owners of the property after the original family) opened it as a bed and breakfast inn shortly after their purchase in 1981.

For four years previous to their purchase, the Walkers had watched the operation of the Sutter Creek Inn while serving its clientele from the Palace, a restaurant they own across the street. This "inn-spiration" proved worthy, and their culinary talents are not wasted here. A typical breakfast starts off with a beautifully displayed fresh-fruit salad of watermelon, cantaloupe, pineapple, blackberries, and grapes served on English bone china. This is followed by scrumptious lemon-cinnamon coffee cake with hot applesauce, coddled eggs, a stemmed glass of fresh orange juice with a slice of banana, coffee, and sweet apple-spice tea. Fresh flowers and a white lace tablecloth grace the formal dining table. Breakfast commences at the stroke of 9:00.

Of special interest are the more than one hundred clocks Frank has collected over the past twelve or so years. Included are grandfather clocks, shelf clocks, and wall clocks, from points as distant as Germany and France and as close to home as Sutter Creek. A Santa Fe railroad clock that once hung in the Albuquerque, New Mexico, telegraph office now passes the time of day in the inn's Parlor Room.

Gate House Inn's most popular guest room (in terms of price and size) is at the top of the stairs — the Brass Room, aptly named for its queen-size brass and onyx bed. My favorite, though, was the Woodhaven Suite, which according to Ursel is the room of choice of the journalists, feature writers, authors, and inn reviewers who come through. This wood-paneled suite that resembles a loft intimates seclusion. Its brass bed with a delicate floral-print comforter in beige and brown, and a large oval braided rug enhance the cozy, tucked-away feeling. It also has a separate sitting room with red-rose wallpaper, a leather sofa-bed to accommodate a third person, and a display of shelf clocks.

Assorted niceties I particularly liked: starched and ironed bed linens; bubble bath and a rubber ducky; a swimming pool, a barbecue, and a greenhouse; and four fine restaurants, all within walking distance of the inn.

The Heirloom

214 Shakeley Lane
Ione, California 95640; (209) 274-4468

INNKEEPERS:	*Patricia Cross and Melisande Hubbs.*
ACCOMMODATIONS:	*Four rooms, two with private bath; twin, double, queen-, and king-size beds. A two-guest-room adobe cottage.*
RESERVATIONS:	*Two to three weeks recommended.*
MINIMUM STAY:	*None.*
DEPOSIT:	*First night's lodging.*
CREDIT CARDS:	*Not accepted.*
RATES:	*Inexpensive to moderate.*
RESTRICTIONS:	*No pets.*

P art of California's fascination is due to the diversity of its people. This is reflected in its variety of architectural styles — particularly in the Gold Country, where people from many parts of the country converged at once. A good example of this is the Heirloom, a bed and breakfast inn in Ione. Obviously built by a Southerner, this two-story brick Colonial mansion with an antebellum arch replicates perfectly the prevailing fashion in the South before the Civil War.

Built in 1863 by a Virginian (who also built another Southern-style mansion in Ione), the structure was soon purchased by Dr. Luther Brusi, who in 1870 was a veteran of the Confederacy. He must have felt very much at home in this lovely dream house, with its stately columns, verandas, and white-wood balconies. Some time later it was sold to James and Catherine Browning (Catherine remained here until 1923); James was associated with the famous Browning rifle company.

The house was purchased by Patricia Cross and Melisande Hubbs in 1980. Both had been looking around Sonoma and Carmel for a dwelling appropriate for a bed and breakfast, when they heard of this place. Ione is somewhat off the tourist track; it was never a boom town, but served as a supply center for the mining camps. Yet when they saw this undeniably breathtaking structure, they knew it was the right one for them.

All windows are deep-set in the Southern style. (The house and garden are completely hidden from public view by shrubs and trees.) The front entrance boasts a fan transom. The living room is completely paneled in wood painted off-white, as was the custom in early days. The high ceiling and paneled windows (draped in gold brocade), stained pine floor with area rugs, and Colonial staircase and mantel are an elegant background to the antique furnishings in this very livable mansion.

One of the pieces Pat and Melisande are most proud of is their grand piano, once the possession of Lola Montez, famed "Gold Rush queen" of Grass Valley. This instrument has an offset keyboard and heavy, beautifully carved rosewood legs.

The rooms are named for the seasons. The Winter Room has a fireplace; burgundy and pale blue tones predominate. The Spring Room, in yellow and green, has lovely handmade quilts, an old-fashioned rocker, and a nice Queen Anne desk. The Autumn Room has a brass bed, a comforter, and pillow shams with matching duet ruffles. The Summer Room features pink rose wallpaper and a double Eastlake walnut bed. (This room also has a private bath.) Guest rooms in the handcrafted adobe cottage offer the campfire aroma of a woodburning stove and the romance of moonbeams dancing across the skylights.

Pat and Melisande are quite flexible toward guests; one is not encumbered with a surfeit of rules and regulations here. "I like to see the tension melt out of people's faces after they've been in the country a while," says Melisande.

Refreshments are served in the afternoon, and guests find fresh flowers, fruit, and candy in their rooms. Breakfast is full — and very generous. On a typical morning you will receive fresh-squeezed orange juice, crêpes with fresh fruit topping, popovers and croissants, Brie cheese, and gourmet coffee. In keeping with the Southern theme, Pat and Melisande usually serve breakfast wearing long aprons and skirts, adding to the sense of calm and antebellum luxury that is so much a part of the Heirloom.

Dunbar House

271 Jones Street, P.O. Box 1375
Murphys, California 95247; (209) 728-2897

INNKEEPERS:	*Bob and Barbara Costa.*
ACCOMMODATIONS:	*Five rooms share two baths; double and queen-size beds.*
RESERVATIONS:	*Three weeks recommended.*
MINIMUM STAY:	*None.*
DEPOSIT:	*First night's lodging.*
CREDIT CARDS:	*MC, VISA.*
RATES:	*Inexpensive.*
RESTRICTIONS:	*No children under 10. No pets.*

This lovely Italianate Victorian with its white siding and blue shuttered windows, wraparound veranda, and white picket fence reminds one of a set from an old western and was, in fact, used in filming the TV version of MGM's *Seven Brides for Seven Brothers*. It reflects the character of Willis Dunbar, a man of means who built the house for his bride, Ellen, in 1880. Dunbar was a prominent citizen in the community, a superintendent of the water company, and at one time served a turn in the State Assembly. Murphys was a boom town then, a magnet drawing fortune seekers who discovered some of Calaveras County's richest placer gold claims here. Today historical Main Street, just steps from the inn, affords seekers of a different sort a well-preserved glimpse into the past of this "Queen of the Sierra."

For Bob and Barbara Costa the move to Murphys killed two birds with one stone. They both wanted to live in the Gold Country and, having inn-hopped their way around the world, wanted to own a b&b. When this property, which was already a bed and breakfast inn, came up for sale, they couldn't resist. Coincidentally, Bob, like former innkeeper John Carr, is a fireman. In fact, Bob is senior marine pilot for the San Francisco Fire Department. Barbara formerly worked at Lawrence Livermore Lab.

The five guest rooms here have country antiques and treasured family pieces. Flowers and doilies are much in evidence; beds are turned down while guests are out to dinner. Electric blankets and fluffy comforters keep you warm in winter; there is air conditioning in summer. Pine-needle baskets, handicrafts, and original watercolors scattered throughout the house show off the talents of local artists. Books, games, and a stereo are located in the parlor. Old photographs of the Dunbar family and of historical events pertinent to the house grace the walls of the entryway.

Breakfast is served between 8:00 and 9:15, but the coffee is on by 7:00. Egg dishes — from crêpes to frittatas — are accompanied by bacon or sausage, fresh fruit turnovers, juice, and coffee or tea. Guests have the option of being served in either their room or the dining room, on the porch, or in the garden.

A side table full of brochures advertising area attractions sits by the door. Pick up a few on your way out, as I'm sure you'll want to get a good start on the day. I'd recommend a couple of hours at Calaveras Big Trees State Park; stop at the Quyle Kilns on your way up to buy some local pottery. Moaning Cavern and Mercer Caverns offer guided tours; Stevenot Winery is open for winetasting; downhill and cross-country skiing is just forty-five minutes away; antique and gift shops, as well as fine dining, are just a block away. Annual celebrations include St. Patrick's Day, the Murphys Homecoming in July, an Oktoberfest, and performances by the Black Bart Players in April and November.

Llamahall Guest Ranch

18170 Wards Ferry Road
Sonora, California 95370; (209) 532-7264

INNKEEPER:	*Cindy Hall.*
ACCOMMODATIONS:	*Two rooms, each with private bath; twin and queen-size beds.*
RESERVATIONS:	*Two to three weeks recommended.*
MINIMUM STAY:	*None.*
DEPOSIT:	*First night's lodging.*
CREDIT CARDS:	*Not accepted.*
RATES:	*Moderate.*
RESTRICTIONS:	*No pets.*

Now *here* is a stay with a difference — Llamahall Guest Ranch, home of Cindy Hall, her two children, and their eleven pet llamas.

Don't expect to be pampered and doted on here. This is not to say that the accommodations aren't pleasant — they are. It's just that this is Cindy's home, and guests sometimes become the secondary consideration rather than the primary. Breakfast, for example, was served *after* Cindy had got the kids off to school.

Not to be dismayed, though, as there is much to enjoy in this wholesome country environment: the quietude, the lovable llamas, a barbecue pit, a hot tub and sauna, a piano and a guitar, fishing and gold-panning on the creek that borders the property, a virtually untraveled road for jogging, lawn darts, and a sandbox. A dog, two cats, croaking frogs, and a host of other animals (squirrels, gophers, lizards, ducks, and geese) will keep you company. A red-tailed hawk lives here and blue heron frequent the pond. And you can not only bring the kids, you're encouraged to. Need I say more?

Guest rooms are on the lower level of the house, ideally situated for a family vacation. Each has its own private entrance, private bath, and both queen- and twin-size beds. Flora, the room that faces the garden, is papered with a deep green raspberry-bramble pattern. Its ceiling fan revolves at a snail's pace, and the tub was especially sculptured for two. Fauna, the room I called my own, had a brass bed with a white eyelet comforter and matching pillow shams, a marble-topped table, chairs, and an armoire. The bath featured a claw-foot tub with brass fixtures and shower head. Long-range plans include two additional guest rooms upstairs.

This all-redwood ranch house, built just twenty some years ago, is a showpiece of area craftsmanship. Its living room, which is open to overnight guests, is stocked with puzzles, games, and books as well as toys, musical instruments, and a stereo. An antique dental cabinet holds liqueurs for the guests' enjoyment. There is a rocking chair and a fireplace; oak paneling and a beamed ceiling complete the warm, homey scene.

The substantial breakfast of granola, hard-cooked eggs, bran muffins with butter, jam, and cream cheese, and a fresh-fruit platter is served family style. Beverages include coffee, tea, and freshly squeezed orange juice.

Llama pack trips may yet be in store at Llamahall Guest Ranch. Their slogan? Y'all haul with Llamahall.

Oak Hill Ranch

18550 Connally Lane, P.O. Box 307
Tuolumne, California 95379; (209) 928-4717

INNKEEPERS:	*Sandy and Jane Grover.*
ACCOMMODATIONS:	*Five rooms, one with private bath; double and queen-size beds.*
RESERVATIONS:	*Three to four weeks recommended.*
MINIMUM STAY:	*None.*
DEPOSIT:	*First night's lodging.*
CREDIT CARDS:	*Not accepted.*
RATES:	*Inexpensive to moderate.*
RESTRICTIONS:	*No children under 15. No pets.*

A visit to Oak Hill Ranch is like living a day in the life of an old TV classic —"Lassie," for instance — without having to do any of the chores. In fact, segments of "Little House On The Prairie" were shot just a mile away from this yellow farm house that only *looks* like it is a century old. Its saga began in the 1950s when Sandy Grover, who was then a school counselor, and his wife, Jane, a teacher, dreamed of building their own Victorian-style home. For twenty years, they scoured old houses as far away as Canada for anything that someday might be useful as vintage detailings — a turn-of-the-century mahogany fireplace, Victorian turnposts, ornate stairs, redwood doorways, railings, balconies, and other relics.

This is one dream that came true. In 1979 Jane, Sandy, and their son, Don, began building the four-bedroom house from the ground up on the site of a dairy ranch. Because of all the paint stripping that had to be done on the salvaged parts, it was a job that would take two long, painstaking years. But when they were through, the Grovers had themselves a nearly exact replica of a Western farm from 1880 crowning an oak-topped hill.

Still unabashedly devoted to nineteenth-century traditions, the Grovers, in particular Jane, love to surprise guests by occasionally dressing in vintage clothing. They also own an antique car — a 1908 two-cylinder Maxwell.

Genuinely nice people, the innkeepers, as much as

their inn, exude peace and warmth. And when you are surrounded by this much country, it's hard *not* to feel like you are "down home." Rimmed by fifty-five acres of pines and a view of the snowcapped Sierra Nevadas, the ranch-house features fireplaces in the sitting room and den, one with a 120-year-old gingerbread mantel, plus a wonderful Victorian pump organ. If you're longing to hear old-time music but can't play it yourself, look to the player piano just off the front hall.

There are two bedrooms downstairs. The Canopy Room has a canopied maple double bed, an armoire, and a balcony that looks over two duck-filled ponds. The balcony sports a white wicker love seat, table, and chair. This room shares a bath with the Rose Room, which holds an antique queen-size bed, armoire, and a wedding picture of Jane Grover's namesake, Calamity Jane.

Even more Calamity Jane memorabilia is upstairs in the Calamity Jane Room, which has a white iron bed, white wicker dresser, and a view of the farm's garden. It shares a bath, complete with an old-fashioned claw-foot tub and marble top basin, with the aptly named Eastlake Room, which brims with a queen-size bed, an armoire, and other Eastlake-style pieces.

A fifth bedroom is in the cottage down the knoll from the main house. Called Cow Palace, it used to be a barn. Today, it holds a slate fireplace, a full kitchen, and enough beds — two queens and a rollaway — to sleep five.

In *their* kitchen Jane and Sandy make a full gourmet breakfast: eggs fantasia, crêpes Normandy, a River Ranch soufflé, or an omelette with ham, bacon, or sausage; fresh orange juice; banana, blueberry or pecan muffins; biscuits with homemade jelly; coffee; tea; and melon or other fresh fruit.

Fueled by such a feast, you'll be ready to explore the surrounding countryside. The ranch is an excellent stopping off point for Yosemite National Park, some sixty miles away; Pinecrest Lake, thirty miles distant; or, just a twelve-mile drive, the Railtown 1897 State Park. With its miles of hiking and horseback riding trails and its frequent rodeos and fairs, Tuolumne County is sure to keep you busy.

Meadow Creek Ranch

2669 *Triangle Road*
Mariposa, California 95338; (209) 966-3843

INNKEEPERS:	*Bob and Carol Shockley.*
ACCOMMODATIONS:	*Four rooms, one with private bath; twin and queen-size beds.*
RESERVATIONS:	*Four weeks recommended.*
MINIMUM STAY:	*None.*
DEPOSIT:	*Half of full amount.*
CREDIT CARDS:	*AE, MC, VISA.*
RATES:	*Inexpensive.*
RESTRICTIONS:	*No children under 12. No pets.*

D own the road, a brown dog named "Mister" romps with two cats. Grey squirrels scurry into holes as a red-tailed hawk soars overhead. And a horse whinnies next to a two-story, Western farmhouse that looks like it hasn't changed much in the last hundred years or so.

This is Meadow Creek Ranch. Located some eleven miles "out of town" (Mariposa is just to the north), the ranch wasn't always so placid. Built as a stage stop in 1858, it offered weary stagecoach riders a place to stay overnight. One of them, Jessie Fremont, wife of General John C. Fremont, slept in the barn, which, in 1859, she called "a haven of rest." The structure has also served as home to some of the first ranch families of California's fertile Central Valley. In later years, a lumber mill clanked away on the sprawling grounds.

Today the stagecoach and mill are gone and a four-guest room bed and breakfast inn stands in their place. Started in 1983, the inn was bought in 1985 by antique collectors Bob and Carol Shockley. "We'd always wanted a fine house, a repository for our collectibles, and a business where we could serve the public," said Bob. "We wanted to work together, too. Running a b&b fulfills all these goals."

Within these walls the Shockleys have made some great changes. They've placed many small period pieces throughout, but they're proudest of an antique you'll find in the very first room you enter. As you come into the big, airy, country living room, look for the 120-year-old French carousel horse above the stone and brick fireplace. By the time you've had a chance to admire it, Carol will probably have slipped a nice, cold beverage in your hand.

Your tour continues to the upstairs bedrooms. Decorated with a queen-size, step-up bed, a matching oak dresser, and lots of green house plants, the Meadow Breeze Room's tone is warm and friendly. Bright, patchwork quilts cover two twin-size iron beds in the Sunrise Room. The Wildrose Room, whose most prominent feature is a century-old, European leaded glass window, is also pleasant. It has a queen-size bed on a simple frame against the window. All three rooms share the downstairs bath.

For total privacy, you may want to stay in what was once the chicken coop of the old ranch — don't worry, the hens are long gone. Transformed over the years into a bunkhouse for hired hands and a rental unit, this cottage next to the barn has been repainted, recarpeted, and filled with amenities by Carol and Bob. Among them: a queen-size, canopied bed made of handcarved Austrian mahogany; a private bath; and sitting area with Queen Anne droptop desk.

The dining room of the main house has its own comfortable ambience. Guests are seated around a long, sturdy trestle table for meals which are prepped by Bob and cooked by Carol. One morning you might be served French toast, ham, orange juice, coffee or tea, and a big bowl of strawberries, cantaloupe, and apples. The next day, light, fluffy pancakes, baked eggs, bacon, and applesauce may be offered.

Well sated, you'll be ready to take a stroll on the ranchland to check out its pastoral vistas, or use the inn as a jumping off point for trips to Yosemite National Park or the Badger Pass ski resort. Great summer rafting is available on the Merced River. All these attractions are less than an hour's drive from the inn.

Rockwood Lodge

5295 West Lake Boulevard
Homewood, California 95718; (916) 525-4663

INNKEEPERS:	*Connie Stevens and Lou Reinkens.*
ACCOMMODATIONS:	*Four rooms, two with private bath; double and queen-size beds.*
RESERVATIONS:	*One month recommended for summer weekends.*
MINIMUM STAY:	*Two nights.*
DEPOSIT:	*Full amount.*
CREDIT CARDS:	*Not accepted.*
RATES:	*Moderate to expensive.*
RESTRICTIONS:	*No children. No pets.*

"This, you think, is the way a mountain chalet ought to be, the way it always looked in your dreams," brags *Ski Magazine* about the Rockwood Lodge's three stories of knotty pine and stone that were crafted by Austrian carpenters and stonemasons back in the 1930s. Complete with a roof that slopes at a sixty-degree angle, Rockwood looks as though it was suddenly plucked out of the Swiss Alps and magically moved to Northern California. But then, its transformation into a bed and breakfast inn also seems to be a tale right out of a storybook.

In 1984 Connie Stevens, a flight attendant, and Lou Reinkens, an aerospace consultant, were looking for a vacation home when they spotted a "for sale" sign on a house that was only 100 feet (not yards) from Lake Tahoe on the area's elegant west shore. "We put down a silly bid, and much to our surprise, the owners said yes to it. So we had to decide what to use this big house for," remembers Lou. Because the property came with its own business license, the couple opted to start a b&b lodge.

Like they say, the rest is history. As Lou and Connie soon found out, Rockwood is imbued with the spirit of "old Tahoe." Part of *The Godfather* (Part II) was filmed just down the road at the Kaiser Estate. Across the street is historic Obexer's Marina, where the plush yachts of the rich and famous are docked. Some seventeen ski resorts also ring the area.

The sprawling, four-bedroom, Craftsman house was built in 1939 for Carlos Rookwood, a wealthy dairyman from Vallejo who used it as a summer home. In the forties, the retreat became a guest lodge. In 1949 the new owners decided the name Rookwood was too hard to remember, so they cut the lodge's iron "O" into a "C" and renamed it Rockwood. By the time Lou and Connie found it, the house was being used as a real estate agency.

For nine months, this married couple sandblasted walls, cleaned ceilings, tiled bathrooms, and put new carpets on the floor. Finally, they filled the lodge with European and Early American antiques.

Guest raves include the warm atmosphere that emanates from the lodge; the hand-hewn pine beams and panels that have been restored to their original golden color; and the Laura Ashley fabrics used throughout the decor.

Each guest room is named after a different location along the lake: Carnelian Bay contains an eighteenth-century American woodworker's bench, an antique armoire, and a queen-size feather bed. Secret Harbor sports Carlos's original built-in secretary and a queen-size four-poster. Emerald Bay harbors a feather bed, an antique nightstand, and a pleasant view of the lake and woods. Upstairs is Zephyr Cove, the only bedroom on the third floor — so high up you feel like you're in a treehouse. A stately white fir stands just outside the window. This room, too, has a queen-size feather bed.

Still, the main draw of Rockwood isn't its history or decor. It isn't even the food, which you can have served in the sitting area of your room, in the dining room, or outside on the terrace. (Breakfasts include juice and fruit, a selection of muffins and croissants, granola, yogurt, and special entrées ranging from Lou's Dutch Babies to Connie's fresh fruit crêpes.) The biggest attraction is the pampering you get at Rockwood. Special touches like chocolate truffles on the nightstand, down comforters and pillows, complimentary body oils and shampoos, and terry bathrobes hanging right in the closet, are just waiting for the two of you.

Mayfield House

236 Grove Street
Tahoe City, California 95730; (916) 583-1001

INNKEEPERS:	*Joanne Neft and Janie Kaye.*
ACCOMMODATIONS:	*Six rooms with shared baths; twin, queen-, and king-size beds.*
RESERVATIONS:	*Two weeks recommended.*
MINIMUM STAY:	*Two nights on weekends.*
DEPOSIT:	*Half total amount.*
CREDIT CARDS:	*MC, VISA.*
RATES:	*Moderate.*
RESTRICTIONS:	*No children under 10. No pets.*

This reasonably priced and very special bed and breakfast began as the private residence of Norman Mayfield, who built it in 1932. The rooms reflect its history as a residence: Julia's Room commemorates Julia Morgan, a frequent visitor; the Mayfield Room, the builder himself; and the Den, the Study, and Mrs. Hinckle's Room are remembrances of the first principal of a local school who lived here while she pursued her teaching and administrative career.

Joanne Neft once owned and operated a travel agency, and initially envisioned the Mayfield House as an office. In the meantime she traveled as part of her job, and was consistently struck by the way so many hotels overlooked the little "extras" that make one's stay memorable (or even tolerable). The idea of using this warm and stylish home as a bed and breakfast seemed a good one, but at first Mr. Mayfield was not interested in selling. In late 1978 he changed his mind. Joanne took possession on May 1, 1979, and opened on June 27 — Mr. Mayfield's ninety-first birthday.

The furnishings are mostly original to the house. None are Victorian, but there are some striking Queen Anne and oak pieces, as well as some handsome Empire Revival ones. There is a large stone fireplace and, in winter, an ample supply of wood. There are no telephones, radios, or televisions in the rooms, but you'll find beamed ceilings and plenty of rare stonework. Each room has its

own library; and down pillows, fresh flowers, and brass and copper accents are the rule. I also liked the original water-colors by Margaret Carpenter. (And the His and Hers velour robes!)

This inn caters to both summer and winter activities — in fact its proximity to skiing is one of the features that make it distinctive. Both cross-country skiing and golf are possible in season just across the street, and guests are within thirty minutes of seventeen downhill ski areas and ten Nordic ski areas. In the summer guests are just a half block from Lake Tahoe and Commons Beach, as well as shops and restaurants; there is gambling at the state line.

Breakfast at the Mayfield House is exquisite — and different every day. The day I was there, that "something different" was Portuguese toast (sweet bread, pan-fried, with fresh fruit sauce), fresh mint from the garden, Danish Havarti cheese, freshly squeezed orange juice, freshly ground coffee, tea, and milk. Mayfield House is also known for its apple strudel, sweet potato muffins, and Finnish pancakes with strawberry topping and sour cream. A newspaper accompanies breakfast — a small but very accommodating extra.

The Feather Bed

542 Jackson Street, P.O. Box 3200
Quincy, California 95971; (916) 283-0102

INNKEEPERS:	*Chuck and Dianna Goubert.*
ACCOMMODATIONS:	*Six rooms, all with private bath; double and queen-size beds.*
RESERVATIONS:	*Two weeks recommended for spring and summer weekends.*
MINIMUM STAY:	*None.*
DEPOSIT:	*$50.*
CREDIT CARDS:	*AE, MC, VISA.*
RATES:	*Inexpensive.*
RESTRICTIONS:	*No children under 12. No pets.*

C huck and Dianna Goubert, owners of historic Huskinson House in the tiny town of Quincy (population 5,000) are specialists in the arcane art of teaching people how to relax, unwind, and enjoy life country style. Their 1893 Queen Anne, built by Englishman Edward Huskinson, is equally instrumental in transporting one back to another point in time.

The slowing-down process begins as you enter the home where Edward, a merchant who also owned a gold mine, a bank, and a saloon, lived with his wife, Jeannie, and their children, Barrett and Gladys. It has five bedrooms in the main building and one guest room in the cottage in back. (The Feather Bed, by the way, does not *have* feather beds, but is instead named after the Feather River from which Los Angeles gets part of its water supply.)

The focal point of the Morning Room is a private balcony overlooking quaint downtown Quincy. There is also an antique English double bed. A spacious front bedroom known as Edward's Room includes the home's original turn-of-the-century colored-glass windows, its own sitting room, a queen-size bed, and an antique armoire. Vintage, claw-foot tubs are found in Jeannie's Sewing Room (which also has an antique, oak double bed), Barrett's Room (where an early American oak fireplace mantel has become the headboard of a queen-size bed), and the Gladys-Reid

Room (Gladys loved it for its fine view of 7,600-foot high Mt. Claremont).

The gardener's cottage, so secure and secluded, is perfect for sweethearts. It comes with private deck, love seat, antique armoire, and wood-burning stove.

To help unwind jangled city nerves, Chuck and Dianna pour complimentary sherry in the Victorian parlor. The antique oak chairs and tables, brass fixtures, lace curtains, and flowered wallpaper whisk you away to what country living must have been like when the Huskinsons arrived on the scene only forty years after Quincy was founded.

Now settled and ready to explore? Follow the Gouberts' suggestion, take a walk around town — or bike. If you give your hosts enough advance notice, they will not only supply you with an old touring bike, but even pack you a box lunch. I chose to follow the town's "Heritage Walk" past the county courthouse, Quincy's first schoolhouse, and the memorabilia-packed Plumas County Museum.

As much as I liked Quincy's unpretentious book stores, art galleries, cafes, and the vistas of the adjacent Plumas National Forest, my first love was the inn's shady porch.

Dianna and Chuck are sure to tell you about the rivers to fish, water holes to swim, and gold to be panned. But for your time here, you may just enjoy reading on the landing on a lazy, summer afternoon, or slowly savoring the goodies from the breakfast basket delivered to the door of your room.

Breakfast, which is also served on the brick patio, includes juice or flavorful yogurt smoothies, fresh fruit, fresh baked pastries, coffee or tea, and sometimes such delights as baked pears and bundt cake.

Needless to say, I left recharged, already anticipating my next visit. I felt, as most guests do, that this was the town where I grew up — the town I would most like to come home to.

Green Gables

The Central Coast

1
17
Watsonville
101
Santa Cruz
Castroville
Pacific Grove
1
Salinas
Gosby House
Green Gables
68
101
House of Seven Gables Inn
Old Monterey Inn
Monterey
Holiday House
Sea View Inn
Stonehouse Guest Lodge
1
Big Sur
Heritage Inn   Templeton
Rose Victorian Inn   *Country House Inn*
Cambria   *J. Patrick House*

House of Seven Gables Inn

555 Ocean View Boulevard
Pacific Grove, California 93950; (408) 372-4341

INNKEEPERS:	*John, Nora, Susan, Ed, and Fred Flatley.*
ACCOMMODATIONS:	*Fourteen rooms, all with private bath; queen-size beds.*
RESERVATIONS:	*Six to eight weeks recommended.*
MINIMUM STAY:	*Two nights on weekends.*
DEPOSIT:	*Full amount.*
CREDIT CARDS:	*Not accepted.*
RATES:	*Moderate to expensive.*
RESTRICTIONS:	*No children under 12. No pets.*

P erched on a rocky promontory overlooking scenic Monterey Bay, the three-story House of Seven Gables was one of a parade of large, showy homes built in the area around the turn of the century.

Completed in 1886 for a Mrs. Page of Oakland, the structure was sold in 1906 to Henry and Lucie Chase, who added the gables and a sun porch. Their fond memories of their Salem, Massachusetts, roots led them to name the house after Nathaniel Hawthorne's multi-gabled home and classic novel *The House of Seven Gables*.

But it wasn't just this house that was so unusual. Lucie was quite a character herself. A generous philanthropist, she amazed civic leaders by plunking down $20,000, a small fortune in the 1930s, to help build the Museum of Natural History in Pacific Grove. She also liked to purr around town in one of Monterey's first electric cars. Her nephew inherited the house and in 1971 sold it to John and Nora Flatley.

Today, Lucie's old home bubbles not only with history, but also with the hospitality of a family-run operation. When John and Nora decided to restore and refurbish the home with their collection of elegant antiques and open it to the public, they gave their adult children a chance to participate too. Daughter Susan handles personnel matters as well as the bookkeeping and promotion work, sons Ed and Fred do yardwork and repairs, Nora is the guest receptionist and cook, and papa John is supervisor of all this activity, or, as he describes himself, "Chief Drone."

Filled to the brim with French furniture, crystal chandeliers, and Persian and Oriental rugs, the home also has the sun porch with a marble pedestal honoring the "Three Graces" and a parlor loaded with antiques. The latter features a Victorian chaise longue, a French mantel clock, and a sampling of the fine art glass collection from the 1860s to 1880s that is scattered throughout the house.

Each of the seven guest rooms in the main house is also decorated in an eclectic but pleasing mix of Victorian-era pieces and antiques from as far away as Europe, China, and Brazil. Of the five upstairs rooms, my favorite is the Breakers, which holds a queen-size ceiling canopy bed, an armoire of seashell carved wood design, a Federal-style bull's-eye mirror, a small refrigerator, and, over by the bay window, a marble-topped table and two chairs.

Some of the nicest rooms are to be found in the Guest House, which is the newest addition to the property. Its four bedrooms (Cypress, Ocean Mist, Victoria, and Mayfair) all have modern baths and built-in refrigerators. All of the inn's guest rooms feature exceptional ocean views.

Also special at the Seven Gables is the 8:00 to 10:00 A.M. breakfast that's served around the inn's ten-seater dining table: platters of fresh fruit, three types of croissants (cinnamon walnut, cinnamon apple, and boysenberry), gourmet muffins (such as mincemeat, cream cheese–pumpkin, or buttermilk bran), strawberry shortcake or apple cobbler, fresh orange juice, and freshly brewed coffee or tea. The presentation is on antique serving pieces from the family treasure trove. Afternoon "high tea" commences at 4:00 P.M. Among the goodies usually included are delicate imported cookies and Nora's homemade fudge.

Would Lucie Chase be proud of the job the Flatleys are doing? You bet she would. I'm sure even Nathaniel Hawthorne would approve. He would probably rechristen this friendly, family-oriented place the House of the Five Flatleys Inn.

Green Gables

104 Fifth Street
Pacific Grove, California 93950; (408) 375-2095

INNKEEPERS:	*Roger and Sally Post.*
ACCOMMODATIONS:	*Six rooms, two with private bath; queen-size beds (one double). Five-room carriage house.*
RESERVATIONS:	*Six to eight weeks recommended.*
MINIMUM STAY:	*None.*
DEPOSIT:	*First night's lodging.*
CREDIT CARDS:	*AE, MC, VISA.*
RATES:	*Moderate to expensive.*
RESTRICTIONS:	*No pets.*

William Lacey of the prominent Monterey Laceys, created this Queen Anne–style mansion in 1888, literally by the water's edge. A Judge Wilbur used it as a summer home in the 1890s. In this century the Gerrard family was responsible for the intelligent and systematic improvements that have kept Green Gables in mint condition. Always an impressive residence, with its wide-angle view of Monterey Bay, this relatively small but elegant dwelling has been an inn since 1958.

Roger and Sally Post were living in Pasadena when they first stayed here on a visit to the area. They told their astonished hosts that they would like nothing more than to buy it; and sure enough, when it was finally put on the market, it was to the Posts that the owners first turned. "It was one of those things that just happens," Sally says. "Call it luck—or providence."

They add that Pacific Grove has many of the advantages of a small town, but isn't isolated: the Monterey Peninsula has all the activities and attractions of any large metropolitan area. Shopping, tennis courts, boutiques, golf courses, bike paths, swimming, and the world-famous Seventeen-Mile Drive are all close; many are within walking distance.

The living room features cozy blue and mauve print love seats by a fireplace, a gay carousel horse, and silk

flowers. In the formal dining room there is a panoramic view of the coastal shoreline. Here also there is a fireplace and several fine Oriental rugs. Photos of the inn grace the stairway.

The Garret Room has a gabled roof, floral wallpaper, and an iron bed with comforters; an appealing little hideaway, this. The Balcony Room has a delightful closed-in balcony with a stupendous view of the ocean. The Gable Room contains a queen-size bed, a large desk, and blue and white wallpaper; the bed has an eyelet lace comforter.

The breakfast is a full buffet including quiche or poached eggs, fresh fruit, granola, homemade bread or croissants, juice, and coffee or tea served in the dining room from 8:00 until 10:00. There are fine gourmet restaurants situated in other historic homes in Pacific Grove; the Posts or their manager are more than happy to help with reservations and directions.

The Gosby House

643 Lighthouse Avenue
Pacific Grove, California 93950; (408) 375-1287

INNKEEPERS:	*Roger and Sally Post.*
ACCOMMODATIONS:	*Twenty-two rooms, twenty with private bath; double and queen-size beds.*
RESERVATIONS:	*One week for weekdays, six weeks for weekends.*
MINIMUM STAY:	*Two nights on weekends.*
DEPOSIT:	*First night's lodging.*
CREDIT CARDS:	*AE, MC, VISA.*
RATES:	*Moderate to expensive.*
RESTRICTIONS:	*No pets.*

T he Gosby House Inn, which like Green Gables is owned by Roger and Sally Post, is one of those fascinating places that have been inns right from their inception. The founder of this inn was one J. F. Gosby, an industrious native of Nova Scotia who made his way to the sunnier climes of California in 1853. He had learned the shoemaking trade at an early age and soon became the town's only cobbler. In the meantime he kept his eyes open for the big break—which came in 1875, when the Methodist Church established religious conference grounds in a secluded area near the ocean. The shrewd Gosby, a Methodist himself, decided that an inn was needed to house the visitors and participants in the many religious and cultural activities that took place there.

So in 1887 Gosby built this comfortable, rambling inn and began almost immediately renting rooms to visitors attending the various meetings sponsored by the church. Civic minded and gregarious, Gosby was a member of many lodges and a town council member from 1892 to 1896. Meanwhile the Southern Pacific railroad extended its tracks to Monterey and built the beautiful Del Monte Hotel, also during the 1880s (building the smaller El Carmelo Hotel to handle the overflow). This brought even more visitors.

Just as the area had become firmly established as the place of choice for vacations and religious retreats, the Del Monte burned to the ground. The demand for accommodations was now overwhelming; Gosby's fortunes soared. He added a round corner tower and bay windows (late 1890s), as well as electric wiring, indoor plumbing, and connecting doors (early 1900s). In the 1920s the irrepressible cobbler changed the name of his inn to the El Carmelo Hotel, no doubt to take advantage of the more famous caravansary's name.

From 1930 onward the inn changed hands several times, and was finally purchased by the present owners in 1976. It has now been rehabilitated in a manner that reflects its original glory, and is once again called by its original name. Fresh paint, brass fixtures, marble sinks, and antique furnishings throughout reflect the over twelve thousand hours necessary for restoration.

Look for the rare doll collection in the entry parlor when you arrive (and the old photograph of Mr. Gosby in front of his shoe shop). There are fresh flowers and fruit in all rooms, and complimentary tea, sherry, wine, and hors d'oeuvres in the afternoon. But the real distinction of the Gosby is in the many extras one does not often find in a bed and breakfast. Shoes left outside your door are shined by the "Boots" (shades of an English inn). The morning newspaper arrives with your breakfast. A hall porter will arrange theater tickets and dinner reservations. Bicycles are available for riding along the Pacific Grove shoreline. (Watch for migrating grey whales from December to March, plus sea otters, pelicans, and other shore birds.)

Breakfast here is a bountiful feast sure to please every palate. Special services at the Gosby include an iron and ironing board, a sewing kit, alarm clocks, and a very thoughtful policy of celebrating special occasions such as birthdays, weddings, and anniversaries.

Old Monterey Inn

500 Martin Street
Monterey, California 93940; (408) 375-8284

INNKEEPERS:	*Ann and Gene Swett.*
ACCOMMODATIONS:	*Nine rooms and a cottage, all with private bath; twin, queen-, and king-size beds.*
RESERVATIONS:	*Two to three months for weekends.*
MINIMUM STAY:	*Two nights on weekends.*
DEPOSIT:	*In full.*
CREDIT CARDS:	*Not accepted.*
RATES:	*Expensive to very expensive.*
RESTRICTIONS:	*No children. No pets.*

No doubt about it, the Old Monterey Inn is special. The only word that works here is *elegance*. And what a pleasure it is — particularly because the elegance is achieved without a hint of ostentation! Located in a quiet area near the heart of Monterey, the inn is surrounded by lovely gardens that create the illusion of an English country house. Architecturally it is in fact English Tudor, and owners Ann and Gene Swett have given it many of the characteristics of the finest English and Scottish inns.

The dwelling was built in 1929 by Carmel Martin, a former mayor and civic leader of Monterey. After passing through several hands, it was purchased and restored by the Swetts, and used exclusively as a private residence until the last of their six children flew the nest. A visit to the Sutter Creek Inn caused the Swetts to consider the possibility of creating a country-style bed and breakfast inn in the heart of Monterey. They have most definitely succeeded — to the lasting delight of the hostelry's many regular guests, including visitors to the world-famous Monterey jazz festival.

Typical of the careful architectural detail to look for at this inn are the huge timber beams and posts in the vestibule. Hand-carved designs on the stairs were done by August Gay, an artist in the community who is also responsible for the window valances.

Besides its sensational setting, it was the extras that won me over at the Old Monterey Inn. The beds aren't just beds — they're experiments in total relaxation. There are soft *and* firm pillows for each guest, and European goose down comforters. Free soft drinks and juices are stored in a refrigerator on the second floor. Breakfast is served on fine china. In the bathroom medicine cabinet I discovered the following: shampoo, nail polish remover, toothpaste, a razor, safety pins, hairspray, and deodorant; a hair dryer, a curling iron, and electric rollers are also available (ask if you need them). Rose petals from the garden are used to make potpourri that guests may take with them as a gift.

Branches from an old oak tree frame an enchanting view from the window of the room called Brighstone. Guests in the Library Room enjoy both a sun deck and a fireplace in this book-lined hideaway that was once actually a library. Visitors in the Dovecote room can relax by a fireplace in shadows cast by a skylight. The Cottage features a sitting room with stained glass; it also has a cozy seat in the bedroom bay window with a view of the garden.

Breakfast here is generous — and very good. The day I was there the following was available: fresh fruit, orange juice, a delicious quiche, croissants, and whole-wheat muffins, as well as coffee, tea, and brewed decaffeinated coffee. Popovers and cheese rolls (said to be the house specialties) are served other mornings. Those who wish may have their morning meal delivered to their room or served to them in bed. On pleasant mornings breakfast is served in the garden, a perfect setting for daydreaming or romancing. Complimentary wine and cheese are served every afternoon at 5:00 P.M.

The Swetts are firm believers in a quote from Boswell's *Life of Johnson:* "There is nothing which has yet been contrived by man by which so much happiness is produced as by a good tavern or inn." This is one of those rare places that delivers this total serenity and pleasure. It is also one of the few that must be experienced to be believed.

Sea View Inn

Camino Real between Eleventh and Twelfth, P.O. Box 4138
Carmel, California 93921; (408) 624-8778

INNKEEPERS:	*Marshall and Diane Hydorn.*
ACCOMMODATIONS:	*Eight rooms, six with private bath; queen- and king-size beds.*
RESERVATIONS:	*Three weeks recommended.*
MINIMUM STAY:	*Two nights on holidays and weekends.*
DEPOSIT:	*First night's lodging.*
CREDIT CARDS:	*MC, VISA.*
RATES:	*Inexpensive to moderate.*
RESTRICTIONS:	*No children under 12. No pets.*

H ere's an economical bed and breakfast where one can park the car and take it from there on foot. (It's three blocks from the beach; five from Ocean Avenue, Carmel's main street.) This country-style Victorian, built in 1906, is one of the oldest guest houses in this artists'-colony-by-the-sea. Yet it is well out of the tourist crush; in this residential neighborhood there are no traffic noises or other distractions associated with congested downtown areas.

The Sea View is popular as a honeymoon haven; don't be surprised if you meet guests returning for their anniversaries. (One couple who had spent their wedding night here fifty years ago returned recently on their fiftieth anniversary.) It is also patronized regularly by visitors to the jazz and Bach festivals, both annual events in Monterey and Carmel, respectively. (Book a room early if you are attending either; accommodations are hard to get during the festivals.)

Proprietors Marshall and Diane Hydorn first visited Carmel looking for a vacation house. (Marshall was flying for TWA and Diane was occupied as a homemaker, raising the couple's children.) More as a joke than anything else, they asked the real estate agent if there were any "little inns" for sale. "As a matter of fact, there is one," was the sobering reply. The Hydorns were hooked as soon as they saw it.

This is an adult hideaway where privacy is everything, but children over twelve are allowed as long as they are reasonably well behaved. The Sea View is furnished with antiques blended in with newer pieces; a great many belongings of the hosts are to be found around the house, too, adding to the personal feeling of the inn. The Hydorns try to give their guests as much attention as possible. They are well informed about local happenings and attractions, including good local restaurants.

The Continental breakfast is served in the living room, before the fireplace, and varies from day to day. When I visited there were assorted cold cereals, juice, fresh fruit, whole-grain toast, and muffins. (And, of course, a choice of hot drinks: tea, coffee, herb tea, and cocoa.) A tasty coffee cake is served other mornings, and on certain Sundays Diane has been known to make quiche as a special treat. Complimentary sherry is served in the afternoon.

Holiday House

Camino Real at Seventh, P.O. Box 782
Carmel, California 93921; (408) 624-6267

INNKEEPERS:	*Dieter and Ruth Back.*
ACCOMMODATIONS:	*Six rooms, four with private bath; twin, double, and queen-size beds.*
RESERVATIONS:	*Eight weeks for weekends.*
MINIMUM STAY:	*Two nights on weekends.*
DEPOSIT:	*First night's lodging.*
CREDIT CARDS:	*Not accepted.*
RATES:	*Moderate.*
RESTRICTIONS:	*No infants. No pets.*

A few years ago, Dieter and Ruth Back found themselves stopping over in Carmel frequently on trips between Los Angeles and San Francisco. Eventually this amiable couple moved to the Monterey Peninsula, and when they heard that Holiday House was up for sale, they decided to give the bed and breakfast business a try. The Backs were not total strangers to the accommodations trade, however. They owned and managed apartment houses in Los Angeles and already operated the Acacia Lodge in Carmel Valley. "What we like about bed and breakfast is that it offers a more personal experience — the chance to meet people and get to know them," Dieter told me as we walked the beautifully landscaped lawns of Holiday House.

This brown-shingled dwelling was built in 1905 by a Stanford University professor as a family summer home and as a retreat for students and faculty. The living room has a stone fireplace and opens onto the sun porch, where there is a marvelous ocean view. Books and games are available. There are also gardens for guests to enjoy: all of the six bedrooms look out to sea or onto a garden. The house is perfectly located; it is a five-minute walk to the beach or to village shops, galleries, and restaurants.

Holiday House has been furnished with antiques and collectibles, most purchased locally. There is no television or swimming pool here; the Backs feel that such conveniences defeat the objective of a bed and breakfast inn, which is rest and relaxation. There is a small pond on the grounds, with a terrace and a stone bench, that adds to the introspective mood of the place. Not that it is without whimsy: all rooms have fresh flowers, and are also stocked with a full supply of jellybeans! Some rooms are directly under the sloping roof, which imparts a cozy, hidden-away feeling. Most are furnished in decor appropriate to the turn of the century; some of the art work is by local artists.

The Point Lobos room features a fine view of Point Lobos and has a queen-size bed. Rustic paneling, decorative shades, and blue, red, and beige patterns on both wallpaper and bedspread set an upbeat mood. Terrace South, with its private back entrance, offers a queen-size and a twin bed — perfect for a family of three or as a third-party set-up.

A hearty breakfast is served buffet style between 8:30 and 9:30 in the dining room or on the sun porch. There is a selection of cold cereals, coffee cake, and English muffins (occasionally bagels with cream cheese); a quiche or a ham-and-cheese casserole; fresh fruit; and coffee, tea, and orange juice.

Since Holiday House has been a guest house since the 1920s, staying here has become a family tradition with some guests. Its pronounced order and cleanliness, its relaxed atmosphere, and its reasonable rates all make it a real find — particularly for those who must watch their budgets, but still wish to avoid the impersonality of the big hotels and faceless motels that have proliferated in the area.

Stonehouse Inn

Monte Verde and Eighth, P.O. Box 2517
Carmel, California 93921; (408) 624-4569

INNKEEPER:	*Virginia Carey.*
ACCOMMODATIONS:	*Six rooms, all with shared bath; double and king-size beds.*
RESERVATIONS:	*Four to six weeks for weekends.*
MINIMUM STAY:	*None.*
DEPOSIT:	*Full amount.*
CREDIT CARDS:	*MC, VISA.*
RATES:	*Moderate.*
RESTRICTIONS:	*No children under 14. No pets.*

S tonehouse was built in 1906 by Josephine Foster, Carmel's resident bohemian. She was a great friend of the arts — of writers particularly — and among her guests were the brightest literary lights of her time: Jack London, Sinclair Lewis, Mary Austin, poet George Sterling. (In those days one didn't have to write, drink, or throw wild parties to be considered bohemian — all one had to do was be a patron of the arts.) Josephine was known affectionately as "Nana" by her friends, of whom there were many on the Monterey Peninsula.

Nana's family was artistic. Her grandfather built the first Cliff House in San Francisco (destroyed later by fire). Stonehouse reflects her idiosyncratic taste. All the stones are carefully arranged and mortared together in the manner of the stone houses of Pennsylvania; creeping vines cover its exterior. Records show that the stones were hand shaped by local Indian craftsmen, and the unique star-shaped window in the front of the dwelling may have been fashioned by one of these men.

Stonehouse is furnished with country-flavored antiques throughout. The living room features a large stone fireplace (sherry, wine, and hot cider are served to guests here before they leave for dinner in the evenings). All guest rooms have handmade quilts, silk flower arrangements, fluffy pillows, and complimentary fresh fruit.

The bedrooms are named after authors. The one

named after George Sterling (it was he who wrote that San Francisco was a "cool gray city of love") contains a handsome king-size canopy bed with a floral comforter, a dust ruffle, and pillow shams. There's an antique dresser, and a comfortable rocking chair and a reading lamp for quiet moments with a book. The Jack London room has an antique armoire and a queen-size bed with a wrought-iron and brass frame, as well as a single bed. Both rooms have good views of Point Lobos.

My favorite room was the Sinclair Lewis. Large and airy, with a huge brass bed, this room's big windows overlooking the rooftop and trees reminded me of the rooms at my grandmother's house when I was a very small child.

The full breakfast includes a hot entrée (baked eggs with bacon, crustless quiche, seafood crêpes), fresh fruit, homemade muffins, juice, and coffee. Breakfast is served from 8:30 to 10:00 A.M., and guests may eat either in the dining room, or—in good weather—on the patio.

One interesting legend about Stonehouse: Nana Foster is reputed to have placed "important papers" within the stone walls on the left-hand side of the fireplace. Writings by her accomplished literary friends? Some of her own literary efforts, perhaps? We may never know. No one's been able to tear the fireplace apart to find out—it's too beautiful.

The J. Patrick House

2990 Burton Drive
Cambria, California 93428; (805) 927-3812

INNKEEPER:	*Molly Lynch.*
ACCOMMODATIONS:	*Eight rooms, all with private bath; twin and queen-size beds.*
RESERVATIONS:	*Three to four weeks recommended.*
MINIMUM STAY:	*None.*
DEPOSIT:	*Full amount.*
CREDIT CARDS:	*MC, VISA.*
RATES:	*Moderate.*
RESTRICTIONS:	*No children under 16. No pets.*

For good reason, Jerry Hulse, longtime travel editor of the *Los Angeles Times*, calls the J. Patrick House "without question the prettiest b&b on the entire Central California coast." Woodsy and tucked away in a grove of fragrant pines, the log cabin–style inn offers warmth, hospitality, soothing American country furnishing, and a great locale just six miles south of Hearst Castle.

But above all, it's the proprietress who makes this inn come alive. A fiery redhead, vivacious but gentle, Molly Lynch has infused a good dose of her own personal style into her inn. From the music she plays on the phone recorder ("Greensleeves") to the name of her hostelry (which honors her Irish dad), Molly's inn is as Irish as Irish can be.

Each of the eight bedrooms (all with wood-burning fireplaces and all the same price) is christened after an Irish county: there's Galway, Tipperary, Dublin, Limerick, Donegal, Kerry, Kilkenny, and, newest of the clan, the Clare. Decorated with pine antiques and willow reproductions, the spacious living room is the place where you "check in" and, if you wish, partake of the complimentary wine and snacks (a recent serving was loaded with three cheeses, fresh vegetables and dip, ham and cheese rolls, smoked almonds, crackers, cherries, and strawberries, as well as soft drinks) from 5:30 to 6:30 P.M.

Both the living room/parlor, with its willow-branch chair; navy and coral floral print sofa; braided, heart-shaped rug; dried flower wreaths; and modest library; and the dining room/sun porch, with tables covered by gay blue and white checked tablecloths, are unpretentious and inviting. "We're not filled with sterling silver and major antiques; we strive to make our guests comfortable," professed Molly as she served a visitor some mineral water.

The Clare, which is located upstairs in the front of the Main House, contains a queen-size bed, log walls with a brick fireplace, pale blue carpets, and windows that overlook stately conifers.

The path to other guest rooms passes through a colorful garden. It includes thick plantings of pungent lavender and a long, flowing passion flower vine with scarlet flowers instead of the usual yellow and white mix.

Of the seven rooms in this cedar-sided lodge behind the Main House, the Limerick and Kilkenny are real items. The former has a reproduction of an Amish willow rocker, a queen-size bed with willow headboard, a brick fireplace, and a window seat covered in brown and white plaid. The latter is dressed in three patterns of pale blue wallpaper and also has a tile-front fireplace, a willow rocker, and a willow headboard for its queen-size bed.

For the 7:30 to 9:30 A.M. Continental breakfast on the sun porch, Molly serves up a bowl of fresh fruit, two types of baked goods, such as apple bread and oatmeal-coconut muffins with jam centers, fresh juice, yogurt, granola, teas, and freshly brewed coffee. (A "don't miss" for vacationing chocoholics willing to indulge their whims is Molly's plateful of homemade chocolate chip cookies, featured nightly in the kitchen pantry.)

Refreshed and unhurried, you'll leave this pseudo-Irish roadside inn with a twinkle in your eye and a smile in your heart. Farther up the coast is Big Sur, farther down is Morro Bay. Also beckoning are nearby beaches great for seashell hunting and tidepooling, hiking trails at Las Padres National Forest, a local berry farm that sells pies and homemade jams, and lots of little wineries.

Country House Inn

91 Main Street
Templeton, California 93465; (805) 434-1598

INNKEEPER:	*Dianne Garth.*
ACCOMMODATIONS:	*Four rooms, two with private bath; queen- and king-size beds.*
RESERVATIONS:	*Three to four weeks for weekends.*
MINIMUM STAY:	*Two nights on holiday weekends.*
DEPOSIT:	*First night's lodging.*
CREDIT CARDS:	*MC, VISA.*
RATES:	*Inexpensive.*
RESTRICTIONS:	*Children by arrangement. No pets.*

The smell of Mexican quiche and zucchini bread hot out of the oven along with the sight of cups of caramel custard and baked peaches with raspberries and cream filled my senses as I popped my head in the back kitchen door of the Country House Inn. Apparently I was just in time for breakfast. "Sit down and make yourself comfortable," said Dianne Garth as she offered me a choice of orange juice or coffee. Dianne had bought Country House just a year before my visit (it was already an inn) after previewing the property in an edition of *Country Living* magazine.

Built in 1886 by C. H. Phillips, founder of the town of Templeton, the house's Victorian country charm was clearly in evidence even though it was in the throes of a complete facelift the day I stopped by. The exterior was being painted a light grey and white with rose trim. Finished interiors in a country French style were quite lovely and offered a taste of what was yet to come. New rose-colored carpeting had been laid down. Of the four guest rooms my preferences ran to Garden View, with its bay window with rose-patterned window seat, crystal chandelier, nice wardrobe, and king-size bed smothered in a white and pink floral comforter, and the Summer Cottage (former servants quarters) done in yellow, blue, and white Laura Ashley prints. A quilt wall hanging and braided heart-shaped rug basket caught my eye as did the queen-size bed with brass headboard and bright, white walls.

Having formerly worked as an interior decorator, Dianne describes herself now as "homebody, mother of two children, and inn proprietor." She has her degree in art and also once owned an art gallery. "It's quiet here, restful you might say. Of course, there's winetasting in the area, and hot air balloon rides. But most people who stop here are on their way to Hearst Castle, just a forty-minute drive."

A good place to relax, the living room at Country House holds a fireplace and a blue and white–patterned sofa. Peachy pink walls are accented by a blue border. Games like Monopoly and backgammon are also on hand. French double doors in the inn's dining room open onto a deck. White lace curtains frame the windows and a quilt hangs on the wall. The pecan wood table and chairs are occupied by guests gathered for breakfast anytime between 7:30 and 10:00 A.M. Dianne named French toast and baked apple pancakes with sausages as other main dishes she serves. Oh well, that's another day!

Located halfway between Los Angeles and San Francisco, Templeton is an old western town with many finely restored buildings. Templeton's Country House Inn is a Designated Historic Site.

Heritage Inn

978 Olive Street
San Luis Obispo, California 93401; (805) 544-7440

INNKEEPERS:	*Jim and Zella Harrison.*
ACCOMMODATIONS:	*Nine rooms, one with private bath; twin, double, and queen-size beds.*
RESERVATIONS:	*Three weeks recommended.*
MINIMUM STAY:	*None.*
DEPOSIT:	*Full amount.*
CREDIT CARDS:	*MC, VISA.*
RATES:	*Inexpensive.*
RESTRICTIONS:	*No children. No pets.*

T he history of the Heritage Inn in San Luis Obispo sounds more like the *Perils of Pauline* than the usual guidebook fare. The saga began in 1902, when the San Luis Obispo Herrera family (one of the old Hispanic families in the area) built this gracious 3,000-square-foot home as a family dwelling. As its ten bedrooms would indicate, the Herreras were a large family: Manuel was the city's constable; Isbaldo was the custodian at the courthouse; and Juanita, the oldest daughter, worked for the Tribune Printing Company. About 1930 the residence was sold to Frank Barcellos, a local saloon owner who moved it from Monterey Street (then the intersection of Highways 1 and 101) to Santa Rosa Street and used it as a lodging establishment for men.

In 1981 the building was bought by Rob and Kathy Strong, who hoped to renovate it and use it as a bed and breakfast inn. The condition of the sale was that the Strongs move the structure to another location to make way for a parking lot. The couple scheduled the house's dramatic half-mile move, only to be halted at the last moment by a neighboring motel's protesting owner. Some frantic legal maneuvering followed — capped by the court's decision that the Heritage Inn could be moved, just hours before the wrecker's ball would have demolished it forever.

An interesting sidelight: the inn's new location was purchased from another branch of the Herrera family. And where was this new creekside location for Heritage Inn? Once again at the intersection of Highways 1 and 101.

I'm glad the good guys won this round, because this is not just the only bed and breakfast in San Luis Obispo, it is a quality establishment by any standard. Current owners Jim and Zella Harrison maintain the precedents set by the Strongs that make this a success.

The character of the inn is turn of the century, with antique furnishings (most from the area), period wall coverings and draperies, bay windows and window seats throughout, period bath fixtures, and a wide and well-chosen variety of San Luis Obispo memorabilia and photos. Guest rooms are provided with brass, wicker, and oak antiques; fresh flowers; and washbasins.

A Continental breakfast is served in the fireside dining room: croissants, muffins, and nut breads, homemade spreads, fresh fruit in season, juice, coffee, or tea.

The reception room provides a large variety of local tourist information and a menu selection from local restaurants (Heritage hostesses are quite eager to help here also); wine and cheese are served in the parlor in the evening; bubble bath is available in the bathrooms; parking is easy—just a few of the reasons people from San Francisco, Los Angeles, and the San Joaquin Valley are finding Heritage Inn the ideal mid-coast stop during that long drive down El Camino Real.

Rose Victorian Inn

789 Valley Road
Arroyo Grande, California 93420; (805) 481-5566

INNKEEPERS:	*Diane and Ross Cox.*
ACCOMMODATIONS:	*Eight rooms, three with private bath; double, queen- and king-size beds.*
RESERVATIONS:	*Three weeks recommended.*
MINIMUM STAY:	*Two nights on holiday weekends.*
DEPOSIT:	*Full amount.*
CREDIT CARDS:	*AE, MC, VISA (to reserve a room only if there's not time enough to send a check).*
RATES:	*Moderate to expensive.*
RESTRICTIONS:	*No children. No pets.*

"When people ask me what it takes to be an innkeeper," explained Diane Cox, "I ask *them* if they like a Grand Central Station lifestyle, and can function on just six hours of sleep, night after night, for a long period of time."

Diane was born in China of mixed English and American parentage. Her family migrated to the United States and resided in Laguna Beach through the forties and fifties. This is where she met husband Ross. "We met in first grade, dated in high school, married in college, and have been living that Grand Central Station lifestyle I mentioned ever since — Ross has forty-one cousins, I have twenty-nine."

Their inn is a family affair. Ross is a builder by trade. Daughter Shelly serves as part-time innkeeper, and another daughter is responsible for much of the interior design of the inn.

The Rose Victorian is truly classified as a country inn, due to its adjoining restaurant/bar operation. The purchase of overnight accommodations on the modified American plan includes breakfast (a fresh fruit plate, home-baked muffins, eggs Florentine, orange juice with champagne) *and* dinner.

This fourteen-room house, once the homestead of a

large walnut farm, is a classic example of Victorian Italian/Stick architecture, with vertical lines predominating. It is painted in four shades of rose, following the Victorian tradition of picking a color and then painting the house in several shades of that color. Original coal-burning fireplaces heat the living room and parlor.

The eight bed and breakfast rooms for overnight guests are filled with mahogany, oak, rosewood, and walnut pieces that carry out the Victorian decor. Each room is named after a variety of rose and decorated in its color: Sterling Silver, Tropicana, Olé, Brandy, Summer Sunshine. A vase with a rose of the same name, from the over two hundred rose bushes planted on the property, is found in each room.

Celebrities, writers, movie producers, and occasionally government officials come here to stay. And, as Shelly aptly pointed out, that is one of the unique features of the Rose Victorian: once you've arrived there's no need to go anywhere else. You can play croquet on the lawn, sip iced tea and nibble on hors d'oeuvres in the late afternoon, feast on sumptuous steak au poivre, roast duck à l'orange, or shrimp Victoria, enjoy an after-dinner drink, relax in your room, or mingle with other guests in the parlor or in the living room around the grand piano.

But then again it would be a shame *not* to go out, as the area has so many attractions: the Great American Melodrama and Vaudeville Show in neighboring Oceano; boating, fishing, and windsurfing at Lopez Lake; mineral hot springs; wineries; and Spanish missions. It's a forty-five minute drive north to Hearst Castle; San Luis Obispo is just fifteen minutes away.

Seal Beach Inn

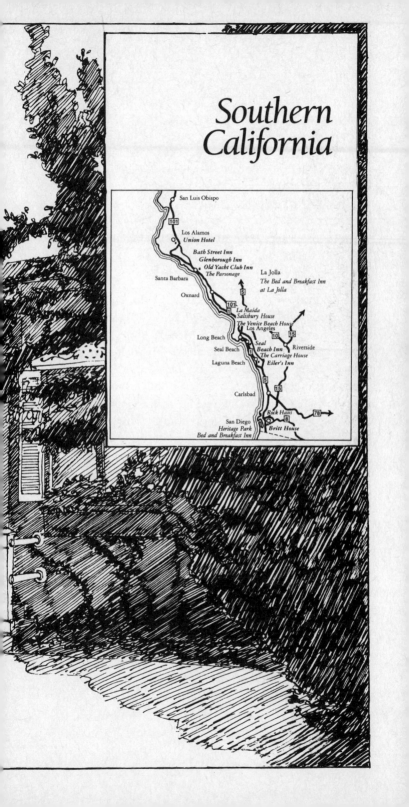

Southern California

San Luis Obispo

101

Los Alamos
Union Hotel

Bath Street Inn
Glenborough Inn
Old Yacht Club Inn
The Parsonage

La Jolla
*The Bed and Breakfast Inn
at La Jolla*

Santa Barbara

Oxnard

101

*La Maida
Salisbury House
The Venice Beach House*
Los Angeles

10   Riverside

15

Long Beach

*Seal
Beach Inn*
The Carriage House

Seal Beach

Eiler's Inn

Laguna Beach

5

15

Carlsbad

Rock Haus

8   **78**

San Diego
*Heritage Park
Bed and Breakfast Inn*

Britt House

Union Hotel

362 Bell Street, P. O. Box 616
Los Alamos, California 93440; (805) 344-2744 or (805) 928-3838

INNKEEPER:	*Dick Langdon.*
ACCOMMODATIONS:	*Sixteen rooms, three with private bath; twin, double, and king-size beds.*
RESERVATIONS:	*Three to six weeks recommended.*
MINIMUM STAY:	*None.*
DEPOSIT:	*In full.*
CREDIT CARDS:	*Not accepted.*
RATES:	*Moderate.*
RESTRICTIONS:	*No children. No pets.*

J. D. Snyder was a New Yorker who came west to make his fortune — and succeeded. In the 1880s he owned the way station in tiny Los Alamos for the stagecoach route between Santa Barbara and San Francisco. In addition to being the local agent for Wells Fargo, he was also involved in farming and a variety of other business ventures in Santa Barbara County. One of them was the Union Hotel, where stage passengers could eat, stay overnight, and wet their whistles before continuing the arduous overland journey.

Fire destroyed the hotel, however, as it did so many other wooden structures of that time. In 1915 it was rebuilt with Indian adobe. Thereafter it was used as a hotel, a rooming house, and a pool room, after which it was boarded up and forgotten. Until it was discovered by Dick Langdon, that is. It became his dream to rehabilitate — or rather *re-create* — this old western hotel based on original sketches of the Union. Wood from twelve barns was used to re-create the exterior with various craftspeople in the area contributing their talents. The result is a work of art that has attracted comment from western buffs and bed and breakfast enthusiasts alike.

Antiques here are imaginative and provocative: two-hundred-year-old Egyptian urns; a pair of swinging doors from a New Orleans house of ill repute; dining room furniture from a Mississippi plantation; an 1880 Brunswick pool table. My room was a masterpiece of whimsy: a ceiling fan, an antique trunk, hats hanging from a coatrack! (I kept waiting for the owners of those hats to come back and claim them.) There is an old crank telephone in the upstairs hall, and guests who listen carefully to the earphone are often surprised by mysterious (taped) voices.

Overnight guests dine together at 7:30 P.M. — the homecooked meal is served family style. Then everyone gathers in the old saloon for an evening's worth of entertainment: there's a Rockola jukebox full of old 78s, a Ping-Pong table, shuffleboard, and a collection of old radio tapes.

One of the most interesting architectural and design triumphs of this inn is the swimming pool. There were no such conveniences in the 1880s, so Dick concealed this one in the guise of an old-fashioned reflecting pond. The grounds also include streetlights, park benches, flower gardens, and manicured lawns. There is a lovely Victorian gazebo with a secret Jacuzzi inside, large enough to accommodate a dozen guests.

A full breakfast is served, and it is as special as everything else about the place. It has been known to include such diverse delights as gingerbread cake, chocolate chip cookies, pound cake, and brandy. After breakfast guests are treated to a tour of Los Alamos in a 1918, fifteen-passenger touring car.

This distinctive adventure in lodging is only open on Friday, Saturday, and Sunday (year-round). "Three days a week is fun," Dick is often quoted as saying. "After that, it becomes work."

The Old Yacht Club Inn

431 Corona Del Mar
Santa Barbara, California 93103; (805) 962-1277

INNKEEPER:	*Nancy Donaldson.*
ACCOMMODATIONS:	*Five rooms, one with private bath; queen-size beds. The Hitchcock House (next door) has four rooms, all with private bath; queen- and king-size beds.*
RESERVATIONS:	*Two months for weekends.*
MINIMUM STAY:	*Two nights on weekends.*
DEPOSIT:	*First night's lodging.*
CREDIT CARDS:	*AE, MC, VISA.*
RATES:	*Inexpensive to moderate.*
RESTRICTIONS:	*No children. No pets.*

*T*ake four independent career women. Add a historic structure crying out for tender loving care. Stir in a need to try something new and different, and you have the highly successful ingredients of one of Santa Barbara's most comfortable bed and breakfast inns.

The Old Yacht Club Inn was built in 1912 as a private residence on Cabrillo Boulevard overlooking the beautiful Pacific. In the 1920s Santa Barbara's yacht club was completely destroyed by a disastrous storm. The present structure was pressed into service as the headquarters for the club; later it was moved to its current location on Corona Del Mar.

Nancy Donaldson, the dean of a Los Angeles high school, and three female friends — also educators and administrators — cooperated to buy, renovate, furnish, and finally operate the Old Yacht Club Inn. Just a short distance from lovely Cabrillo Beach, the OYCI has five tastefully decorated guest rooms.

Rooms that share baths come with washbasins; there is a small decanter at bedside for guests whose slumber is improved by a sip or two of sherry. The two front rooms have balconies surrounded by flowers.

The Castellamare room is my favorite: hardwood

floors, a window seat, bedspread and drapes with a brightly colored flower print. (I also liked the Portofino room, with its queen-size canopy bed, and shades of baby blue, tan, and cream.) All rooms are decorated with antiques, and the front rooms catch the sun and a delicious afternoon breeze.

Guests are invited to share the living room as well as the spacious front porch. (Arriving guests are given a glass of wine or a cup of tea in the living room.) There is a fireplace here, but no television. As a native of the area, Nancy is well equipped to steer guests to the best restaurants and nearby attractions. Bicycles are available to guests, as are beach chairs and towels. Those who arrive on Amtrak or at the airport can be picked up.

The breakfast is fuller than most, usually featuring egg dishes, with fresh fruit, juice, homemade breads (zucchini and banana), and coffee cake. Nancy will also cook dinner for guests who request it in advance (mainly on weekends). Request it—she's an *excellent* cook!

Bath Street Inn

1720 Bath Street
Santa Barbara, California 93101; (805) 682-9680

INNKEEPER:	*Susan Brown.*
ACCOMMODATIONS:	*Seven rooms, all with private bath; twin, queen-, and king-size beds.*
RESERVATIONS:	*Six weeks recommended.*
MINIMUM STAY:	*Two nights on weekends.*
DEPOSIT:	*First night's lodging or half the full amount for longer stays.*
CREDIT CARDS:	*AE, MC, VISA.*
RATES:	*Moderate.*
RESTRICTIONS:	*No pets.*

From the time Vizcaíno entered the harbor on the eve of Saint Barbara's Day in 1602 (and so, appropriately, named the channel for her), Santa Barbara has been a magnet for adventurers, visionaries, entrepreneurs, and most of all, people irresistibly attracted to its mild climate and scenic beauty. Both newcomers and old Santa Barbara hands have found the Bath Street Inn ideally located for maximum enjoyment of the city's rich cultural and resort activities.

Bath Street Inn began as a private residence in 1895, and was called the House of the Three Sisters by local residents. (At least partly because of the huge *Pittosporum* tree with three trunks that stood outside, it would seem.) When Susan Brown found it with the aid of a realtor, the old dwelling was badly in need of some sisterly attention. And it got it—with the help of a local architect who supervised much of the renovation.

A common theme among owners of bed and breakfast inns is a desire to leave an environment of cutthroat ambition and enter a service-oriented world. Susan—a personnel manager in Anaheim for ten years—was no exception. This charming and intelligent woman pronounced herself "somewhat disillusioned with the business world." Or at least its most competitive and least reflective aspects.

At the same time, she offers a service that businesses of all descriptions find eminently helpful: seminar facilities and a conference room.

This Queen Anne Victorian has three stories with a small second-story eyelid balcony in front, and is larger inside than it appears from the street. (The third floor — where the common area is located — feels like an entire house in itself.) The rooms are decorated with a nice mix of antiques that enhance the 1895 atmosphere of the original dwelling.

The Continental breakfast is served outdoors on the porch or patio when weather permits — which it usually does in Santa Barbara. It consists of homemade breads, rolls, coffee cake or croissants, juice, fresh fruit in season, and a choice of coffee, tea, milk, or cocoa.

The Glenborough Inn

1327 Bath Street
Santa Barbara, California 93101; (805) 966-0589

INNKEEPERS:	*Jo Ann Bell and Pat Hardy.*
ACCOMMODATIONS:	*Nine rooms, five with private bath; double and queen-size beds.*
RESERVATIONS:	*Two to three months for weekends.*
MINIMUM STAY:	*Two nights on weekends.*
DEPOSIT:	*Full amount.*
CREDIT CARDS:	*MC, VISA.*
RATES:	*Moderate to expensive.*
RESTRICTIONS:	*Children under 12 discouraged. Pets discouraged.*

The Glenborough is a handsome, two-story structure built in 1906 in what is often termed the California Craftsman style. Built by a single craftsman for Louis Brooks, vice president of a local fuel company, it was quite modern for its time, with a decorative brass heater instead of the traditional wood fireplace. But in renovating, the decoration and design have mainly followed the turn-of-the-century mode of the architecture. With few exceptions, furnishings are antiques — even the curtains are of old lace or crochet. Rooms have pictures from the early 1900s, and a very special part of the decor are the Fillmore-signed nostalgic prints of Los Angeles.

Proprietors Jo Ann Bell and Pat Hardy met when they served together on the board of directors of a battered women's shelter in Riverside. Jo Ann has a background in social work as a psychotherapist, and still maintains a small practice. Former director of a crisis hotline, Pat is a people-oriented bundle of creative energy whom Jo Ann describes as "a greeter, a morning person, and a risk-taker." The decorating was done mainly by Pat, with Jo Ann "keeping things from getting out of hand."

The French Rose room is graced by elegant inlaid French furniture and a rose velvet spread; my favorite of all four rooms in the main house, this spacious chamber has a fine mountain view framed by antique embroidered curtains. Aurelia's Fancy celebrates a young woman who once lived here, with a rocking chair, a full queen-size cannonball field bed, accented with rich blue, antique lace curtains, and an heirloom quilt. The Country room projects a cozy ambience, its earthy tones enlivened by the morning sun, with antique golden oak furniture. The Garden room is the smallest but cheeriest. A former sun porch overlooking a garden, it has an antique brass and white iron double bed; furniture is wicker and antique oak, accented by lush plants.

Four of the Glenborough's nine guest rooms are in an early 1880s cottage across the street, with separate entrances, a secluded New Orleans–style garden, and a private bath for each room.

Wine, tea, and hors d'oeuvres are served in a pleasant parlor in the evening; there is a hot tub in the garden that may be reserved for private use.

Breakfast at the Glenborough included a platter of fresh fruit (baked apple in wintertime); homemade coffee cake and nut breads (pumpkin and banana); Moma's egg casserole; orange juice (or a berry and banana smoothie); and tea, cinnamon-laced coffee, or cocoa. The morning meal is served between 8:00 and 9:30, and delivered to the room, if desired, or to the parlor or garden.

"We don't necessarily emphasize a homey atmosphere," says Pat. "We believe many of our guests come here for privacy or romance."

The Parsonage

1600 Olive Street
Santa Barbara, California 93101; (805) 962-9336

INNKEEPER:	*Hilde Michelmore.*
ACCOMMODATIONS:	*Six rooms, all with private bath; queen- and king-size beds.*
RESERVATIONS:	*Two to six weeks recommended.*
MINIMUM STAY:	*Two nights on weekends.*
DEPOSIT:	*First night's lodging.*
CREDIT CARDS:	*MC, VISA.*
RATES:	*Moderate.*
RESTRICTIONS:	*No children under 14. No pets.*

*I*f you need some tender loving care, plan to spend a day or two with Hilde Michelmore at The Parsonage. "TLC" is Hilde's specialty, and perhaps it was the similar orientation of the former residents that drew her to this house, once a parsonage for the Trinity Episcopal Church. "I just loved the house when I first saw it," she says of this Queen Anne Victorian built in 1892. "I looked at it one month, and moved in the next."

The Parsonage is now very much a home for Hilde, and a home-away-from-home for her guests, many of whom find such an instant rapport with her that they invite her out to dinner. From the television in the living room to the generous but informal breakfast served on the sun deck (cheese soufflé, apple-bran muffins, a slice of watermelon, coffee, and juice), you find the owner/operator school of philosophy. As Hilde insists, "When you lose that, you lose the whole concept of what bed and breakfast is all about."

The house sits on the corner of Olive and Arrellaga streets on Santa Barbara's upper east side. A wrought-iron gate leads to the large front porch that invites you into the high-ceilinged parlor and library, once used for church business. Redwood moldings are in evidence, as is a bird's-eye redwood fireplace. Hilde has incorporated her personal furnishings with pieces she purchased especially for the house.

Each guest room has its own bathroom, although

some are larger than others and one or two are closet size. The Rosebud Room and the Versailles Room are the only downstairs bedrooms and unfortunately I didn't get to see them, as they were occupied at the time. Of the four upstairs rooms, however, I can highly recommend the Honeymoon Suite, which runs the entire length of the front of the house, with a gorgeous view of the ocean, palm trees, and the downtown area. The suite consists of a bedroom with a king-size canopied bed and an antique armoire, a bath (with a marble-topped washstand and a pedestal sink), and a solarium with an abundance of light filtering through its many clear and stained-glass windows. The other rooms, Lavender and Lace, Las Flores, and the Peacock Room, carry out the various themes suggested by their names.

Santa Barbara's lovely beaches, botanical gardens, golf courses, art galleries, and fine restaurants make for a great L.A. getaway weekend or an unhurried stopover before heading south to the City of the Angels.

La Maida House

11159 La Maida Street
North Hollywood, California 91601; (818) 769-3857

INNKEEPER:	*Megan Timothy.*
ACCOMMODATIONS:	*Seven rooms and five suites, all with private bath; twin, double, queen-, and king-size beds.*
RESERVATIONS:	*Three weeks recommended.*
MINIMUM STAY:	*Two nights.*
DEPOSIT:	*First night's lodging.*
CREDIT CARDS:	*Not accepted.*
RATES:	*Moderate to expensive.*
RESTRICTIONS:	*No pets.*

All the great things you've been hearing about La Maida House are true. This twenty-five-room, 7,000-square-foot Italian villa is the crème de la crème of the small inns. Its marble fireplace, spiral staircase, French doors, beveled glass mirrors, and bubbling fountains are reminiscent of the glamorous Hollywood of the thirties and forties. The house was actually built in 1926 by one T. G. La Maida, a fruit and vegetable rancher. The largest guest room, Cipresso, overlooks the cypress trees along La Maida Street. Its canopied bed, ceiling fan, and wicker furniture remind one of warmer climes—perhaps Zimbabwe, which is where innkeeper Megan Timothy hails from.

Other touches I like here: AM/FM clock radios, refrigerators, and private-line telephones in the guest rooms; down comforters and wool blankets; a copy of the *Los Angeles Times* delivered to the door; bathroom scales for the weight-conscious; full laundry and dry-cleaning service on request—and Megan will even prepare lunch or dinner for a tired and weary traveler with a little advance notice.

"Our guests are guests in the true sense of the word," said Megan. "In Africa when we had house guests we catered to their every little whim. That's what I'm striving to re-create here."

A woman of many talents, this Megan. A caterer by profession, a patron of the arts, a sculptor in stained glass, a photogapher extraordinaire, an interior designer, and even a one-time professional folk singer.

Everything here is homemade, right down to the blended yogurt–fruit juice beverages served at breakfast and the *padkos* (an African tradition of food for the road) Megan gives guests as a parting gift. What for many other innkeepers is the lull in their day, is for Megan the busiest part; she was baking oatmeal cookies when I arrived in the early afternoon. Megan keeps chickens for fresh eggs, grows her own fruits, vegetables and herbs, and makes her own jams and preserves.

Writers, producers, directors, and celebrities are entered on La Maida's guest list. Part of the reason is that the inn is so close to most of the major studios (Universal, Burbank, Columbia, Warner Brothers, NBC). La Maida has even seen a little moviemaking of its own. The house was featured in scenes of "Quincy" and the popular television series "Simon and Simon."

Other nearby attractions include the Hollywood Bowl (Megan will provide a picnic basket or pre-concert supper), the Huntington Library and gardens, the Norton Simon Museum, and the Los Angeles County Museum. (La Maida is a quick ten minutes from the Hollywood/ Burbank airport.)

Speaking of art, Megan's breakfast is a feast of edible art. The fare includes freshly baked breads (scones, brioches, or oatmeal muffins), an attractive carved-fruit platter with Tunisian oranges (sprinkled with rosewater and cinnamon), and a refreshing fresh fruit–yogurt drink such as peach-rosewater-honey or mint-pepper. (Bing cherries partially dipped in bittersweet chocolate were served at bedside.)

So the question is: Is it Hollywood or Zimbabwe? Perhaps it's the best of both.

The Venice Beach House

15 Thirtieth Avenue
Venice, California 90291; (213) 823-1966

INNKEEPERS:	*Philip and Vivian Boesch.*
ACCOMMODATIONS:	*Eight rooms, four with private bath; double, queen-, and king-size beds.*
RESERVATIONS:	*Two weeks recommended.*
MINIMUM STAY:	*Two nights on weekends.*
DEPOSIT:	*Half total amount.*
CREDIT CARDS:	*AE, MC, VISA.*
RATES:	*Inexpensive to moderate.*
RESTRICTIONS:	*No children under 10. No pets.*

A bbot Kinney made his fortune in the thriving tobacco industry of his day. Around the turn of the century he bought up some marshland on the coast of California near Los Angeles, and in an attempt to re-create Venice, Italy, he constructed piers, boardwalks, bathhouses, and canals. Kinney was called a dreamer by some, but his project (dubbed "Kinney's Folly") soon brought the rich and famous to his door. Venice experienced its heyday as a resort town through the early 1900s. Then a series of disasters and misfortunes started it on a long, slow decline.

Today Venice is as much a state of mind as anything else. People either love it or shun it—there's nothing in between. Most of the action is found on the beach boardwalk, where vendors ply their wares in an open-air market, punk rockers on roller skates command one's attention, and muscle men strut their stuff.

If you're one of those who love it (or are perhaps just a bit curious), then you'll adore the Venice Beach House, a California bungalow-style bed and breakfast inn opened in 1984 by Philip and Vivian Boesch. Needless to say, this perky young couple love this zany beach town. Philip is a communications industry attorney; Vivian, a Louisiana transplant who should be properly thanked for bringing Southern hospitality to Southern California.

The inn's guest rooms recall Kinney's Venice of

America in both name and decor. Warren Wilson's Room commemorates the newspaperman who built this retreat in 1911. Tramp's Quarters honors Charlie Chaplin, the original Venice tramp who created his famous character here in the film *Kid Auto Races at Venice Beach*. Of course there's Abbot Kinney's Room and the Pier Suite. Finally, there is James Peasgood's Room, lest we forget this rascal who changed the history of Venice forever by embezzling from the city treasury in 1922.

A light Continental breakfast of fresh fruit, muffins, coffee, and juice is served from 8:00 to 9:30 A.M.; wine and cheese from 5:30 to 7:00 P.M. Gourmet picnic lunches are available on request.

Washington Street's shops and sidewalk cafes are just a block away, as is the beach itelf. The inn provides bicycles and beach chairs. In quiet moments you can curl up by the fire in the spacious living room with its beamed ceiling and bay windows, or sit out on the patio with a glass of sun tea and read the inn's copy of the colorful history of Venice, *Venice California 1904–1930*, by Jeffrey Stanton.

Venice has been described as "a city that's striving to make a comeback." I applaud Philip and Vivian Boesch, who are certainly doing their part to help.

Salisbury House

2273 West 20th Street
Los Angeles, California 90018; (213) 737-7817

INNKEEPERS:	*Kathleen and Bill Salisbury.*
ACCOMMODATIONS:	*Five rooms, three with private bath; twin, double, queen-, and king-size beds.*
RESERVATIONS:	*Three to four weeks recommended.*
MINIMUM STAY:	*None.*
DEPOSIT:	*First night's lodging.*
CREDIT CARDS:	*AE, MC, VISA.*
RATES:	*Inexpensive to moderate.*
RESTRICTIONS:	*No children under 10. No pets.*

K athleen Salisbury's idea for a b&b evolved from an interest in old houses, a background in interior design and furniture sales, and an obsession with good food. Ten years in public welfare work as both a case worker and a supervisor also helped motivate her in this people-oriented project.

Just minutes from downtown Los Angeles and the freeway, Salisbury House has developed a clientele that is primarily business oriented. But the inn is also centrally located for day trips to Disneyland, the Los Angeles area museums, Beverly Hills shopping, Santa Monica and Venice beaches, and Universal Studios tours.

Bargain prices, down comforters and feather pillows, televisions and telephones available for guests, an amply stocked wine rack in the upstairs hall, and freshly baked chocolate chunk cookies supplied to the rooms, make for other good reasons to stay here.

The California Craftsman–style home, built in 1909, had only two previous owners before Bill and Kathleen came along. The first, a physician whose office was downtown, reputedly owned one of the first automobiles in the area. This pocket of stable family homes on wide streets with big old trees finds friendly neighbors sitting out on the porch.

The living room of Salisbury House is made cozy

by a piano and pendulum clock, tile fireplace with wood mantel, deep blue floral print sofa and matching love seat, corduroy-covered armchairs, and Oriental motif carpets. Clusters of family pictures sit atop the piano. Also evident is a family of stuffed toy animals. Original stained and leaded glass windows are found throughout the house, as are wood-beam ceilings.

Three of the guest rooms are named for their predominant color: the Rose, Green, and Blue rooms; the fourth is the Sun Room where white and citron yellow hues combine with sunshine rays to give the room its bright, cheery look. The fifth accommodation is the Attic Suite. Covering the home's entire third floor, the suite's 600 square feet contain a spacious sitting area with wing-back settee (as well as a table and chairs), a king-size brass bed, and a private bath with antique claw-foot tub. An American country theme prevails.

Breakfast in bed is available on request. Otherwise, it's served in the dining room on weekdays between 7:30 and 9:00 A.M. or on weekends between 8:00 and 9:30. Coffee is usually out by 7:00. The buffet includes freshly squeezed orange juice, vanilla nut cream–flavored coffee, a variety of teas, and entrées like chicken crêpes, puffed apple pancakes, or grilled sausages with a corn soufflé. The fruit accompaniment might be as simple as a fresh fruit and yogurt parfait, or as intriguing as poached pears stuffed with dark chocolate cream resting on a bed of raspberries. Homemade granola is always on hand, as are the highly regarded house breads: walnut streusal coffee cake and chocolate chip–macadamia nut bread. Occasionally there is an apple cobbler or Kathleen's own fresh pear pie.

The Seal Beach Inn

212 Fifth Street
Seal Beach, California 90740; (213) 493-2416

INNKEEPERS: *Marjorie and Jack Bettenhausen.*

ACCOMMODATIONS: *Twenty-two rooms, all with private bath; twin, double, queen-, and king-size beds.*

RESERVATIONS: *Two weeks recommended.*

MINIMUM STAY: *Two nights on weekends.*

DEPOSIT: *First night's lodging.*

CREDIT CARDS: *AE, MC, VISA.*

RATES: *Moderate to expensive.*

RESTRICTIONS: *Children discouraged. No pets.*

The Spanish called it Rancho Los Alamitos; the German burghers who followed knew it as Anaheim Landing. Bay City was the rather slick monicker cooked up by developers in the 1920s. Today this sleepy coastal village is known as Seal Beach (after the many seals that once flocked to the beaches here), but it is in many ways just as quiet now as it was in former days—which for those of us who wish to get away from it all is a big plus. Yet the nearby convergence of four major freeways makes Los Angeles and destinations in Orange County easy to get to when it's time to return to the real world.

The style of the Seal Beach Inn is French Mediterranean, a perfect choice for this part of the state. When one first hears of its twenty-two rooms, one imagines that this might be a motel that serves breakfast. Not a bit of it! The rooms are equipped with antiques and warm, quality furnishings, carefully designed to impart a Continental country inn flavor. (All rooms have private baths, and kitchen-bars are available in most.) Prints, objets d'art, collectibles, and books abound in most rooms. There is a pool, as one might expect in Southern California; and there is also an attractive garden with roses, geraniums, hibiscus, and begonias (among scores of other flowers).

Seal Beach Inn began as a motel in the 1920s, when Seal Beach was a wide-open gambling and resort area, which makes the European feeling of this place all the more remarkable. ("The closest thing to Europe since I left there," reads one encomium in the register.) Hardwood floors and wood paneling are everywhere. Antique lamp posts and a brick courtyard, blue awnings and yellow-painted fence, and an ancient British telephone booth all add to the ambience.

Proprietors Marjorie Bettenhausen and physician husband Jack go out of their way to provide those little extras that make a bed and breakfast different from any other kind of accommodation. Current magazines and the *Los Angeles Times* are available in the library; there is even an ironing board and iron available for guest use. Just one block from the ocean, Seal Beach Inn is also close to the Old Town section of Seal Beach (the high percentage of artists and craftspeople living in the area is obvious in the boutiques and shops), the Long Beach marina, and a total of four shopping areas on various waterfronts. (And the inn is just fifteen to twenty minutes by car from the *Queen Mary*, Knott's Berry Farm, and Disneyland.)

Breakfast in the Tea Room begins at 7:30 and lasts until 10:30. The croissants, freshly baked muffins, breads and tortes, homemade granola, fresh fruits and juices, cheeses, egg casserole or quiche, freshly ground coffee, and selection of imported teas make this a wonderful morning meal.

Marjorie and Jack enjoy what they do, as becomes obvious when one talks to them about their work. "Every day it's something different," Marjorie told me. One interesting moment came when two attractive French girls admitted sadly that they had run out of money. What to do? Before a call could be placed to the French Embassy, two French pilots checked in, and *voilà!* . . . the next day the two young women were flown back to Paris free of charge. A charming story, and one that might have an interesting follow-up. . . .

Eiler's Inn

741 South Coast Highway
Laguna Beach, California 92651; (714) 494-3004

INNKEEPERS:	*Henk and Annette Wirtz.*
ACCOMMODATIONS:	*Twelve rooms, all with private bath; twin, double, queen-, and king-size beds.*
RESERVATIONS:	*Four to five weeks recommended.*
MINIMUM STAY:	*Two nights on weekends.*
DEPOSIT:	*First two nights' lodging.*
CREDIT CARDS:	*AE, MC, VISA.*
RATES:	*Moderate.*
RESTRICTIONS:	*Children discouraged. No pets.*

*E*iler Larsen was a Danish immigrant with a passion for wishing people well — an agreeable eccentricity (if eccentricity it really is) that made him a well-loved local figure in Laguna Beach. The colorful Dane simply loved to say hello to people, and each day strode up and down Laguna Beach greeting residents and strangers alike. In the 1960s he was made the town's official greeter by the municipal government, and as the irrepressible old gentleman grew older and declined in health, the tabs for his meals and lodging were quietly picked up by government and business people. When he passed away in 1975, he left a warm memory of a man who represented perhaps the highest form of hospitality: a desire to make others feel good with no reward for oneself except the company of one's friends.

Following closely on the heels of this tradition is Eiler's Inn, owned and operated by Henk and Annette Wirtz. ("Henk and I came as guests of the inn in 1979 and bought it in 1981," says Annette.) Eiler's is a small establishment, despite its twelve rooms, arranged around a marvelous fountain courtyard that is definitely more Hispanic than Scandinavian. Cheese and a fruit board greet the newly arrived guest, as do complimentary champagne or sparkling cider. (Afternoon tea is also served around the courtyard fountain.) There is often live music during the wine hour on Saturdays. Both Annette and Henk are well acquainted with the area and are happy to recommend local eating and entertainment spots.

There is a fireplace in the parlor, and a library is generously stocked with games and puzzles; there is also an attractive sun deck on the second floor. Rooms are decorated with a Southern California 1940s motif (the premises began as a hotel in the early 1940s): rose-patterned rugs and speckled linoleum floors look as though they might have been part of a film set for *Chinatown*. (All rooms have a private bath.)

The buffet-style breakfast is served in the courtyard between 8:30 and 10:30. It includes fresh fruit in a basket, cereal and milk, tomato or orange juice, hard-cooked eggs, pastries, and freshly ground coffee. The courtyard at Eiler's Inn is one of the most pleasant places imaginable to begin one's day, and in the bright smiles and good company of Henk and Annette one is assured that the tradition of friendliness personified by Eiler Larsen is very much alive.

The Carriage House

1322 Catalina
Laguna Beach, California 92651; (714) 494-8945

INNKEEPERS:	*Vernon, Dee, and Tom Taylor; Rik Lawrence.*
ACCOMMODATIONS:	*Six suites, all with private bath; twin, double, queen-, and king-size beds.*
RESERVATIONS:	*Three to four weeks recommended.*
MINIMUM STAY:	*Two nights on weekends.*
DEPOSIT:	*First night's lodging.*
CREDIT CARDS:	*Not accepted.*
RATES:	*Moderate.*
RESTRICTIONS:	*None.*

S outhern California has its own unique style when it comes to bed and breakfast — especially when contrasted with the inns of the North Coast. Perhaps the climate evokes a more casual atmosphere; perhaps it has something to do with the architectural styles of the area as well. Take the Carriage House as a case in point. Here you have six suites surrounding a central brick courtyard in a horseshoe-shaped fashion. (This arrangement is similar to Eiler's Inn, the other Laguna Beach bed and breakfast.)

Each suite features its own parlor, separate bedroom, and fully equipped kitchen. Room decors play on themes like Green Palms (forest-green walls and carpet, white woodwork, white wicker furniture, a ceiling fan, and, as one would expect, potted palms), Lilac Time (cranberry and lilac tones, French doors that open to the courtyard), Primrose Lane, Mockingbird Hill, Mandalay, and Home Sweet Home (calico and gingham).

The focal point of the inn is Grandma Bean's dining room, where guests of the inn enjoy a buffet-style breakfast from 8:30 to 10:00: hot and cold cereals, coffee cake and English muffins, fresh fruit, two different juices (orange is one), coffee, and tea.

This is a family-owned and -operated affair (Dee Taylor and husband Vernon are the resident innkeepers; son

Tom and Rik Lawrence are co-owners) located on a quiet residential street just two blocks from the beach and a few more from the heart of the village.

Laguna is a town people fall in love with as well as in. Hand holding is as popular here as jogging and cycling, and stealing a kiss as common as stealing the show — in this case the show is the annual Festival of Arts and Pageant of the Masters held each year throughout July and August.

Rock Haus

410 Fifteenth Street
Del Mar, California 92104; (619) 481-3764

INNKEEPERS:	*Tom and Carol Hauser.*
ACCOMMODATIONS:	*Ten rooms, four with private bath;* *twin, queen-, and king-size beds.*
RESERVATIONS:	*Two to three weeks recommended.*
MINIMUM STAY:	*Two nights on weekends, Memorial* *Day through Labor Day.*
DEPOSIT:	*Full amount.*
CREDIT CARDS:	*MC, VISA.*
RATES:	*Moderate to expensive.*
RESTRICTIONS:	*No children. No pets.*

"The realtor who showed me this house said the original architect must have had a bed and breakfast in mind," Tom Hauser said jokingly as we shared a cup of coffee and some banana-nut bread on the sun porch of the Rock Haus one Thursday morning.

We were alone. All the other guests had chosen to sleep in; I had been tempted to do the same myself. What made Tom's remark so amusing was the fact that the Rock Haus was built at the turn of the century, long before bed and breakfast as we know it in this country today was established — let alone fashionable. But I could see that the notion wasn't too far afield, as the house (with its ten bedrooms and five baths) is perfect for a bed and breakfast — one of the finest on the South Coast, I might add.

This California bungalow sits perched on a hill overlooking the Pacific. The quaint village of Del Mar with its outdoor cafes and shops and unspoiled beach is just two blocks below. The living room, which has been both a gambling parlor and a church sanctuary, is now filled with traditional furnishings, a player piano, a rocking horse from England (although Tom has always wanted a racehorse), and a brick fireplace with a backgammon board in the inglenook.

I occupied "Top o' the Rock," a very private hideaway with a cooling ocean breeze. The delicately patterned gold, green, and white wallpaper was accentuated by white woodwork; a white eyelet comforter with matching pillow shams and dust ruffle covered the queen-size bed. The love seat provided an ideal spot for cuddling and cooing. Old photographs of a young Bing Crosby at the Del Mar race-track added a touch of interest. Another popular accommodation is the Huntsman's Room, masculine in decor with its fireplace, king-size bed, and private bath. But no matter which room you choose (Whale Watch, the Wicker Garden, Court Room, Wren's Nest, Pine Needles, Triple Crown, or South Lawn), you can't go wrong.

After breakfast (which also includes fresh fruit, cheese, orange juice, and coffee), plan to spend the day at the beach or an afternoon at the renowned Del Mar race-track (the season runs from July to mid-September), stroll around town, or drive south to San Diego to visit the zoo, Sea World, or Balboa Park.

"I try not to take all this for granted," Tom continued as I prepared to be on my way. "Without exception people love this place — and after all, how many other professions can you think of where you get stroked every day?"

The Bed & Breakfast Inn at La Jolla

7753 Draper Avenue
La Jolla, California 92037; (619) 456-2066

INNKEEPER:	*Betty Albee.*
ACCOMMODATIONS:	*Sixteen rooms, fifteen with private bath; twin and queen-size beds.*
RESERVATIONS:	*Three to four weeks for weekends.*
MINIMUM STAY:	*None.*
DEPOSIT:	*First night's lodging.*
CREDIT CARDS:	*MC, VISA.*
RATES:	*Moderate to expensive.*
RESTRICTIONS:	*No children under 12. No pets.*

The only bed and breakfast inn in La Jolla, this lovely dwelling was built in 1913 by architect Irving Gill, who for many years had worked side-by-side with his better-known contemporary Frank Lloyd Wright. Gill was a pioneer of modernism—his work known for its machinelike quality and precision detail. It has been said that this stucco boxlike structure with its prominent arches best exemplifies his "Cubist" style.

In the 1920s John Philip Sousa lived here. By the time Betty Albee came along in 1983, the property had been abandoned and was in a sad state of disrepair. "I could see the Irving Gill design just begging to be redone," she explained, and reported that the purchase price of the house, $750,000, was just the down payment of the over $1 million that was then sunk into building and renovation.

Sitting pretty in the heart of La Jolla's cultural complex (surrounded by the Museum of Contemporary Art, a school, church, hospital, and the Woman's Club), the inn harbors sixteen guest accommodations: eight in the original structure, eight in the addition (a matching new building dovetailed to the old). Rooms are charmingly appointed, and all but one come with private bath. My evening was spent in The Shores, a twin-bedded room just off the upstairs guest parlor and sun deck. There was a decanter of sherry in the room and a basket filled with apples and oranges. A fortune cookie on the bed pillow yielded what I truly hoped was my fortune — it read: Your future looks bright. Other niceties included floral print comforters with matching pillow shams and dust ruffles on the beds, a pedestal-base breakfast table with two chairs, a supply of current magazines of interest, a digital alarm clock, fluffy towels, and European lotions and soaps in the bath. (A television set, VCR, and ice maker were located in the combination parlor/library. Umbrella tables and chairs as well as a chaise longue were found on the deck.)

Pacific View is another room that commanded my attention with its fireplace, antique mantel clock, corner bookshelves, double French doors, a "pineapple post" bed, blue upholstered love seat, and fine writing desk. The premier attraction, however, is the Holiday Suite with its canopied four-poster, eight-foot-high armoire, tile and brick fireplace, tailored white chintz sofa and wing-back chair, Oriental carpet, view of the Pacific, and abundance of healthy green plants.

Breakfast spots are many and varied: the dining room, the garden, the sundeck, or your bedroom. If you choose the latter, a delightful tray holding freshly squeezed orange juice, coffee and tea, and a basket filled with croissants, muffins, and Danishes accompanied by sweet butter and jam is delivered to the door of your room. Breakfast hours span 7:30 to 9:30 A.M. The inn stocks an ample supply of sightseeing literature and res-taurant information; there is a pay telephone for guest use in the downstairs hall.

A picnic of sandwiches, fresh fruit, chocolates, and champagne or sparkling cider can be prepared for your day out with a little advance notice. The possibilities in and around this seaside community include a visit to the nearby Scripps Aquarium or the University of California at San Diego campus. Main street shops and restaurants are within easy walking distance, and the beach is just one block away. Wine hour is scheduled back at the inn at 4:00 P.M.

Britt House

406 Maple Street
San Diego, California 92103; (619) 234-2926

INNKEEPER:	*Daun Martin.*
ACCOMMODATIONS:	*Ten rooms, one with private bath; double and queen-size beds.*
RESERVATIONS:	*One week for weekdays, six weeks for weekends.*
MINIMUM STAY:	*Two nights on weekends.*
DEPOSIT:	*First night's lodging.*
CREDIT CARDS:	*AE, MC, VISA.*
RATES:	*Moderate.*
RESTRICTIONS:	*No pets.*

*I*t was not only San Diego's first bed and breakfast inn, but is still one of the best anywhere. "From Mendocino to the stormy coast of Maine," raves the *Los Angeles Times*, "it is without a doubt the most perfectly restored Victorian serving America's travelers today." Such tributes by a large metropolitan newspaper do not come every day; and when one visits this romantic gabled and turreted Queen Anne delight, one begins to understand what all the shouting is about.

Set in a neighborhood experiencing an extensive renovation of Victorians, Britt House was built in 1887 for Eugene Britt, an attorney active in civic and state affairs. (It was later owned by the Scripps family, prominent in newspaper publishing.) It was discovered by Daun Martin, who sank over $100,000 into restoring the proud old mansion. One of its most impressive — and justly famous — features is a stained-glass window two stories high, backing a winding staircase. Screens of wooden beads grace the doorways; hardwood floors and old wood paneling are used with the utmost imagination and taste.

The furnishings in the guest rooms enhance the romantic mood. The Windsor Room contains a queen-size bed with an ornately carved wooden canopy draped in velvets of cerise and crimson. The Governor's Room overlooks a garden, and its blue and white color scheme is enhanced by the personal furniture of Gov. Robert Waterman, the state's seventeenth governor. The Eastlake Room is done in caramel, cream, and burgundy; one can see the ocean while sitting at its gateleg table, and its Belgian rug, carpet-backed reclining rocker, and Eastlake dresser add to the sense of luxury. Fresh fruit, homemade cookies, and candy kisses are available in all rooms, and one bath has a pair of matching claw-foot tubs.

Breakfast is both full and imaginative. On weekends, for example, Daun fixes her famous baked eggs over tomatoes with salsa on the side. The daily homebaked yeast bread is accompanied with sweet butter and jam. The Viennese roast coffee is prepared filter-drip style. Weekday fare also includes a variety of egg-based dishes and choice of teas.

Heritage Park
Bed & Breakfast Inn

2470 Heritage Park Row
San Diego, CA 92110; (619) 295-7088

INNKEEPER:	*Lori Chandler.*
ACCOMMODATIONS:	*Nine rooms, three with private bath; twin, double, and queen-size beds.*
RESERVATIONS:	*Three to four weeks on weekends and holidays.*
MINIMUM STAY:	*Two nights on weekends.*
DEPOSIT:	*Half of full amount.*
CREDIT CARDS:	*MC, VISA.*
RATES:	*Moderate.*
RESTRICTIONS:	*No children. No pets.*

Two blocks from Old Town San Diego, the first permanent Spanish settlement on the California coast—now filled with museums, art galleries, and restaurants—sits Heritage Park Bed & Breakfast Inn. Just imagine the setting: a quiet seven-acre park formed solely for the preservation of endangered Victorian homes. Among the cobblestone walkways and gardens stand seven classic Victorian structures from the 1800s. Built in 1889 for Harfield and Myrtle Christian, this particular Queen Anne is characterized by a variety of chimneys, shingles, a two-story corner tower, and an encircling veranda. Featured in *The Golden Era* magazine in 1890, it was called "an outstandingly beautiful home of Southern California."

This inn, too, is family run. Lori Chandler, who acts as hostess and operations overseer, along with her mother, two sisters, and their husbands, spent two years trying to convince the County of San Diego to approve a bed and breakfast permit. Hundreds of hours went into research, and the original blueprints had been uncovered by the time the county finally gave the project its approval. The result of the remodeling job that took the house back to its original floor plan was called "one of the most enchanting projects we've seen and a major contribution not only to the park, but to the city as well" by a panel of judges for San Diego's "People in Preservation" awards.

The Chandlers have completely decorated the nine-room inn with antiques and collectibles of the 1800s. The formal front parlor contains period settees, Eastlake parlor tables, a 1901 Victrola with a brass horn, and a mahogany Eastlake-style fireplace with moss green tiles against a backdrop of William Morris wallpaper. Carpet reproductions from the 1800s blend with Oriental rugs designed to match Tiffany glass patterns.

Breakfast, served between 8:30 and 10:00 A.M., is "packed to go" for business people or travelers who need to get on the road early—another considerate touch. Heritage Park specialties include huevos rancheros and stuffed quesadillas served with sausage links (there's a chili cheese bake for Sunday morning brunch), Victorian sweet bread with a cream cheese filling, orange muffins with orange butter, a carved melon with yogurt-tossed fruit and trail mix, coffee, tea, and fruit juice.

Guest chambers follow themes in both name and decor. The Garden Room boasts a "Floral Basket" wall covering from the American Folk Art Collection, a sunflower-motif burled walnut Eastlake bed, and an 1880 triple-style vanity mirror with built-in corner curios. The Victorian Rose Room has a white and brass iron bed and a pink rose motif. The Turret encompasses the home's turret tower with its 180-degree view. Country Heart is the least expensive room with stenciled-heart walls and towel racks, heart-shaped pillows, and a tiger oak Bombe bed. The largest room, Queen Anne, contains a four-poster with a hand-crocheted, tassled canopy; an 1890s fainting couch; and a walnut armoire. Other rooms are Coral Tree Lookout, Morning Glory Room, Forget Me Not (white iron and brass bed), and the Bay Room.

A film from the inn's collection of old classics is shown in the parlor each night at 7:00 P.M. Popcorn is included. *Magnificent Doll* starring Ginger Rogers and David Niven was playing the day I visited, but *It's A Wonderful Life* with Jimmy Stewart and Donna Reid is said to be the most popular with the guests.

Special occasions come often at this inn. Lori puts

together packages of champagne, chocolates, roses, and bubble bath for honeymoon or anniversary couples. Her coup, however, is a very romantic five-course candlelight dinner served to the room by a butler or chambermaid in period 1880s costume. Also offered is a Victorian Country Supper with lighter fare of barbecued chicken or ribs, two gourmet salads, crusty sourdough bread, and custom-baked desserts.

The inn celebrates Christmas with an annual Victorian candlelight tour that runs the entire month of December. The house has trees laden with candles, bows, and heirloom ornaments. Antiques and gift items are offered for sale. Strolling minstrels and hot wassail complete the time-honored scene. During the rest of the year, the ornaments of the house are the congenial friends who frequent it. Heritage Park Bed & Breakfast Inn — what a hit!

Bed and Breakfast Reservation and Referral Services

Following is a list of agencies that book reservations and refer travelers to bed and breakfast inns as well as to accommodations in private homes. These services are gaining in popularity, and the rooms in private homes include breakfast along with overnight lodging at very affordable rates (from $20 up per night).

Operations vary. Some services charge the traveler an annual membership fee, while others take their commissions from the host providing the lodging. In some cases the agencies provide lists or directories of the homes they contract with and leave the arrangements up to you.

American Family Inn/Bed & Breakfast San Francisco
(415) 931-3083
P.O. Box 349
San Francisco, CA 94101

A reservation service with homes in San Francisco, Marin County, Monterey/Carmel, the Wine Country, and the Gold Country (also some Los Angeles locations). Rates range from $45 to $125 per night; no membership fee.

Bed & Breakfast International
(415) 525-4569
151 Ardmore Road
Kensington, CA 94707

A reservation service with homes in all areas of travel interest in California. Rates from $38 to $125, double occupancy; no membership fee. Send a self-addressed (legal-size) stamped envelope or call for a free brochure.

Rent-A-Room International
(714) 638-1406
11531 Varna Street
Garden Grove, CA 92640

Represents homes in southern California; $30 to $60 per night.

Digs West
(714) 739-1669
8191 Crowley Circle
Buena Park, CA 90621

A reservation service for California homes from Santa Barbara to San Diego; the company also books bed and breakfast inns all over the state. Rates run from $30-plus single, $38-plus double.

Northwest Bed and Breakfast
(503) 243-7616
610 S.W. Broadway
Portland, OR 97205

A reservation service for California homes from Anchor Bay to San Diego as well as Western states and western Canada referrals. Annual membership fee $15 single, $20 double; includes directory listing over 350 accommodations. Room rates $20 to $40 single, $25 to $65 double; family rates available.

Bed & Breakfast Exchange
(707) 942-5900
1458 Lincoln Avenue, #3
Calistoga, CA 94515

A referral service for Napa, Sonoma, and Mendocino counties as well as the Gold Country and San Francisco. Room rates start at $55 per night.

Bed & Breakfast Homestay
(800) 447-6667 (in California)
(805) 927-4613
P.O. Box 326
Cambria, CA 93428

A reservation service for bed and breakfast lodging in private homes. Geographic coverage: "Hearst Castle Country" and the central California coast. Room rates $45 to $85.

Megan's Friends
(805) 544-4406
1776 Royal Way
San Luis Obispo, CA 93401

A membership organization that provides a reservation service: $10 one-time membership fee. Listings include private homes and guest houses on the central coast (primarily in San Luis Obispo and Santa Barbara counties). Room rates from $30 up.

Eye Openers Bed & Breakfast Reservations
(213) 684-4428 or (818) 797-2055
P.O. Box 694
Altadena, CA 91001

A reservation service for homes throughout California. Rates from $30 per night; one-time membership fee $5.

Carolyn's Bed & Breakfast Homes of San Diego
(619) 422-7009
416 Third Avenue
Chula Vista, CA 92010

A reservation service for San Diego County, with several homes located around Los Angeles (Pasadena, North Hollywood, Palm Springs, and Catalina Island). Rates from $25 up.

Bed and Breakfast of Los Angeles
(818) 889-7325/8870
32127 Harborview Lane
Westlake Village, CA 91361

A reservation service for private homes and a few small inns in southern California; also handles a limited number of coastline properties from San Diego to San Francisco. Room rates from $30; $5 reservation fee. Directory available for $2.

Napa Valley Tourist Bureau
(707) 944-1557
P.O. Box 3240
Yountville, CA 94599

A reservation service for bed and breakfast inns, homes, hotels, and country clubs in the Napa and Sonoma valley areas. Rates from $55 to $225; no fee.

American Historic Homes
(714) 496-6953
P.O. Box 336
Dana Point, CA 92629

A nationwide reservation service that provides bed and breakfast in private homes and inns of historic significance; many California locations. Room rates $35 to $85, double occupancy.

Inland Empire Bed & Breakfast
(714) 739-1669
8191 Crowley Circle
Buena Park, CA 90621

A reservation service for homestays in San Bernardino, Riverside, and east Los Angeles counties. Rates from $30 up.

Tahoe North Visitors and Convention Bureau
(916) 583-3494
(800) 822-5959 (in California)
(800) 824-8557 (from outside California)
P.O. Box 5578
Tahoe City, CA 95730

A reservation service for the north Lake Tahoe–Truckee area which represents over 100 lodging properties, five of which are bed and breakfast inns. Room rates start at $60.

San Diego Bed & Breakfast
(619) 560-7322
P.O. Box 22948
San Diego, CA 92122

Reservation service for host homes in San Diego; rates in the $40 to $60 range.

Travelers Bed & Breakfast
(714) 627-7971
P.O. Box 1368
Chino, CA 91710

Reservation service for U.S. inns, cabins, and condos; $45 and up, double occupancy.

Bed & Breakfast Hospitality Reservation Service
(619) 722-6694
P.O. Box 2407
Oceanside, CA 92054

Handles homes and inns all over California. No fee; room rates from $35 up.

Bed & Breakfast Approved Hosts
(805) 647-0651
10890 Galvin
Ventura, CA 93004

Reservation and referral service for b&b homes in Ventura County. Rates from $55 to $125.

Bayhosts
(415) 337-9632
1155 Bosworth Street
San Francisco, CA 94131

A reservation service for gay people with bed and breakfast homes in San Francisco, Sausalito, and Berkeley. Rates
from $28 to $50 per night. No membership fee.

Wine Country Bed & Breakfast
(707) 578-1661
P.O. Box 3211
Santa Rosa, CA 95403

Reservation service for homes within a thirty-five mile
radius of Santa Rosa: Healdsburg, Kenwood, Sebastopol,
Santa Rosa, and vicinity. Rates in the $50 to $70 range.
No membership fee.

Hospitality Plus
(714) 496-7050
P.O. Box 388
San Juan Capistrano, CA 92693

Homes and some inns from San Francisco to San Diego;
rates from $35 up.

Christian Bed & Breakfast of America
(714) 496-6953
Box 388
San Juan Capistrano, CA 92693

Homes offering bed and breakfast to Christian-oriented
people. Reservations made inside California; referrals outside the state. Rates from $35 up.

Cohost, America's Bed & Breakfast
(213) 699-8427
P.O. Box 9302
Whittier, CA 90608

A reservation service with homes throughout California.
Rates from $40 to $85; no membership fee. Specializing
in considerations for the disabled, senior citizens, and families with children.

Wine Country Reservations
(707) 257-7757
Box 5059
Napa, CA 94581

Reservation service for the entire Napa Valley. Room rates
from $65 up; no fee to client. Brochure available.

Carmel Tourist Information and Roomfinder Service
(408) 624-1711
Box 7430
Mission Street between 5th and 6th
Carmel, CA 93921

Handles accommodations in bed and breakfasts, hotels,
motels, and cottages in northern California. Specializes
in the Monterey/Carmel area. Free service; room rates from
$60 up.

Monterey Peninsula Reservations
(408) 373-0155
(800) 822-8822 (U.S.)
546 "C" Hartnell Street
Monterey, CA 93940

Pacific Grove, Carmel, and Monterey reservations at bed
and breakfast inns as well as motels and hotels. Room rates
start at $60; no booking or membership fee.

Bed & Breakfast Reservations
(800) 443-6082 (in California)
(800) 634-1370 (outside California)
1834 First Street
Napa, CA 94559

A reservation service with homes throughout northern and central California. Rates from $50 up; brochure sent on request.

Napa Valley Reservations Unlimited
(707) 252-1985
(800) 251-NAPA (in California)
1598 Yajome Street
Napa, CA 94558

Reservation and referral service for Napa Valley accommodations (bed and breakfasts, hotels, resorts). No booking or membership fee. Average b&b rate is $75 for two.

Bed and Breakfast Society International
(512) 997-7150
407 Cora
Friedrichsburg, TX 78624

Referral and reservation network; publishers of the *Bed & Breakfast World Directory and Travelguide.* Handle host homes and inns worldwide; many California listings and locations. Room rates start at $40; $35 annual membership fee (includes a $7.50 b&b directory, news bulletins, and unlimited referrals and bookings).

InnServ
(317) 369-2245
Route #1, Box 47
Redkey, IN 47373

A nationwide reservation service for bed and breakfast and country inns with many California locations. Average room rates for two are around $60; the range is from $25 to $200. Annual membership fee is $9.95 (includes InnServ reservation guidebook, a quarterly newsletter, and a toll-free "800" number for reservations at any of the accommodations represented).

Bed and Breakfast Associations

Regional associations assist the traveler with information on bed and breakfast accommodations in their geographic area by providing group brochures and central telephone referral services. The associations listed below welcome your call or letter.

Association of Bed & Breakfast Innkeepers
of San Francisco
737 Buena Vista West
San Francisco, CA 94117
(415) 861-3008

Brochure available; send legal-size, self-addressed, stamped envelope.

Bed & Breakfast Innkeepers of Santa Cruz
and Half Moon Bay
P.O. Box 464
Santa Cruz, CA 95061
(408) 425-8212

An association referral service. Phone or send for free brochure with self-addressed, stamped envelope.

The Inns of Point Reyes
P.O. Box 145
Inverness, CA 94937
(415) 663-1420

An information and referral service. Free brochure available.

Bed & Breakfast Innkeepers of the Monterey Peninsula
598 Liane Street
Monterey, CA 93940
(408) 372-4777

Send $1 for brochure.

Bed & Breakfast Inns of Sonoma Valley
316 East Napa Street
Sonoma, CA 95476
(707) 996-5339

Telephone referral service for five member inns. Send for free brochure with self-addressed, stamped envelope.

Wine Country Bed & Breakfast Inns
of Sonoma County
P.O. Box 51
Geyserville, CA 95441
(707) 433-INNS

Booklet, wine road map, and calendar of events available for $1.

Bed & Breakfast Association of Upper Napa Valley
P.O. Box 2147
Yountville, CA 94599
(707) 944-1222

Central referral service. Send $1 for brochure.

Bed & Breakfast Innkeepers of Napa Valley
1834 First Street
Napa, CA 94559
(707) 224-4667 or (800) 443-6082

Send for free brochure.

Mendocino Coast Innkeepers Association
P.O. Box 1141-LB
Mendocino, CA 95460

Handy pocket guide depicting twelve Mendocino Coast inns; available for $1.50. (Comes with photo-packed map/brochure of the eighty-mile Mendocino Coast).

Bed & Breakfast Inns of Humboldt County
P.O. Box LB-40
Ferndale, CA 95536
(707) 786-4000

Free county brochure available; $1 for a set of individual inn brochures plus information on the area.

Bed & Breakfast Inns of the Gold Country
P.O. Box 462
Sonora, CA 95370
(916) 626-6136

Send legal-size, self-addressed, stamped envelope for free brochure.

Amador County Bed and Breakfast Inns
P.O. Box 322
Ione, CA 95640
(209) 274-4468

Send for free brochure with self-addressed, stamped envelope.

Gold Country Inns of Tuolumne County
P.O. Box 462
Sonora, CA 95370

Send for free brochure.

Historic Country Inns of the Mother Lode
P.O. Box 106
Placerville, CA 95667

Send self-addressed, stamped envelope for free
brochure.

Inns of Grass Valley and Nevada City Association
P.O. Box 1983
Nevada City, CA 95959
(916) 477-6634

Telephone referral service for ten member inns.

Sacramento Innkeepers' Association
2209 Capitol Avenue
Sacramento, CA 95816
(916) 441-3214

Free brochure.

Yosemite Bed & Breakfast of Mariposa County
2669 Triangle Road
Mariposa, CA 95338
(209) 966-2456

Send for free brochure.

Bed & Breakfast Innkeepers Guild of Santa Barbara
P.O. Box 20246
Santa Barbara, CA 93120
(805) 682-3199

Send for free brochure.

Bed & Breakfast Innkeepers of Northern California
P.O. Box 766
Calistoga, CA 94515

Send $1.50 for brochure covering inns in Northern
California from Carmel/Monterey north to Humboldt
County and east to the Sierras.

Bed & Breakfast Innkeepers of Southern California
P.O. Box 15425
Los Angeles, CA 90015-0385

Send legal-size, self-addressed, stamped envelope for free brochure.

Bed and Breakfast Publications

Guidebooks to bed and breakfast inns, homestays, and reservation services.

(Most are available, or can be ordered, through your local bookstore.)

Country Inns of the Far West: California $8.95
    by Jacqueline Killeen
101 Productions
834 Mission Street
San Francisco, CA 94103

Reviews of country inns and bed and breakfast inns.

The Great American Guest House Book $8.95
    by John Thaxton
Burt Franklin & Company
235 East Forty-fourth Street
New York, NY 10017

The Complete Guide to Bed & Breakfasts,
Inns & Guesthouses $12.95
    by Pamela Lanier
John Muir Publications
P.O. Box 613
Santa Fe, NM 87504

Bed & Breakfast in California $9.95
    by Kathy Strong
The Globe Pequot Press
Old Chester Road, Box Q
Chester, CT 06412

Bed & Breakfast, American Style $10.95
    by Norman T. Simpson
The Berkshire Traveller Press
Stockbridge, MA 01262

Bed & Breakfast Homes Directory—West Coast $9.95
    by Diane Knight
Knighttime Publications
890 Calabasas Road
Watsonville, CA 95076

Lists bed and breakfast accommodations in private homes
in California, Oregon, Washington, and British Columbia.

Bed & Breakfast U.S.A. $9.95
    by Betty Rundback and Nancy Kramer
E.P. Dutton, Inc.
RD 2, P.O. Box 355-A
Greentown, PA 18426

Bed & Breakfast Inns of Northern California
The San Francisco Bay Guardian
2700 19th Street
San Francisco, CA 94110

Annual guide issued the first Wednesday of April each year.
Free on the newsstand; $2.00 by mail, year-round.

Bed & Breakfast Almanac $4.50
B&B Productions
P.O. Box 295
St. Helena, CA 94574

A guide to accommodations and activities in the Napa
Valley wine country. Order by mail.

Bed & Breakfast North America $13.95
   by Norma Buzan
Betsy Ross Publications
3057 Betsy Ross Drive
Bloomfield Hills, MI 48013

A directory of bed and breakfast reservation services, small inns, and individual guest houses in the U.S., Mexico, and Canada.

The Bed & Breakfast Guide
for the U.S. and Canada $11.95
   by Phyllis Featherston and Barbara F. Ostler
The National Bed & Breakfast Association
P.O. Box 332
Norwalk, CT 06852

Lists over 1,100 individual bed and breakfast homes and family-run inns and provides access to 8,000 more through a Reservation Service section.

Fodor's Bed & Breakfast Guide $9.95
   by Mary Winget
Fodor's Travel Publications, Inc.
Division of Random House
201 East 50th Street
New York, NY 10022

Guide to bed and breakfast homes booked through reservation services.

A Treasury of Bed & Breakfast $14.95
The American Bed & Breakfast Association
P.O. Box 23294
Washington, D.C. 20026

Descriptions of over 3,000 homes offering bed and breakfast in North America. Order by mail.

California B&B Inns   FREE
California Office of Tourism
1121 L Street, Suite 103
Sacramento, CA 95814

A statewide listing of more than 200 bed and breakfast
inns. For a free copy send a stamped (39 cents), self-
addressed, legal-size envelope to the above address.

The Bed and Breakfast Traveler:
Touring The West Coast $10.95
    by Lewis Green
Pacific Search Press
222 Dexter Avenue North
Seattle, WA 98109

A combined travel guide and bed and breakfast inn directory to the West Coast, from San Francisco, California,
north to Vancouver, British Columbia.

Favorite California Inns $9.95
    by Bobbi Zane
2445 Northcreek Lane
Fullerton, CA 92631

Review of fifteen choice inns from the publisher of the
newsletter *Yellow Brick Road*. Order by mail; add $2.50 for
postage and handling.

The West Coast Bed & Breakfast Guide $12.95
    by Courtia Worth and Terry Berger
Prentice Hall Press, Div. of Simon & Schuster
Gulf & Western Building
One Gulf & Western Plaza
New York, NY 10023

Covers California, Oregon, and Washington.

Bed & Breakfast Coast to Coast $12.95
   by Bernice Chesler
The Stephen Greene Press — Publisher
Viking Penguin, Inc. — Distributor
40 West 23rd Street
New York, NY 10010

A guide to some 200 bed and breakfast reservation and
referral services throughout North America.

Frommer's Bed & Breakfast North America $8.95
   by Hal Gieseking
Prentice Hall Press, Div. of Simon & Schuster
Gulf & Western Building
One Gulf & Western Plaza
New York, NY 10023

A directory of b&b reservation services that book stays in
private homes; some individual inns.

Bed & Breakfast Directory for San Diego $3.50
   by Carol Emerick
Keystone Publications
P.O. Box 3292
San Diego, CA 92103

Includes information about bed and breakfast homes and
inns located throughout San Diego County. Order by mail;
postage included.

Bed and Breakfast Directory   FREE
AAA-California State Automobile Association
Attn: Touring Department
150 Van Ness Avenue, P.O. Box 1860
San Francisco, CA 94101-1860

Directory of bed and breakfast inns for central and northern California, free to members of the American Automobile Association. For a copy, drop in to your nearest AAA
district office and show your membership card, or write
or phone with your membership number.

West Coast Bed and Breakfast Inns
Country Inns of America — California $12.95
    by Andrews, Allen, Gardner, and Berger
Holt, Rinehart and Winston
383 Madison Avenue
New York, NY 10017

Bed & Breakfast World Directory and Travelguide $9.00
Bed & Breakfast Society International
407 Cora Street
Friedrichsburg, TX 78624-4213

Access to thousands of host homes and inns worldwide
through this guidebook which is updated each year.
Includes photos and features about hosts, guests, and traveling "b&b style." Order by mail; $9 postpaid. Payment
applies to membership fee for the Bed & Breakfast Society International (see Reservation Service section for
details).

Newsletters

California Inns
Toby Smith, Publisher
P.O. Box 3383
Santa Rosa, CA 95402

Reviews of bed and breakfast and country inns throughout California. $25/year. Special reports on bed and break-
fast inns in specific areas of the state also available at $7.50
each; send for list.

Yellow Brick Road
Bobbi Zane, Publisher
2445 Northcreek Lane
Fullerton, CA 92631

Reviews of bed and breakfast inns along with news of areas
and events of travel interest. Published monthly; $36/year.

Inn Review
Norman Strasma, Publisher
P.O. Box 1789-L
Kankakee, IL 60901

Covers b&bs, country inns, and small hotels throughout the United States and in Canada. Published ten times a year. $27/year; sample copy: $2.

Cookbooks from B&Bs

The American Bed & Breakfast Cookbook $12.95
   by The Bed Post Writers Group
East Woods Press
Old Chester Road, Box Q
Chester, CT 06412

More than 200 recipes from b&bs across the U.S.

Bed & Breakfast Cookbook $9.95
   by Pamela Lanier
Running Press Book Publishers
125 South 22nd Street
Philadelphia, PA 19103

A collection of breakfast, brunch, and teatime recipes from America's foremost bed and breakfast inns.

Bread & Breakfast: Best Recipes from North America's Bed & Breakfast Inns $7.95
   by Linda Kay Bristow
101 Productions
834 Mission Street
Suite 202
San Francisco, CA 94103

Regional specialties and treasured family favorites including Fresh Peach Soup, My Great Aunt Fanny's Date Cake, Minnesota Wild Rice Waffles, and Virginia Ham and Apple Pie.

Cooking INN Style $9.95
    by Sonnie Imes
Bed and Breakfast Innkeepers of Northern California
P.O. Box 766
Calistoga, CA 94515

A combined bed and breakfast inn guide to Northern California and breakfast recipe cookbook. When ordering by mail, add $2.50 for postage.

Grant Corner Inn Breakfast & Brunch Cookbook $10.95
    by Louise Stewart
Grant Corner Inn
122 Grant Avenue
Santa Fe, NM 87501

Includes Southwest regional specialties for breakfast and brunch; tried and true recipes. Order by mail; add $3 for postage and handling.

The American Country Inn and
Bed & Breakfast Cookbook $22.95
    by Kitty and Lucian Maynard
Rutledge Hill Press
513 Third Avenue South
Nashville, TN 37210

Over 1,700 recipes from 500 inns; hardcover volume.

Publications on How to Open/ Operate a Bed and Breakfast Inn

So, You Want To Be an Innkeeper $10.95
    by Davies, Hardy, Bell, and Brown
101 Productions
834 Mission Street
Suite 202
San Francisco, CA 94103

Contains a wealth of information for the novice or veteran — everything from balancing the budget to balancing the teacup — plus how-tos, anecdotes, and case histories based on the authors' (all innkeepers themselves) own experiences.

How To Open and Operate a Bed & Breakfast Home $10.95
  by Jan Stankus
The Globe Pequot Press
Old Chester Road, Box Q
Chester, CT 06412

A step-by-step look at the challenges and rewards of setting up and operating a bed and breakfast home.

How To Open (and Successfully Operate)
a Country Inn $8.95
  by Karen L. Etsell
The Berkshire Traveller Press
Stockbridge, MA 01262

innkeeping
Mary Davies, Publisher
P.O. Box 267
Inverness, CA 94937

A newsletter for owners/operators of bed and breakfast and country inns. Subject matter ranges from inn promotion to policies and procedures. Issued monthly; $48/year.

Index

Tues - SF
Weds S.F → NAPA
Thurs - mendocino
Fri Mendocin